Unemployment

Unemployment

PERSONAL AND SOCIAL CONSEQUENCES

EDITED BY STEPHEN FINEMAN

Foreword by Adrian Sinfield

TAVISTOCK PUBLICATIONS

London and New York

First published in 1987 by
Tavistock Publications Ltd
11 New Fetter Lane, London EC4P 4EE

© 1987 Tavistock Publications Ltd

Printed in Great Britain by
Richard Clay Ltd, Bungay, Suffolk

British Library Cataloguing in Publication Data

Unemployment: personal and social consequences.
—(Social science paperbacks ; no. 348)
1. Unemployment — Great Britain
I. Fineman, Stephen
331.13'7941   HD5765.A6
ISBN 0-422-60080-6

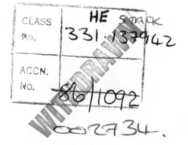

Contents

List of contributors

Editor

Stephen Fineman Senior Lecturer in Organizational Behaviour, School of Management, University of Bath.

Anne-Marie Bostyn Post-graduate social anthropologist, Department of Social Anthropology, University of Edinburgh.

Sarah Buckland is a Research Fellow on the Alvey DHSS Demonstrator Project in the Department of Sociology, University of Surrey.

Claire Callender Lecturer in Social Policy, Department of Social Policy and Health Services Studies, University of Leeds.

David Y. Clark Temporary Lecturer in Sociology, Ealing College of Higher Education, London.

Yvonne Dhooge Research Officer, Responding to Unemployment: a Training Initiative for Health and Social Services, Department of Social Sciences, South Bank Polytechnic, London.

David Fryer Lecturer in Psychology, Department of Psychology, University of Stirling.

Jean Hartley Lecturer in Occupational Psychology, Department of Occupational Psychology, Birkbeck College, University of London.

Leo B. Hendry Senior Lecturer in Education, Department of Education, King's College, University of Aberdeen.

Susanne MacGregor Senior Lecturer in Political Sociology, Department of Politics and Sociology, Birkbeck College, University of London.

Stephen McKenna Lecturer, Stannington College, Sheffield.

Roderick Martin Professor of Industrial Sociology, Department of Social and Economic Studies, Imperial College of Science and Technology, London.

vii

Jennie Popay Research Officer, Thomas Coram Research Unit, University of London Institute of Education, University of London.

Jeremy Seabrook Writer and journalist, with special interests in poverty and unemployment, West Norwood, London.

Daniel Wight Post-graduate social anthropologist, Department of Social Anthropology, University of Edinburgh.

Foreword

Shortly after unemployment reached half-a-million in 1963, I began my first piece of research interviewing men out of work in the north-east of England. I felt pleased when many people who heard about the study said how valuable my research would be – but then they added, not for policy-makers or contemporary analysts, but for historians, because never again would Britain experience what was seen as an appalling level of unemployment. The presumption of both an accepted commitment to full – or at least high – employment and its achievement seemed as strong and as pervasive then as its opposite is today. It is worth noting how assumptions about the level of unemployment have changed, for they do much to shape other assumptions about what it is reasonable to expect and to hope for, about what can and should be done. On the same statistical basis as applied in the 1960s, the rate of unemployment was 15 per cent in 1985 compared with an average of less than 2 per cent for the whole twenty-five years between 1946 and 1970. Those days of low un-employment are now seen as the abnormal ones, almost to be dismissed as some economic aberration, and comparison is made much more easily with the recession between the wars, and particularly the doleful 1930s. The fact that in 1948 the Labour Cabinet seriously discussed banning the football pools in order to take the women checking the coupons into the labour-starved textile industry seems unbelievable to many today (Deacon 1980).

As unemployment has remained high in the 1980s, the sense of shock and outrage at the social and economic waste of so many millions without jobs seems to have abated. The peak of this may have come in the autumn of 1980, as the number out of work rose swiftly past two million with no sign of any reversal in it or the government's policies. The three-million total, which was reached more slowly, was less of an event. With reduced expectations of change there has been a decline in the scrutiny of the reality behind the monthly count. 'The unemployed' have become 'un-employment' again, an aggregate which only attracts attention when it is changing size – or recurrent statistical sleight-of-hand by the govern-ment leads to debate about its proper measurement.

This book sets out to rescue the unemployed from such impersonal aggregation, and reveals them and their many different experiences in terms of their daily lives as members of British society. It throws valuable light not only on the people who have been subjected to being out of work, but also on the variety of its impact and their individual responses. In 1938 the Pilgrim Trust provided a vivid illustration of this theme: 'Unemployed men are not simply units of employability who can, through the medium of the dole, be put into cold storage and taken out immediately they are needed. While they are in cold storage, things are likely to happen to them' (Pilgrim Trust 1938: 67).

In 1986 there are two major differences. Unemployment shows no sign of falling from the peak of the recession as it had by 1938: indeed recent months have seen further increases. And long-term unemployment is much higher. Even by the official figures the number who have been claimants for a year or more without any break is just short of 1,400,000 – two out of every five unemployed. Very many of these have been without work for more than three years and their chances of coming out of 'cold storage' must be very remote. Although there are difficulties in making exact comparisons with the duration data of the 1930s, there is no doubt that long-term unemployment is very much higher today. And the contrast with the 1950s and 1960s is more dramatic and much less debatable. During that whole period the number registered unemployed for a year or more averaged less than 50,000 – only one twenty-eighth of the present total.

Another objective of this book is to examine the picture of unemployment as a uniform and negative experience which tends to dominate most of the literature. Unemployment, like any other major crisis, challenges people's ability to participate in the daily life of society in ways in which they have been accustomed. The chapters which follow offer a wealth of evidence of people's efforts not only to survive but also to give sense to their new situation, to transcend or exploit it. In this as in any other society most people do not sit back when confronted by unemployment. 'Life goes on' is a truism of the fatalist, but the reality is that people make it go on. The contributors to this volume succeed in conveying the vigour and ingenuity of many responses and the spirit of determination, if not defiance, with which many people carry on their lives.

The evidence of successful escapes from unemployment, and from the unsatisfactory employment which often preceded it, raises searching questions about the present organization of our society, where so much of life is dependent upon access to employment and is shaped by its experience, rewards, and constraints. However, in correctly revealing the many facets of the experience of unemployment, the authors seem to me to underline that this *is* an essentially negative experience for the very great majority, however varied its impact and people's responses to it may be. Even the more innovative diversions from the problems and pressures indicate the very limited range of alternative opportunities at present available for the three to four million out of work and reveal that many have costs which may come to weigh more heavily as people grow older.

The problems of unemployment are made more evident by the application of good research methods. 'Keeping it in the family', the title of one section in the final chapter, summarizes neatly the many ways in which the full impact of the experience of continuing unemployment remains concealed from the rest of society. It is a matter of self-respect for a family and its individual members that they can cope, and that coping often includes playing down difficulties before a passing interviewer. Contact over a longer period, and with different members of the family, or living in a small community and observing its daily life, reveals much more clearly and fully the many separate ways in which being out of work changes relationships and routines. The second or third interview allows comparisons to be made over time that throw light on the extent to which the ability to cope is often dependent on the opportunity to hope that things can change for the better. It is remarkable how much more revealing – and often angry – are the accounts of being out of work given by those now back at work when the pressure to present oneself and the experience acceptably is reduced.

What Sennett and Cobb (1973) have vividly called 'the hidden injuries of class' emerge in the frequent contrast between the rich and eloquent accounts of those made redundant after years of security and the laconic responses of those whose jobs made them vulnerable to recurrent periods out of work even when unemployment generally was low. What might be called the hidden injuries of youth also become evident in the often less articulate frustration of those who have yet to establish themselves in the labour force and are wondering if they ever will.

The general direction of the evidence presented in this book becomes all the more significant in the light of government evidence on the changing impact of unemployment – at least among men, since comparable data on women are not available. Despite many assumptions to the contrary, the burden of unemployment has become more, not less, unequally distributed as the numbers out of work have risen during this recession. In 1983 one-third of the men from semi-skilled or unskilled jobs had spent some time out of work in the previous twelve months – four times as many as among men in non-manual work. In 1975–77 the difference had only been three times as great (Central Statistical Office 1980, Tables 5.18 and 5.19 for the mid–1970s and 1985; Table 4.26 for 1983).

Those who have now become even more vulnerable to unemployment are also likely to have the fewest resources to protect themselves and their families from their loss of earning power. Future historians may be better placed to explain why, therefore, the level of income support provided to the unemployed has been reduced by this government – and present proposals to reform social security are likely to reduce it even further. Part, at least, of the explanation lies in the very different perception of unemployment and the unemployed held by the present government compared with at least the administrations of the first decades after the war. There is a marked contrast between the assumptions of the recent Reviews of Social Security and the Beveridge Report of 1942. In the latter, unemployment was seen as the problem which governments must take action to reduce and control in order to make the nation more socially secure; in the former the unemployed are themselves seen as part of the problem. There are many references in the Green Paper on the Reform of Social Security to the need to improve incentives among those out of work (DHSS 1985; Forrester 1985: 13–14). This view is consistent with the general emphasis in government policy. Whatever the economic impact of 'supply-side' economics, frequent ministerial emphasis on 'workers pricing themselves out of jobs' is likely to help create or maintain a climate which rejects arguments for action to help the unemployed.

In its valuable contribution to the better understanding of the social-psychological consequences of unemployment, this book provides important evidence which is needed to inform political and economic debate.

Adrian Sinfield
Department of Social Policy and Social Work
University of Edinburgh

References

Beveridge, W. H. (Chairman) (1942) *Report on Social Insurance and Allied Services.* Cmd. 6404. London: HMSO.

Central Statistical Office (1980) *Social Trends 1980.* London: HMSO.

—— (1985) *Social Trends 1985.* London: HMSO.

Deacon, A. (1980) Spivs, Drones and Other Scroungers. *New Society*, 28 February.

DHSS (1985) *The Reform of Social Security.* Vol. 1, Cmnd. 9517. London: HMSO.

Forrester, D. B. (1985) The Fowler Reviews – An Initial Response. In *The Welfare State and the Fowler Reviews – A Christian Response.* Nottingham: The Shaftesbury Project.

Pilgrim Trust (1938) *Men Without Work.* Cambridge: Cambridge University Press.

Sennett, R. and Cobb, J. (1973) *The Hidden Injuries of Class.* New York: Vintage Books.

1. Introduction

Stephen Fineman

Perhaps the dominant image of unemployment is the one we receive from our newspapers, television, and radio. We are informed of the closure of manufacturing plants, the necessary 'rationalization' of certain industries, and how poorly competitive Britain has become. Each month one television news programme offers us a tableau of new jobs created (in reassuring green) compared with jobs lost (in worrying red). We see politicians and trade union officials squabbling over whether we have 3¼, 3½, or maybe over 4 million unemployed. A politician of one hue will explain to us that the latest unemployment figures are a promising sign of a 'deaccelerating trend', while another is keen to demonstrate that it is nothing of the kind.

For those of us left somewhat confused by this picture, we have at least two ideological positions to consider. The first, and at present regnant, is that increased unemployment is a natural consequence of overpaid labour, making British goods less competitive. We must therefore tolerate growing unemployment until the more commercially viable jobs thrive and expand. The second suggests that any significant unemployment is indefensible and we must create jobs regardless of their immediate economic contribution. An upturn in the world economy will eventually get us out of our difficulties. The political and economic debates weave about these perspectives, enhanced and accentuated by the image that a particular political party wishes to portray – in the interests of its own popularity and survival.

Yet it is the very language of this political and economic discourse, and the remote level of abstraction within the term 'unemployment', that moves us a safe distance from the people unemployed. It insulates us from the human realities behind the rhetoric and statistics. It is hoped that this book may help close this gap.

Shifting attention to the unemployed serves several purposes. The first is a descriptive one; it tells something of life without work, such as:

1

* the problems that people encounter as they seek to make meaning and purpose for themselves;
* the way that they cope without earned income;
* how well agencies of help function;
* the roles and tensions between nearest and dearest;
* what happens to families and communities as more and more people lose work;
* the way that joblessness penetrates the lives of those of very different social backgrounds;
* how unemployment rubs off on the employed.

The second purpose is an interpretative one. Observations at the rawer edges of society expose the inadequacy and fragility of structures that we readily take for granted. The unemployed, from their 'disenfranchised' position, offer us unusual clues as to what work, as we have come to know it, contributes to our psychological and sociological integrity. They jolt us into questioning the inevitability, and desirability, of 9 a.m. to 5 p.m. existence for around forty years of life. Their viewpoints soon raise questions about the nature of the educational, industrial, and political systems of which they are a product and part.

The third purpose is one of challenge and potential action. What, from our descriptive and interpretative work, are our possible futures? What can we design differently, and 'better'? If we are to develop features of our society from the realities of those who live it, in ambiguity, what advice can we offer to those who struggle to design and implement social policy?

For certain social researchers these are very important issues. In this volume some of them have their say.

The overall aim of this book has been to explore unemployment in terms of the aforementioned purposes, but through the eyes of professional researchers and writers who are close to the 'firing-line' of unemployment. As it happens, a number of them were actually inside the battle, being unemployed at the time of writing. I sought out those who had a distinct penchant for qualitative research, which I viewed as critical to the essence of the endeavour. I was also keen to serve the subject-matter, not one particular academic discipline. So psychologists here rub shoulders with sociologists, social anthropologists with organizational scientists and analysts of social policy. One or two of the contributors eschew any particular academic allegiance.

I solicited original contributions from new and 'established' writers. I invited them to offer a thoughtpiece or empirical study in one of the following focal areas: the individual experience of unemployment; issues facing women; the long-term unemployed; the jobless middle class; school-leavers without work; family-related concerns; the effects of unemployment on a whole community; helping strategies; educational responses; issues of industrial relations. I saw this as a broad slice through the social context of unemployment, and a necessarily partial one for a single volume such as this. My predilections in no way implied the insignificance of other areas of unemployment, such as amongst the disabled, blacks, or other minority groups.

I asked two more things of the contributors. Firstly, that they should attempt to appeal to an audience that would include people outside of their particular discipline; they could therefore loosen up on some of their customary reporting conventions. The student of unemployment, though, should find food for thought, if not inspiration, in what they write. Secondly, I asked them to try to reflect the spirit of my third 'purpose' – to take their descriptions and interpretations, where relevant, into directions for new thought, action, or policy. As it turned out, some grasped this point with vigour and eloquence, while others preferred a more cautious and conservative line.

The book took shape from these beginnings. All of us met together for a day, before writing. We exchanged outlines, negotiated content, and confronted each other with a flood of exciting ideas. Thereafter, those with closely associated chapters kept in contact with one another, while I nagged and co-ordinated things from Bath. I also provided feedback for final revisions.

The results are in the following twelve chapters, which are organized in four parts:

Part 1, 'Inside experiences', reveals some of the 'guts' of being unemployed, and special issues facing those struggling to survive, the poor, and women in search of work. There is also a chapter which reminds us that joblessness is now not a class discriminator: professionals, and others of the well educated, are solidly represented in the unemployment statistics.

In Part 2, attention moves to 'Families and communities'. The immediate social context of unemployment is highlighted through accounts of family structures and relationships. We are shown that household matters buffer and complicate an individual's unemployment, to the extent that joblessness creates problems and challenges within all corners of family life. A chapter on a high-unemployment community gives us a glimpse of everyday life outside of people's front doors: how people's social patterns, consumption, and key rituals can get dramatically thrown out of gear.

Part 3 takes a rather different angle by examining some of the broader 'Social responses and structures' associated with unemployment. This includes the way our social services cope, the kind of specialist provision we make for those who fall further and further back in the queue for work, and where our schools fit into an unemployment scenario. In this part of the book we also take a bird's-eye view on how the individual realities of joblessness, and the scarcity of work, have translated into grass-roots industrial relations practice. Is there a new mood about work and employer–union relationships?

In the fourth, and final, part of the book I take a position 'Looking on' to all that has been contributed. I have attempted to highlight some of the emergent themes, and also pursue some of the directions in which they might take us: directions about jobs, work, wealth, assistance, and social change.

Part 1
Inside experiences

2. Surviving

Jeremy Seabrook

A council estate on the edge of a Midland city, where few people are likely to want to buy the houses, even if they could afford to. The ground is marshy and the houses damp; a false cloud from the power-station always attenuates the sunlight. The houses were built soon after the war, exiguous bare sketches of a living place, although well spaced. Muddy expanses of worn grass, gardens run to seed; long-term neglect – faulty drains and broken windows covered with pieces of cardboard; a raw bleak place. There is a male unemployment rate of almost 50 per cent; in some streets there are only two or three people working.

Some of the older people remember the 1930s: the ingenuity that then went into finding the necessities to subsist has changed into ingenuity in finding money. Then, they will tell you, they broke down wooden lamp-posts or fences for fuel, trespassed to catch rabbits, scavenged for wood in the hedge-bottoms; as the men came home from work, their dinner-bags were searched to see if they had stolen anything. As times have changed, so the kinds of petty crime have changed – a length of rubber hose to bypass the gas meter, jump-leads to avoid the electricity meter. On the estate there are two neighbouring houses that have had the electricity cut off; the man next door has rigged up a cable that runs the current for three houses from one meter. This of course meant that a very high rate of electricity consumption was being registered in one house; the meters had to be fixed so that only a plausible amount was being used.

Alex

Alex is from Greenock; in his mid-fifties, he is a fragile man with a delicate face, grey stubble, and skin stretched so tight over his thin face that he looks as if he is perpetually smiling. He sits on the edge of his sofa with its grubby nylon stretch-cover, rolling cigarettes with stained and trembling fingers – thin cigarettes that are used up in a moment if he smokes them to satisfy; they simply go out if he does not. He wears an old pair of pale blue jeans, with a patch of darker blue at the knee, sewn roughly with red and white cotton; shabby shoes, threadbare dog-tooth sportscoat. He came to the city from Scotland in the 1960s to work on the building. He was separated from his wife, and had three children to bring up. He lived in a flat with the three children. The room where they slept had an old-fashioned gas fire that did not have a proper extractor.

'One winter day, it was a cold day, I remember the date, it was the 12th January 1968. It had been a cold day, and when the lad came home from school he said, "Can we have the fire on, Dad?" So I put it on low. It was freezing, there was snow on the ground. It was only a small flat. The boy and girl slept in the living-room. I left the fire on low when they went to bed. But they must've felt cold in the night and turned the fire up. When I got up in the morning, the fire was blazing away; and I couldna wake them. They were both unconscious. He was only six, she was five. I rushed out into the street with them, and the neighbours came out and we rolled them in the snow to bring them round. They sent for the ambulance. The girl came to; but by the time they got the lad to hospital, he was dead. The Gas Board had known since 1950 that the extractors they were using were dangerous, and they should have been changed a long time before. The room was full of carbon monoxide. I was told by a solicitor that I should sue. When my wife heard what had happened, she came back to me. She said after a loss like that, we should be together, make a go of it. She left the bloke she was living with and moved down here with me. But I wasna interested in claiming against the Gas Board. The wife said we should sue for every penny we could get. But I wouldn't. I wanted my bairn back! So she left me again. She'd only come back to get her hands on the compensation money. So I was left with the girl and the oldest boy to bring up.

'I've had no work for six years. I've done odd jobs. I was doing paving-stones for a cottage outside town. While I was working, the woman next door comes and asks me if I'll do the same for her. I was getting the stones cheap so I could do it for a good price. She said, "Oh, that's cheap. The firm I got a quotation from wanted five times as much." Well, I'm working there a few days, say hello to her husband. Anyway, next time I go down Social to sign on, bloke behind the counter looks at me and says, "Don't I know you?" I thought, "Oh hell, here we go." I said, "I don't know, you ought to. I've been coming down here for two years." It was the bloke I'd done the flags for in his garden. He never said anything. He never stopped my money.'

Alex travels to Rampton (a 'secure' hospital) every month to see his eldest son. He is in there for an indefinite period. 'He's not ill,' Alex says defensively:

> 'He's there because him and his mate lured some poof into the house one night. They were pissed. They were hard up and wanted some money. They were only gonna take his money off him. So they take him back home for a drink; and, well, he hasn't got any money or he turns funny. So they start on him. Only my boy got all the blame. Both of them said the other hit him first. They cut him up with a garden scythe. Rampton. It's not a prison. It's a hospital. He doesn't have any drugs. A sleeping-tablet at night, that's all.'

Gail and Dave

Gail and Dave moved on to the estate six months ago. For Gail, at twenty-six, this was one of many new starts; but for Dave, at twenty-five, this is his first adult home. Gail is the only woman he has wanted to live with. Gail has changed her image as a pledge that it really *will* work this time. Her hair is bronze-gold. She has tried to remove the tattoos from her arms, which has left them red and smudged. She wears two pieces of metal sculpture around her neck, one with a mock amethyst in the centre.

The furniture has been provided by Social Services: it does not match. The plastic armchairs are torn in places, exposing yellow spongy foam. But the house is warm: some drawings of fantasy-bikers and two metal peacocks over the fireplace. Gail would like to have it done in stonework, 'when we get on our feet'.

She and Dave have now been together for seven months. Dave has black curly hair, tight under a knitted navy-blue hat; combat jacket, ancient oily jeans, and Doc Marten boots: wide warm smile. From Newcastle originally, he spent three years in the army, but has not worked for the past two years. Outside, on the grass verge, is parked a maroon Cortina, which he is repairing. Dave loves cars. 'If only I had a hundred quid. I'd start my own business.' He would buy cars from the city scrap-yard for £20 each: one with worn-out bodywork but a reasonable engine, another with clapped-out engine but bodywork that could be patched up. Transfer the engine, a few basic repairs, couple of hundred profit, 'no sweat'. He says: 'You want to leave something for your kids. You don't want to pass through this world with nothing to show at the end of it.'

Dave is hard. He says he is not afraid of anything. He was in the Parachute Regiment. 'Once the 'chute got caught on the aircraft wing. I thought, "If this is it, what can you do?" I got away with two broken ankles and a broken nose.' Nothing hurts him. Gail stabbed him one night. 'Go on, do it again.' He says:

> 'One night I was coming out of the pub with my mate. We were both pissed. Suddenly, I feel somebody grab me from behind. I hate being touched. I turned round. There were two guys. I took a swing at them. One wound up with a broken pelvis, the other a fractured skull, put them both in intensive care. It turned out they were plain-clothes policemen. I got off, because they didn't identify themselves first.'

One night he had borrowed a mate's Ferrari 7.5-litre. He was just pulling away from the lights when he heard the police siren and saw the blue flashing light. He swerved into the park, crossed the park at 150 m.p.h., took the car on two wheels to get through the bollards. They never caught him, but in the chase two police cars were smashed and a police motor bike hit a wall.

'I'm hard. I had to be. My father broke my arm and leg when I was six months old.' Dave says he misses his mother. She died at forty, after years of having been beaten by her husband. 'She died of a heart attack. It was him. I don't know where he is now, but if I get him, I'll break every bone in his body.' Dave was loved by his mother; that is why he is sure he will make it with Gail.

Gail was never loved. Her father abused her sexually. Her mother knew about it, but chose not to know, for fear of losing her husband. Marie, Gail's daughter, who is eight, sits quietly on the sofa, half listening to the adults, sucking at a bag of savoury potato-sticks. She was born when Gail was seventeen. Gail's three other children are in foster homes. She wants them back. She says she wants to start a petition, signed by her friends and neighbours, to declare that she is not an unfit mother. She was sterilized after the youngest was born, but now she would like a baby with Dave. The two oldest are fostered by a well-off family 'who can give them all the things I can't. That's why Dave wants to start a business. Then we could give them everything.'

Gail feels safe with Dave. His reputation will protect her from her husband, who has just come out of prison. He wants her back. He has said that he is coming to get her. 'He used to beat me up. That's why one of my babies was stillborn.'

It is easy to understand how looking for work occupies a low position in their list of priorities. Living is itself a full-time job.

Dave's mate, Greg, arrives; a slight, subdued boy of twenty-two. He is staying with them at the moment. When Dave gets going, there will be a job for Greg. Dave is teaching him all about cars. Greg was living with his father, but his mother left home, and now his father has a girl who is only two years older than Greg. Greg says: 'She spoils everything. They don't want me there. And my mum don't want me with her either.' Greg believes in Dave.

A few days later they were arrested for burglary. They had broken into the weekend retreat of a peer and had stolen a safe, which Dave had left in the boot of the car. The break-in was a botched, clumsy business. Dave got twelve months in prison.

In many of the houses on the estate the husband says to the wife, 'Come on, love, how about some tea?' even when they have nothing to do all day. Their *machismo* is the last refuge of all that redundant energy that was sweated out of them when they were at work; their power over their women is a sort of last refuge for their pride. Mrs Taylor says to her husband, 'Make it yourself.' She says:

> 'My father was like that. He'd sit there, and the kettle'd be boiling on the hob, and he'd fetch her, yell for her to come out of the kitchen, from down the garden, even from off the toilet, to lift it off and make tea. He used to gamble terrible. He was a smelter in the steelworks. He always had good money, only he never gave her enough. I remember once when he offered her some money, she said, "Go and take it to the other family you're keeping." He was most upset. "What other family? I've never looked at another woman." She said, "No, Eddie White's family." He was the bookmaker.'

Colin and Wendy

Colin has moved in with Wendy. Officially, he is living at the probation hostel, and he has to report back at night, but he is allowed one night a week with her. Wendy is in her late thirties; Colin is twenty-two. Wendy was badly beaten by her husband and spent some time in a women's refuge. Her sight was impaired by the injuries she received. Colin is from Norwich, a tall young man with a shock of dark hair; he has been told he looks like Sylvester Stallone. Although it is a chilly day, his torso is bare. He is grating cheese in the kitchen for a potato pie. He has a profusion of multi-coloured tattoos – a dragon, a rose, a gravestone. Wendy stood by him when he was in court last week; she wrote a letter of mitigation, to say she had known him for five years and that she had a long-term relationship with him, even though she has known him less than a month. The judge told him he had Wendy to thank for the leniency with which he was being treated. His offence was burglary. He is not a very efficient criminal. He says regretfully that he does not really have the 'bottle' for it. In fact, he got so drunk before he even dared enter the house that he dropped his address book on the floor; he was picked up by the police a few hours later.

Wendy says she is the first woman who has ever really got through to Colin. For the first time in his adult life he has cried with her. She played the same record over and over on the sound system, an old Jim Reeves number, and eventually he broke down and wept. She says that she started by mothering him a bit, but slowly a sexual relationship developed.

Wendy is in the darts team at the local pub. She is very skilled and can run rings round nearly all the men. She likes to have a good time. They had a party at the weekend, which went on till four in the morning. She got so stoned, her mind is a blank after midnight; the only thing she has to show for it is a bump the size of an egg on her head.

Wendy is worried about Tina her daughter, who is thirteen. She has run away from home several times; she has been drunk several times; she says she has been offered drugs; and she has had sex with older boys. Wendy takes her down the pub with her. 'At least I can keep an eye on her there.' When Tina is bad, Wendy hits her. Colin says that is wrong. He thinks Wendy can see herself in Tina, things she does not like, so she tries to knock them out of her. 'You can't change yourself by hitting somebody else,' he says. Wendy goes up to him and puts her hand down his trousers. 'Isn't he lovely?' she says.

Two weeks later, he had gone. Wendy was tragic. 'Bastard,' she says. 'He was using me. It was just somewhere safe for him to go to keep him out the nick – where he ought to be. Story of my life, that is, being used by blokes till they don't want you any longer. It won't happen again.'

For many people like Colin and Wendy, the idea of work is not an issue. They accept their dependency on welfare, which is a kind of basic income that has to be supplemented in any way that may present itself: looking after some stolen goods, odd jobs, looking after a neighbour's kids for the weekend, keeping your eyes open for anything that can be turned into cash. Wendy says that 'living is a full-time job'; her life is so full of difficulties and anxieties that it takes her all her time to survive from day to day. 'Time', she says bleakly, 'is something you have to get through.'

Lorraine

At Lorraine's one afternoon, just after the pubs have closed, Lorraine brings Tone and Chrissie back with a couple of lagers. Her house is shabby but scrupulously clean and tidy; everything in its place. She has a lot of second-hand ornaments – ancient presents from Skegness, pieces of ironwork, Capodimonte figures, paintings of an angry seascape with a stallion in the foreground, a reproduction of Constable's 'Haywain', and a painting of a little girl crying huge pearly tears.

They talk about the indignities of being 'on the Social', and their triumphs over it. From the point of view of society, this is counter-productive, in the sense that it turns many peaceable people into petty criminals; on the other hand, it is useful to the status quo, in that people do not on the whole attack the system, but find weak points at which it may be exploited. The system is not seen as susceptible to change. Its labyrinthine ways are so tangled that the best that can be hoped for is the avoidance of some of its regulations. A great reservoir of bitterness and resentment often builds up; but it is directed, for the most part, against the administration of welfare, the hardness and unfairness of officials.

Lorraine: 'I went to the Social when my giro never came. I had no money. I had to walk the three miles into town. I said, "How am I going to feed my kids?" "Do they have free dinners at school?" "Yes." "That'll do them till tomorrow." '

Chrissie: 'They gave me a voucher for £10. You have to spend it down the Co-Op. You show yourself up. There's people standing behind you in the queue. They look at you, you can see in their eyes what they're thinking: "What's wrong with her that she has to have vouchers? Can't be trusted with money. She must be an alkie." '

Lorraine: 'They always say, "It's in the post." The universal answer. You've no bargaining power on the Social. You're there to plead, and that's it.'

Chrissie: 'I had a lodger. He *was* a lodger an' all. I wasn't sleeping with him. They sent a letter: "The situation at this address is unsatisfactory, and we cannot accept it." They gave him four weeks to find another address. So we got an address of some friends who were working, and gave that. He still stays with me. As soon as you give somebody else's address, that makes you a criminal.'

Lorraine: 'I know several couples who've split up, say the marriage has broken down. That way they get two lots of money. That's what it does to people.'

Tone: 'I was doing a few odd jobs for my uncle – cars. I'd rather do that than sit at home and rot. I was paid in a couple of packets of fags. Somebody must have seen him give them to me. I was sent for. "You've been working, and been paid in kind. It's a serious charge. If you get a job within eight weeks, we won't bring proceedings against you." It's not the first time. I'm always fiddling about with cars. I do it for my mates, for nothing. So when I go down to sign on, my hands are oily; they always are. They say, "Are you working?" "No." They get someone to follow me, I know it's them. In a Capri. They park at the end of the street. I knew what they were doing. I get into my overalls and start work on my next-door neighbour's car. They sit there maybe half an hour. Who's paying their wages to do that?

'The only thing that keeps you sane is trying to find ways to beat the system. My mate pays somebody £5 for an address, and they say he's having bed and breakfast there; and the Social pay £35 a week. He stays somewhere else for £10; and he's been getting £120 a fortnight. That means he's paying out £30 a fortnight, and that gives him £45 a week. They've changed the rules now, but he's been in the mental hospital because he tried to top himself, so he still gets away with it.

'A lot of people try to fiddle the electricity or gas. I've got a spare meter. I change the meter about three weeks before the reading is due; that means you can cut your bill by two-thirds. The thing is not to overdo it, not make it obvious. If you get a *nil* reading in the winter quarter, they'll be suspicious. People get greedy and push it too far. It's the stupid ones who get smart people like us into trouble.'

Chrissie: 'You used to be able to stop the disc going round with a magnet, but not now they've put plastic discs in.'

Tone: 'The electricity meters are outside now, all cased in. But if you know where to do it, you can drill a hole, put a wire in, and that will stop the meter; a very, very small hole.'

They discuss ways of getting things without paying for them.

'If you buy something through a club agency – say, a video – all you have to do is sign somebody else's name. They deliver the video, then when they send the bill, you ignore it. When they come round you just deny it. It's not your name, you never signed, how can you be liable to pay for it?'

Tone: 'We have a way of getting a music stack, a TV, whatever. A group of you – half a dozen, say – you pool all your money from your giro one week, go over to Coventry, buy a music stack, £250. Then you take the receipt, go over to Birmingham. There's a big hypermarket where the same electric goods store has a concession. You keep the assistants busy while your mate goes and lifts an identical music stack. He takes it to the check-out, you show them the receipt – same date, same price – and you're through. Then you sell both of them, a bit cheaper than the shop price, you can share out the money.

'I'm lucky. My missus works at Tesco's. She knows who the store detectives are, so you can always do a bit of extra shopping, like.'

Chrissie: 'Well, I had a bloke lodging with me. We weren't sleeping together. One Saturday morning, a knock comes at the door. "Mr

Holland?" "Who wants him?" I'm shitting hot bricks. "We've followed him. He has given the firm he's working for this address. You are Chrissie Travis?" "Yes." "Are you are on social security?" "True. Mr Holland does stay here. I don't take any money from him. He gets his own food, does his own cooking. He doesn't sleep with me. Do you want to go upstairs and inspect the beds?" The bastards said they did. And they went upstairs. And they raked about in the dirty washing. I said, "What's wrong, do you get off on doing things like this?"'

Tone: 'I got married twelve months ago. I claimed for Jen as my wife. When the Social Security came they said they didn't believe I was married. "How do you make that out?" "There's no wedding photos up." Then she got a part-time job in the supermarket. I got a letter. They're doing me for fraud.'

Chrissie: 'If you give an address on this estate, you can't get credit, you can't get insurance.'

Lorraine: 'I hate this estate. I wouldn't buy one of these houses in a fit. I know somebody who bought one, had it all tiled, spent £300. All the tiles fell off. The weatherboarding at the front is all warped. They've only been up five years. The wood is all rotten. I can't afford to go and see my parents. I've got to get a bus into town, 35p, then a bus out to their estate, another 35p. That's £1.40. If I take the kids it's £3. It's like going on bloody safari.'

Chrissie: 'I tried for a clothing grant. They say if you have a sudden gain or loss of weight, you're entitled to a grant. Well, I did, I put on a lot of weight. They wouldn't give me anything. I appealed, and they found in my favour. But still the Social wouldn't pay, even though the tribunal had found I was justified.'

Tone: 'I don't see why you can't get credit on Social. What could be more stable than your income, such as it is? Damn sight more reliable than jobs – especially some of these tin-pot jobs they get the youngsters on. Training. If the kids refused to do them, they'd have to pay real wages. The kids are being used to get wages down.'

Lorraine: 'The trouble with being on Social, all your money is spent in advance – rent, food, fuel. You have nothing left for luxuries, like clothes or furniture. If you have a smoke and a drink, Christ, it's the wages of sin.'

Paula

Paula is in her mid-thirties. She left school just before her sixteenth birthday and was married two weeks later. Her husband was a lorry driver, six years older than she was. 'I thought life began when you got married. For me, it was more like the end.' She spent long hours on her own. Sometimes, when he was driving across Europe, he would be away for a week. Paula had two children by the time she was eighteen. She felt tired and frustrated. She had a couple of casual affairs on the estate where she was living. Her husband received an anonymous letter that told him to watch his wife. One day he didn't go to work but waited for the boy-friend to call. There was a fight; afterwards he beat Paula up. Once this had happened, it seemed all his inhibitions were removed. Violence occurred more frequently. Afterwards, she says, he would make love to her, fiercely, even though she was often in pain. She left him and spent a few months with a friend. Her husband wept and promised that things would change. But it started again; so she took the children and came to the city.

She has brought them up on her own; a poor, pinched existence. She lived with a man some years older than herself. Her children were always afraid whenever they saw their mother playing with the boy-friend. 'Don't hit my mummy.' Paula took in a twenty-year-old girl who had been thrown out by her husband. Paula's boy-friend and this girl became lovers. At the same time Julie, Paula's daughter, was sexually assaulted. 'I went to the police. They knew who he was. They said there was insufficient evidence. They did nothing. He went scot-free. I said, "I'll keep watch on the bastard, I'll get even." They said, "You can't take the law into your own hands." I was ill over it, on tablets. I was drinking a lot.'

This was the state Paula was in one night when she and the girl lodging with her fell into conversation with a man they knew slightly. He was looking for someone to 'pay out' his wife, who had walked out on him after fourteen years of marriage. He had been getting his mates to drive their cars at her, give her a fright. But he wanted someone to give her a real scare.

Paula was full of anger at that time. It seemed easy to talk terms; there was a chronic shortage of money. At first they assumed it was just talk. But they saw the man again the following night. He was even more hardened against his wife. He wanted someone to make a 'basket case' of her. Paula and Jackie were offered £100 to give her a beating she would remember. They talked it over with their boy-friends. They agreed to help: the men were to be paid £30 each, the women £20.

A night was set aside for the 'mission', as they called it. They worked themselves up into a sense of conspiracy and excitement. They sat up late into the night, drinking vodka and planning. Suddenly, life offered them a feeling of having something to accomplish, instead, as Paula put it, 'of having to sit on your arse every day, waiting for a giro to come through the door'. They worked up a sense of injury and indignation against the woman they did not know. Paula had never been in trouble before. She is not hard – quite the reverse. In retrospect, she cannot understand what got into her. It became a sort of fantasy of a search-and-destroy mission, a just revenge.

They went to the house late one evening, knocked at the door. One of the woman's children tried to defend her, but she was badly beaten. She had to have several stitches, sustained a broken rib and a partial loss of hearing. When they had finished, they went to the pub. The wronged husband paid over the money. The sense of exhilaration soon fell away. They tried to justify it. They had paid her out all right. But what for? What had they done? Paula went home and wept bitterly. She cuddled the children; she had seen herself in the woman's fear. They were all arrested the next day.

You can feel how it happened. Paula is aware of the vacuum in which her life is lived, without anything to claim her energies and intelligence. The crime of Paula and her friends has a curious resonance: not only in the disgracing of humanity and the sacralizing of money (that is an old story); but in the way it illustrates how the repressed and unwanted energies of people that are not required by society so easily get turned against other people. 'I don't know what possessed me,' said Paula. What makes it all so poignant is that she cannot imagine any other redress for the injuries she has suffered than that blind expression of anger against people who are as unfortunate as she is.

They suffered agonies of remorse and shame. They turned against each other, blamed each other for initiating it. Paula got six months. She was shocked by prison. She had spent time close to a woman in a well-publicized murder case; and this woman had been badly disfigured by an attack inside the prison. Paula's story had been all over the local paper; her photograph had been published. When she came out of prison, she had to be rehoused because her life had been threatened, and she had received what she called 'a load of hate-mail'. Her children had been in care, fostered out in a town thirty miles away. Soon after being rehoused she was in a club one night, and somebody said, 'You know who she is, don't you?' The whole room froze and stared at her. She was soon recognized in the new neighbourhood. People knocked on her door in the middle of the night; there were anonymous letters. She says: 'Punishment doesn't finish when you've done your sentence. That's when the really hard stretch starts.'

Tony

Tony and Barbra have just moved into their house with Lisa, their two-year-old daughter, and Sam, who is from Tony's first marriage. Tony wanted this house, on the outer edge of the estate, because he intends to buy it eventually and sell it for a decent profit. He is a firm believer in what he calls 'playing the system'.

'It's dog eat dog in this world. It's a jungle. I never made it, but I'll play by the rules and get what I can out of it.' He has a sunburnt face, blond hair, white teeth and moustache; bursting with energy and vitality. He is avid and powerful. To learn that he is on invalidity benefit comes as a surprise. He says his first concern is with surviving; and in this society, that means money. Since invalidity benefit is higher than unemployment pay, he calls on a back injury from which he recovered some time ago. 'I'm due to go off invalidity. They examined me and said I was fit for work. But I shall appeal. They never even looked at my back. Compressed spine – lorry driver's complaint. I shall appeal, and I shall win.' Tony works, moonlighting; drives a heavy goods vehicle for firms that prefer not to employ people full time. It suits him not to pay tax or insurance. He will get £25 for a day's work, driving a thirty-two tonner.

It is easy to understand how work becomes casualized, how all the safeguards won by trade unions can be circumvented by collusion between workers and employers. The gain is immediate to people like Tony, but in the long term it is unlikely to help the next generation, who will inherit the effects of broken solidarity. The irony is that Tony says he is doing it all for his son.

'When you're working, legal and above-board, you work Monday, Tuesday and half Wednesday for the government; you don't start making anything for yourself till half-way through the week.

'What we ought to do in this country is boot out all the immigrants for a start. It wants somebody tough. Like Hitler. Human beings are basically tribal. Send the army into Toxteth, Brixton, Handsworth; shoot a few of them, that'd soon stop any trouble. I always say why bother with repatriation; I'd repatriate them all for 75p a time. That's all it'd cost. That's the price of a bullet. Repatriate them to the great spirit up in the sky, whatever it is they believe in. We'll turn them out in the end, it's gotta come. The British lion doesn't mind having its tail tweaked for just so long, but when it's had enough, it'll turn round and bit their fucking heads off. Old Amin, he was a bit loony, but he had the right idea. Kicked out all the Pakis; and what daft buggers took 'em in? We did.

'You might think I'm an ignorant sod. Not so. The resources of this earth will only stretch so far. The population of the world will double in twenty years' time. Our population is stable; but they breed at such a rate, there'll be famine, disease, Christ knows; the horsemen of the Apocalypse will look like a fucking gymkhana.'

The rhetoric, with its violent, aggressive *machismo*, can equally be read as a kind of despair at the de-skilling, the disemploying of male energy. If the poor know how to justify their responses it is because, not so long ago, they were the objects of the same ideology that they now turn on those poorer than themselves.

Tony was married at twenty, divorced while his three children were still under five. He looked after them for six months, and then they went into care. He says: 'I'm going to look after number one. I'll do anything for my wife and kiddie.' He looks down at the three-year-old, a beautiful child, playing with a spoon and fascinated by her inverted image in the concave metal scoop. Tony's eyes soften. 'You have to work the system. I got this carpet for £20. It's worth two hundred. The firm goes bust. I meet a bloke in the pub, and he'll let me have it cheap before the Official Receiver gets his hands on it; it just means I'm an unofficial receiver.' He grins.

'I did a job a couple of weeks ago, frozen chickens. I had to drive them up North. I discover there's a mistake, there's one bag of chickens extra, hundred and fifty of them. I thought, "Fair enough; 150 capons, not bad." When I get home, I go to the pub, say to the landlord, "Want a few capons? They're £7 in the shops. You can have them for a pound." He takes half a dozen; another guy in the pub takes four. I sell about fifty in the pub that night, then put the rest in my mate's freezer. When I get home, there's three fucking panda cars and police motor bikes waiting for me outside the house. One of the blokes who bought a chicken was CID. "You're selling stolen chickens." "They are not stolen." I showed him the invoice. They were surplus to the number on the sheet. As if I'd be so stupid. "Oh, that's different." "Do you want to buy a few?" I sell fifty to the coppers. Next time I'm booked for speeding, nothing comes of it.

'When times are prosperous and there's plenty of work, it's the skilled working class who are on top – all the decent, hard-working, respectable people. But when there's a slump, the best are knocked for six, they don't know what's hit them. They haven't learned the law of the jungle. The hard workers, the skilled blokes – they can't cope. That's when the villains and the survivors come into their own.'

He grins.

People and policies

Only a minority, and perhaps a small one, of unemployed people live like this, on the margin of legality; but they are among some of the most able and most vigorous, the young, intelligent, and energetic. It is not to be expected that such people will face the long empty hours without money with any sense of equanimity. There is something horribly imprisoning about 'being on benefit'. The poor-law Bastilles of the early industrial era have their counterpart in the constant reference that people make to 'Alcatraz' or 'Sing-Sing' when they speak of the poor estates where they live. Each day they come face to face with how little it seems that human beings can do without money. They are victims of a society that has permitted – indeed, made a virtue of encouraging – market transactions to encroach upon every conceivable aspect of our lives, and has then withheld the money essential for the consummation of such transactions. In this context, the only scope for human ingenuity seems to lie, not in making and mending, contriving and creating, making our own amusement and distractions, but simply in getting our hands on the money that alone will enlarge our freedoms. When the Right talks of the Welfare State as having sapped the moral fibre of the people, it is attributing a very real feeling of helplessness and dependency to a false cause. It is the invasive power of money that has impaired people's sense of autonomy, not an absence of fear about paying hospital bills or seeing their children want for basic sustenance.

Capable and energetic people cannot be expected simply to sit passively by and accept. This is one reason why so many of the poor channel their efforts into finding ways of increasing the meagre survival income of the state; not necessarily by 'ripping off' or stealing, but in the twilight zone of 'fiddling', getting a bit extra, a little something in hand.

The government makes a great parade of prosecuting people for defrauding the social security system. Whenever there is an announcement of a clamp-down on 'scroungers', it always wins headlines. The truth is that this is pure mummery. Indeed, the ingenious ways of surviving – for those who do not simply sit waiting for manna from heaven – are a useful safety-valve for the system. Stealing and cheating keep people out of worse (and possibly political) mischief. The snoopers and spies appear as a piece of theatre, a sop to those working for low wages, a device to scare off the respectable and obedient. The people who live by their wits, often off each other, are absolutely necessary to the system. If the crack-down were real, and all alternatives were blocked to the most resourceful among the poor, there would be trouble indeed. And this is directly related to the high moral tone of the law-and-order debate. Rising crime statistics, however embarrassing to a government that has vowed itself to reducing crime and to the relentless pursuit of criminals, have one great, unspoken advantage. They indicate the extent to which the poor fail to channel their energies into the struggle for political change. The actions of criminals do not carry any dangerous germ of political and social alternatives that might be seen as more generally desirable. It is this unavowed secret that makes it possible for a government to go on invoking law and order with increasing emphasis, even while the crime statistics continue to rise.

The fact that political alternatives have not been readily sought by the dispossessed can only strengthen the sense of security of the established order. That a party of Labour is unable to address itself with any conviction to those who have never worked, that most trade unions appear incapable of voicing the sense of exile and suffering of the poor, is a great comfort to those who preside over the current restructuring and disciplining of a working class within the context of a new international division of labour. When the poor take matters into their own hands they tend to do so on an individual basis, in a kind of parody of mainstream values. Their actions can all the more easily be interpreted as individual moral failings, and this offers a further alibi against any suspicion that their misery might be socially produced. It goes even further: the criminal poor, for the most part, turn in their despair upon each other. It is on the poor estates and in the run-down areas that most crimes are committed; and this furnishes the majority of the people with an agreeable sense of security. If the ghettos burn, and the ambulances and police-waggons bring out their sad cargo of mutilated humanity, this is experienced by most people only by means of the television screen and the newspapers. It is not difficult to raise ancient fears of the spectre of the mob, thus insulating even further the mainstream from the incomprehensible disorders of the poor. Rising crime, far from being a threat to a party of law and order, can become an inestimable ally, because the political issue it raises is the need for more coercion, more discipline.

This is how it comes about that there is an unspoken alliance between the high moral tone of official rhetoric, on the one hand, and the culture of surviving, on the other. The enterprise and initiative that take place in the forbidden zone are simply the price to be paid for more legitimate versions of these things, which are enshrined at the heart of, vaunted as the very *raison d'être* of, the society in which we live. Things are seldom what they seem, particularly in a culture that devotes so much of its energy to the manipulation of surfaces and images. If the rich and successful feel vindictive towards the poor, this may well be because the poor illuminate too starkly, not an opposition to their values, but too naked and eager an identification with them. The only question is, as one engaging petty crook said, 'Who is kidding who?'

3. Women seeking work

Claire Callender

This chapter explores the ways a group of women made redundant from a clothing factory look for jobs.[1] The reality of these women's experiences reflects neither the dominant ideas about job search and the unemployed nor the findings of 'malestream' research on job-seeking. This is because influential ideas about employment/unemployment are male dominated and inappropriate for understanding women's position in the labour market. It is argued that women's job-seeking strategies perpetuate their disadvantaged position in the labour market and reinforce dominant conceptions about 'women's work' and their labour market activities.

The chapter addresses a series of questions. What strategies do women use to look for jobs and why? What are their experiences of job search? How effective are these strategies for finding a job and what are their limitations? Are there hidden dimensions to women's searches that have consequences for their participation and location in the labour market?

In our work-orientated society, which condemns idleness, the task of actively seeking paid work is perceived to be an integral part of the experience of unemployment.[2] Indeed, searching for employment is part of the unemployed status; it is a part of the socially constructed identikit of the unemployed person. Not only are there social expectations that an unemployed person will be engaged in job search, but there is also a moral imperative. This is clearly exhibited in popular opinion, the media, and political ideology – especially in the rhetoric of the New Right. Sketching a caricature of the unemployed we see that if they do not hunt industriously and unremittingly for paid work (characterized by the advice of Norman Tebbit, erstwhile Secretary of State for Employment, to 'get on your bikes') then they may be deemed unworthy of respect, labelled as un-deserving, stigmatized as scroungers, and even considered not truly unemployed. The logical corollary of such attitudes is that the unemployed have only themselves to blame for their condition, for if they really wanted to find paid work they would actively engage themselves in job search. It should be evident that this model, which relies so heavily on personal pathology, ignores the considerable structural constraints affecting job acquisition. However, the insistence on active job search does reveal how the work ethic operates as a social value whose character is supposedly decisive for individual and national material and moral well-being.

Is this analysis applicable to women, especially to married women? Paid employment may be a moral imperative for men but questionable as a dynamic for women. This is not to imply that paid work is not a necessity or unimportant for women or, therefore, that they do not engage in job search. Rather the issue is the way prevailing ideas surrounding employment and unemployment are male dominated and thus inappropriate for understanding the position of women in the labour market (Callender 1985b).

The active job-search principle and the issues of the work ethic and work incentives, all of which are rooted in orthodox/neo-classical economic theory, feed into research and studies on job search. This research is in two groups. In the first group there are general studies about the unemployed (Hill *et al.* 1973, Daniel 1974 and 1981, North Tyneside CDP 1978, Marsden 1982, White 1983, Moylan, Millar, and Davies 1984) or about people made redundant (Wedderburn 1965, Martin and Fryer 1973), including discussions of job search. The second group of studies focuses primarily on the activities of job-seekers, employed and unemployed (Sheppard and Belitsky 1966, Rees and Shultz 1970, Reid 1972). Although not all these studies adopt the same view regarding the operation of the labour market, they take for granted notions about job search and the accepted male face of unemployment.

How appropriate is this research for women's experiences of job search and job acquisition? A large number of the studies exclude women and concentrate solely upon men's experiences of looking for paid work. The few studies that do incorporate women are often based on samples that are biased in particular ways: the studies are either gender blind or gender bound. They assume that women's experiences are the same as men's or that they can be explained solely in terms of the sexual division of labour and women's domestic role. These assumptions need to be questioned and empirically verified.

Some women's experiences of job search may be similar to men's. However, unemployment and the seeking of paid work can be understood only within the context of the labour market and how it operates. The demand and supply of men's and women's labour are not the same. Women exhibit distinctive characteristics within the labour market. Their experiences of and relation to waged labour are different from those of men. Women's domestic role and the dominant familial ideology are likely to have some effect on their job-search behaviour and on the securing of paid employment. Nevertheless, their experiences cannot be explained solely in terms of their family role, just as men's experiences cannot be understood solely in terms of their economic role. We have to examine the specificity and reality of women's experiences. The following analysis relies upon both my own empirical research on redundant women and recent studies of non-working women (Chaney 1981, Coyle 1984b, Cragg and Dawson 1984, Martin and Roberts 1984, Martin and Wallace 1984).[3]

Women, job search, and job acquisition

I examined the impact, on a group of married women, of redundancy through the partial closure of a clothing factory in one of the valleys in South Wales. The clothing factory, which opened in 1939, is part of a multinational company and was until recently the major employer of female labour in the area. The factory is located in a sub-region where both male and female unemployment rates are well above the national average. The redundancies, based on the 'last in, first out' principle, operated in stages from 1978 to 1981, reducing the work-force from more than 1,500 to 530 (123 men and 407 women). All the women interviewed had been made redundant involuntarily and had worked full-time in the factory at low-paid manual jobs on the shop floor, jobs that were classified as unskilled. The majority of the interviews took place between nine and twelve months after the women's redundancy.[4]

The redundant women's job-seeking activities, behaviour, and attitudes must be placed within a context. The most important factor governing these was the nature of the labour market, but other significant factors were the involuntary way in which these women entered the job market and the impact of their redundancy. 'The character of post-redundancy careers is a result of a complex interrelation between the assortativeness in the redundancy process and the type of demand for labour in the market' (Harris, Lee, and Morris 1985: 159). The designation of the redundants at the clothing factory was not random because certain types of women were 'selected out' by the redundancy process, and they were characterized by disadvantages, in human capital terms.

The women did try to resist the redundancies, but in a highly individualistic manner (Callender 1986). This resistance is indicative of another context for understanding redundant women's job-seeking behaviour, namely the commitment to continuing in paid employment. None of the women had had any intention of stopping waged work, and many of them had envisaged working at the clothing factory until retirement. When questioned, all the redundant women wanted to work again.

The women were very flexible regarding the conditions and type of paid work they were prepared to accept. Their pay expectations were dictated by their wage prior to redundancy, but many were willing to take, and indeed took, a reduction in their pay packet. Many studies on job search underplay the fact that demand in the labour market, in reality, is structured. They adopt an individualistic view of job acquisition and emphasize the supply side of the labur market, neglecting the demand side. However, these women had an astute appraisal of the state of the labour market and of the way demand structured their 'choices' and opportunities. They realized the meaninglessness of 'choice' when there were no or very few jobs to choose from and when they had limited opportunities to operationalize their 'choices'. Consequently, the vast majority of the women were prepared to accept any job. As one woman, Marlene, remarked:

> 'Anything, probably a factory job, or as I say I've got my name down at the hospitals for auxiliary nursing . . . but there is a two-year waiting-list there . . . or a job in a shop or whatever comes, if something comes. . . . I don't think I have any preferences . . . well, there is nothing, nothing much about. . . . I think people are clinging to their jobs.'

Some women tentatively expressed certain job preferences like doing factory work or working with people; several women said they did not want to do cleaning work, but they were aware of the lack of employment opportunities and of the need to be malleable in the existing economic climate. Other women suggested that some factors constrained their 'choice', such as the hours they were prepared to work and the distances they were willing to travel. These constraints arose out of financial concerns and practical considerations of their domestic responsibilities. However, none of the women with children and dependent relatives specifically mentioned these obligations as an issue or an actual constraint. Although their dual role had been problematic at times, they had organized and marshalled resources for coping with their paid and unpaid work. They made complex and elaborate child-care arrangements, for example. They did not view their family responsibilities as limiting or frustrating because they were an accepted part of their lives. Both caring for the family and paid work were an integral part of these women's lives. What is marked among them is the way the necessity of and commitment to paid employment overrode both their preferences and the constraints such as the location and hours of employment. Thus it is not surprising to find that the women identified the lack of suitable employment and the high levels of unemployment as the main factors restricting their job prospects.

The women's understanding of the notion 'looking for work' and their subjective definitions of their employment status were most significant factors affecting their job-search behaviour. All the women were asked, 'Are you looking for work or have you looked for work?' Interestingly, the majority denied that they were looking for work. But when offered a job they willingly accepted it; or if they heard of a vacancy they vigorously pursued it. Indeed, nearly half of the women who answered in the negative actually gained employment. This is because of the women's very distinct preconceptions as to what counted as looking for work. For most of these women actively seeking work implied direct applications to employers. So the remark by Diana that 'I'm just waiting for the Job-centre. . . . No, I haven't looked for a job . . . I look in the newspaper every week. . . . I do tell people if they hear of a job to let me know' is not a contradiction but a clear statement of the manner in which active job search was pursued and perceived. These women's responses to this question are, therefore, an artefact of the question asked. This has methodological implications for other studies that ask the same question but do not recognize that for some respondents the term 'looking for work' may have a very specific meaning that may be different from the analyst's interpretation of it.

Furthermore, such responses are connected to the women's self-perceptions of their employment status. Many redundant women did not consider themselves as unemployed, and this self-perception had a direct impact on their job-search strategies. Inevitably, it is associated with the blurring of the boundaries for women between employment and economic inactivity, and between unemployment and economic activity, which renders their classification within the labour market problematic (Callender 1985b). This resistance to being labelled unemployed deserves greater attention because the 'malestream' literature assumes that the job-seeker perceives her/himself as unemployed, and therefore measures the extent and seriousness of job-search activities by the intensity and variety of strategies used. The non-identification is supported by the work of Martin and Roberts (1984) and Cragg and Dawson (1984). The former found that many non-working women did not identify with the label 'unemployed' and did not consider themselves thus because they saw working in the home as a full-time job, as *work* in its own right. As Chaney suggests, 'few people thought of themselves as having been actively searching because, as housewives, they did not see themselves as out of work' (Chaney 1981: 35).

The problems and contradictions of these self-perceptions are summed up by one of the women in my study: 'Housewife, that's what I'm doing. . . . Unemployed in a way, yet in another way housework is work, isn't it? It's work really, but to some it's not work. . . . An unemployed housewife, that's me.' Other women associated being unemployed with the official dimensions of unemployment, namely claiming benefit or registering for paid work. A number rejected the label because of the stigma attached to it; they preferred the status of housewife/mother. Moreover, perceiving oneself as a housewife was a way of reconciling the 'pains' of unemployment and the sense of worthlessness. Certain women felt that the label of unemployment was appropriate only for single people or men, while others thought of themselves as retired because they were unlikely to find another job. As Martin and Roberts suggest, 'the terms "unemployment" and "employment" have somewhat different associations and meanings for many women from those they have for men' (Martin and Roberts 1984: 84).

Many women became discouraged from looking for paid work because of the poor state of the economy. As Cragg and Dawson observed:

'There are signs also that women were more prone to let their perceptions of the labour market affect perceptions of their own employment status: the less buoyant the market appears, the weaker the claim they make upon it – irrespective of need.'

(Cragg and Dawson 1984: 70)

Some women did not look for work and did not consider themselves as unemployed because they believed that their claims to a job were not as great as those of men, young people, or some women who had greater financial need. Their attitudes were encapsulated in the queueing principle (Martin and Wallace 1984), namely that in times of high unemployment certain social groups (men and young people) have greater claims to paid employment. The identification of men as primary bread-winners had a direct effect on the women's perceptions of the importance of their own employment needs (Cragg and Dawson 1984: 73). The women's lack of belief in their legitimate right to paid employment was also a reflection of the fact that paid work was not a moral imperative for them, unlike for men. The work ethic, which is primarily directed at men and exerts pressures upon them to search for work, produces dilemmas and contradictions, especially for married women, who are seen by some to have a legitimate role in the home rather than in the labour force. Others felt their age was 'against them' in obtaining paid work (Walker, Noble, and Westergaard 1985) or that they had inadequate skills and qualifications.

So some women defined themselves out of the labour market because they felt that they were unlikely to get paid work, for whatever reasons, or because they believed that they had no rights to waged work. Once again it must be emphasized that even these women took advantage of any opportunity to secure employment.

Job-search strategies

The three main job-search strategies used by the redundant women – direct applications to employers, Jobcentres, and informal social networks – although analytically separate, must be seen together and understood as part of a process of job search. Social networks proved the most effective for gaining employment.

Direct applications to employers

According to the provisions of the redundancy payments legislation (Department of Employment 1984), workers are eligible for paid time off to look for waged work. About half the women took advantage of this and started looking for new employment before they had finished working in the clothing factory. At this stage, and immediately after the re-dundancies, the most common strategy was to call upon employers in person and particularly to visit local factories on the off chance of a job opening. However, no woman actually obtained a job in this manner. Debra sums it up:

'Tried about twenty places. . . . We walked the valleys, me and my mother, we went together. There's three factories over at 'Pandy . . . as you're walking up into Pen-y-Craig there's more. There are about five or six there. . . . So your name is down everywhere but you never hear from them. . . . "Sorry, no jobs going." That's all you got. "Sorry, no jobs." So you would have to say, "Can I put my name down just in case?" You'd fill in an application form and you never hear.'

Some women tried to rationalize this thankless task by going only to factories where they had heard of definite vacancies. However, their efforts were equally fruitless.

The popularity of this strategy is related to five factors. Firstly, in comparison to other approaches – such as newspaper vacancy advertise-ments, the employment service, or informal social networks – it was one of the most accessible and readily available. The only resources required were time, energy, and some knowledge of the local labour market. Secondly, it was one of the least bureaucratic of all strategies, which may have particularly appealed to women who felt uncomfortable or lacked confidence in negotiating officialdom and rigid rules. Thirdly, the choice of face-to-face personal contact may have been indicative of the way women generally prefer to interact. Fourthly, the women could assess the workplace by their visit and ensure that certain domestic constraints were not broken. Fifthly, direct application to employers was one way the women could take control and responsibility for their situation. It was a direct action based upon their individual effort and their own initiative. The attractiveness of this self-reliance is shaped by dominant notions of job search, and is also reflected in research on job search – that the individual should be responsible for obtaining her new employment. As Cragg and Dawson similarly noted in their study:

> 'There was widespread predilection for private, personal initiatives through the small ads in papers or by direct approach. Using these methods tended to be perceived as "finding *yourself* a job", whereas using the Jobcentre was less flatteringly perceived as "*them* finding *you* a job".'
>
> (Cragg and Dawson 1984: 44)

This strategy was grounded in a long tradition of how people obtained paid work and it fitted into the women's understanding of the term 'looking for work'.

The immediacy of results from direct applications to employers had both advantages and disadvantages. It was an exhausting, costly, painful, and frustrating experience, as Marlene, and then Joan, explained:

> 'You can sort of tell by the look on the Personnel's faces that they haven't got anything for you. . . . When they ask how long you've been working and were you made redundant . . . they've got that sort of look . . . "Oh gosh, she's no good then, she was made redundant." They make you feel as if you're begging for it, you're begging for a job.'

> 'Oh God, another day wasted again . . . but it's a queer thing to explain really how you feel when you need a job and you can't get one, frustrating it is. You're looking, you're trying, and you're not getting anywhere. . . . It was as if you were like on your knees like – "Give me a job."'

As with women in Cragg and Dawson's study, this time- and energy-consuming method was used decreasingly and more selectively as the duration of job-seeking increased because of its costs and the feelings of hopelessness and futility it engendered. As Joan continued to explain: 'I didn't bother after that. . . . The way things were going, we were hearing about redundancies, this factory in the balance. . . . So I thought it's idiotic to go looking at places like that for a job when the work-force that were already there were insecure.'

Registering for work and Jobcentres

Once the women were unemployed the most frequently used channel was the Jobcentre. The expansion of the state employment services in the 1970s was evidence of the importance of the notion of active job search. Jobcentres were opened to encourage the unemployed's job-seeking behaviour and to capture more of the job market's vacancies (MSC 1978, 1982). The reshaping of the employment services did lead to an overall increase in the use of the service by women (Daniel 1981). The separation of the functions of registration for unemployment benefit and payment of benefit from those of job counselling and job placement, together with attractive and accessible office premises, benefited women. Women are consequently likely to be one of the groups hardest hit by the current cuts in the employment service.

A little less than half of the women were eligible for unemployment benefit (Callender 1987), and hence they automatically registered for work at the Jobcentre.[5] Several women who received no social security benefits also registered because they saw it as a possible avenue for obtaining a job. Young women were more likely to register than older women, primarily because of their social security eligibility. Unlike with the women in Martin and Roberts' (1984) study, there seemed to be no correlation between registration for work and whether the women wanted full- or part-time employment.

Some women rejected the idea of registration: they desired to be self-sufficient and free from official agencies; while others preferred alternative methods of job search. Many felt a certain nervousness and uneasiness about registering at Jobcentres. For certain women the centres represented officialdom and bureaucracy. Indeed, Jobcentres were part of the state machinery for policing the unemployed and were one way in which the unemployed were socially controlled (DE/DHSS 1981, Hill 1981). Some women preferred to avoid contact with what they considered an alienating agent of the state's authority. This dislike and suspicion were compounded by their confusion over the respective roles and functions of the Department of Employment, the Department of Health and Social Security, the Manpower Services Commission, the 'dole', employment benefit offices, employment offices, and Jobcentres. Not surprisingly, there was a widespread uncertainty about what registration entailed, if they were eligible to register, and whether it was relevant to their needs – as Cragg and Dawson (1984) also discovered. Morphy, who had managed to get new employment, remarked: 'No, I never went to the Jobcentre at all. I thought because I wasn't paying stamp I didn't think I could go to the dole to look for work. That's what I thought.'

Some women did not perceive themselves as unemployed and so felt it not legitimate to register as unemployed. Others either did not want the label of 'unemployed' associated with Jobcentres or did not want confirmation of their unemployed status. There was supportive evidence that 'for some women registering for employment is equated with seriously looking for work and *being unemployed*' (Martin and Roberts 1984: 162, emphasis added). From this the superficiality of the argument that women's non-registration can be understood solely in terms of their eligibility for social security benefits is clear.

Inevitably these factors affected not only the women's registration at Jobcentres but also their general use of the official employment services. So, as with the redundant women in Coyle's study, the women's use of Jobcentres was related to the propensity to register. However, as Cragg and Dawson have also pointed out, there was no significant correlation between registration and success in finding employment. Nor was there evidence to suggest that the use of Jobcentres as opposed to other methods indicated a greater seriousness about job-seeking (Cragg and Dawson 1984: 43).

Although a large number of redundant women did visit the Jobcentre they tended to use it pragmatically and selectively. Few women went regularly to the Jobcentre or made special journeys (which was costly) solely to look at the jobs. They called in when they attended the nearby unemployment benefit office, when they heard of potential job openings, and when they had been offered a job interview directly through the Jobcentre. This behaviour was the result of their perceptions of the Jobcentres' effectiveness. These patterns of usage should not therefore be seen as an indicator of the women's commitment or motivation to finding new employment, as the orthodox literature on job search would lead us to believe. This literature assumes a direct relationship between achievement motivation, job-search behaviour, and actual job acquisition (Sheppard and Belitsky 1966). Rather, their behaviour was a reasoned response to their situation and can be explained.

First, the Jobcentres had adopted a policy of contacting the women directly if a suitable job came up, once they had registered. Secondly, the women, like many unemployed, recognized that Jobcentres were limited in the help they could offer because of the sheer lack of vacancies. As Anita observed, 'if there's nothing about, there's nothing they can do or say'. Debra remarked cynically, 'Oh, the Jobcentre! With the big orange thing outside and six jobs inside on a big notice-board!' Many of the women felt that the Jobcentre did not cater for them. The jobs displayed were unsuitable or inappropriate; they required skills, experience, and qualifications that the women did not possess; they were in the wrong location; or they were considered 'men's jobs'. The women, again like many unemployed (Daniel 1981, Hill 1983), found the Jobcentres' administration inefficient and unreliable. They sent too many people for interviews for the same job, or the women were sent on interviews for jobs that had already been filled. The sparseness of jobs and the nature of the jobs available reinforce the arguments about the women's lack of job choice and the way the demand for labour was structured.

Thirdly, several women expressed ambivalent attitudes towards the Jobcentre staff, who were at times unsympathetic. Others also believed that preferential treatment was given to those people in receipt of benefit and to male job-seekers. Linda commented:

> 'I think unless you claim benefit you find more jobs on your own than you do at the Jobcentre. They help mostly the youngsters, the ones that are single, the ones that have signed on, more than the others. . . . Mind you, if the work is slack, the men should have it before the women, especially if they got families. They're the bread-winners if they got children.'

The attitudes reported of the Jobcentre staff are not surprising, since greater importance is attached to male than to female unemployment (Callender 1985b). Unemployed men are considered more of a problem and more worthy of attention, and such dominant ideas are likely to influence the behaviour of Jobcentre staff. Although there is little or no research that specifically examines their attitudes to their clients, studies on unemployment benefit office staff suggest that they, like all other groups in society, are influenced by dominant ideas and values regarding claimants and the unemployed (Stevenson 1973). However, Daniel (1981) has shown that people in areas of high unemployment receive less help from staff in comparison to those in areas of low-level unemployment.

The women's perceptions of the Jobcentres help explain certain women's use of them. For some, going to the Jobcentre was a way of legitimizing their job search and unemployment status, and a means of expressing their desire to regain paid work. Linda's remark, by contrast, suggests that other women questioned the legitimacy of their unemployment status and doubted whether they were in fact unemployed. Their right to paid employment was questionable to them, and they clung to the queueing principle. It was clear to a number of women that if the Jobcentres were unable to help these 'primary', 'deserving' job-seekers, then they were unlikely to help women with more tenuous claims on paid employment. Brenda sums it up:

> 'I haven't been at all to the Jobcentre. I would like a job but I haven't been. Listening to people saying that there's no work available I thought it's pointless going down there. There is no work about, only for youngsters, nothing for my age group. But I don't think there's

anything to offer even them down the Jobcentre anyway. My oldest daughter has been out for months upon months . . . and she's got qualifications which I haven't got. A factory floor I worked on, but she's got a good head on her.'

Some women were just waiting and hoping that they eventually would be contacted by the Jobcentre. This demoralizing process made them passive, but they felt powerless to do anything else:

'It seems silly to me. You keep going to the Jobcentre and you think, "Oh, perhaps today I'm going to be lucky." But then you go and there is nothing. That's when I start feeling, "Oh well, what's the point of going there when you know there's not going to be anything there?" '

Just under half of all the women who had used the Jobcentre had at least one job interview through the service. A small minority of women gained jobs with the same employer but left after a few days because they complained of exploitative working conditions.

Unlike the women in the studies by Cragg and Dawson (1984), Martin and Wallace (1984), and Martin and Roberts (1984), the women in my study did not rely on newspaper advertisements as a major source of job information. This is probably because there was only one local weekly newspaper, which did not carry many job advertisements, while the jobs advertised in the regional newspapers were unsuitable because of their location. The major other channel for finding employment was informal social networks, to which we now turn.

Social networks

Social networks, such as family and friends, proved the most effective method of job acquisition in this as in other studies on the unemployed (Rees and Shultz 1970, Mackay *et al.* 1971, White 1983, Coyle 1984a and 1984b, Cragg and Dawson 1984, Martin and Roberts 1984, Martin and Wallace 1984, Moylan, Millar, and Davies 1984). However, it has been suggested that strong personal-network ties are more necessary to women than to men as a basis for claiming support, given their inferior quality of existence and conditions. Others have observed that women's networks are important as a means of contesting male power. Women's investment in the family can be viewed either as a register of subordination or as a form of collective insurance (Grieco and Whipp 1984).

Some commentators suggest that informal social networks are the most important form of recruitment, which has significant implications for the structuring of employment opportunities and job-search behaviour (Jenkins 1984). There is certainly evidence to suggest the increasing use by employers of informal networks and internal labour markets as mechanisms for recruitment and the allocation of labour in the present recession, although it is beyond the bounds of this chapter to discuss employers' recruitment channels (Jenkins *et al.* 1983, MSC 1984, Beardsworth *et al.* 1985, Curran 1985). With plentiful supplies of labour, particularly at the unskilled and routine non-manual levels, employers are often able to gain enough applicants without the need to advertise.

Despite this increasing use of informal networks, the standard literature on job search has tended to gloss over or ignore the significance of informal networks, partly because their effectiveness challenges orthodox labour economic theories. These theories stress active job search and assume that the most rational strategy is a systematic exploration of all the opportunities on the demand side of the labour market. Consequently, formal channels for obtaining employment such as employment services are considered more efficient than for example informal networks, which are by their nature restrictive (Addison and Siebert 1979).

The nature of women's networks

The role of the family in labour-market participation and access to employment has been well documented (Bott 1957, Young and Wilmott 1957, Salaman 1974); but as Whipp and Grieco (1983) have shown, these analyses have limitations for gender relations. According to Whipp (n.d.) and Grieco and Whipp (1984), women were able through familial ties to assert themselves and assist each other in the workplace, determining precise features of the organization of work; they could act as employment brokers and recruitment channels, provide guarantees as to the performance of the applicant (Chaney 1981), and play an important part 'in the search for employment and in its counterpart, the search for labour' (Whipp and Grieco 1983: 20). Particularly beneficial to women were the ties between women as opposed to those that link women to men.

Informal ties were particularly important for the redundant women in this study because of the kin-centredness that was especially strong in South Wales (Lee 1985). For the majority, social networks were family-based and located within their community, and this had a direct impact on employment opportunities. Not only did female kin aid job acquisition, but they were also relied upon for domestic help and child care when the redundants were in paid work. The women were accustomed to mobilizing their informal networks. The vast majority of them had secured their original job at the clothing factory in this way.

The character of these informal networks, in particular their spread and location, was essential to women's labour-market experiences. As research on male redundant steelworkers in South Wales has demonstrated, the extensiveness of the steelworkers' networks dictated the patterns of post-redundancy labour-market experience. Social networks influenced not only whether the redundants found new work but also the nature and type of that employment (Morris 1983).

> 'The character of the redundants' social networks . . . would appear to be both an historical outcome and a contemporary determinant of labour-market position. The manifold of relations in which the household is embedded not only determines the effect of post-redundancy labour-market career on the household. It is itself a determinant of the character of that career.'
>
> (Harris, Lee, and Morris 1985: 161–2)

According to Granovetter (1973), job information is more widely diffused where the links between individuals are not close. Where highly connected networks exist the same information is likely to be available to all. Granovetter attributes an important role in the informal provision of job information to what he refers to as the 'strength of weak ties' – ties measured in terms of a combination of time, emotional intensity, intimacy, and reciprocal services (Granovetter 1973). Weak ties are more significant than strong ties for job acquisition.

The nature and quality of women's social networks, in contrast to men's, need scrutiny. We should not allow the effectiveness of women's social networks in helping them to get work to overshadow the limitations and disadvantages of those female networks as a source of employment.

The women's social networks were characterized by strong ties. They were local, and this proximity was essential for the character of the ties and the job-search outcome. All of the redundant women were born and bred in the area, as were their families. Together with the relatively static nature of the local community, the women's social networks were stable but geographically limited. The women had much more frequent contact with their kin than with friends and neighbours. The focus of their lives was home and the family, and most socializing was concentrated within their homes or the homes of their female kin with other women and children. Unemployment just exacerbated these existing conditions. Once unemployed, the redundant women rarely met or visited their ex-workmates from the clothing factory, irrespective of whether or not the workmates were still employed in the factory. With the financial constraints imposed by unemployment, one of these women's first economies was a reduction in their social life and going out to pubs and clubs. By contrast their husbands' social life was less restricted by the onset of their wives' unemployment. This severe reduction in social relations and contact led to isolation and loneliness (Martin and Wallace

1984) and inhibited the development of weak ties. These restrictions in social horizons also partly contributed to an increased reliance on female kin, the relationships being characterized by active and strong moral ties. Thus, for the majority of redundant women, their constricted social networks were primarily female-centred.

The women's informal networks are related, firstly, to the privatized nature of women's working lives and the strong and restrictive boundaries that existed, particularly for women, between home and work (Purcell 1982); and, secondly, to the discontinuity of women's employment patterns. Although the domains of the family and paid work are linked (Siltanen and Stanworth 1984), there appeared to exist divisions between the public and private spheres. So even when in paid employment the women rarely saw their workmates outside the factory gate. Going out with the 'girls' was a special occasion and infrequent. With the pressures of their dual role they had little time to socialize with neighbours, and some had lost contact with friends as a direct result of being engaged in full-time paid work. Formal socializing was often crowded out of their lives. The women's lives tended to be compartmentalized, and their work and social networks did not overlap. The women relied on female kin rather than on workmates or men for their emotional support, within the confines of the private, domestic sphere.

Husbands and wives had separate lives and separate social and work networks. Their lives exhibited strong sexual segregation, which is very characteristic of close-knit social networks (Bott 1957, Campbell 1984). However, many men's work and social networks tended to overlap (Harris, Lee, and Morris 1985). They, unlike the women, had access to the public realm of clubs and pubs, the institutions that served as a focus for their social interaction (see also Bostyn and Wight, Chapter 8, this volume) and as the base upon which men's networks were founded (Lee, Morris, and Harris 1983). This is not to suggest that men's access to public networks necessarily led to an advantaged labour-market position (Morris 1983) but it widened the scope of their networks compared to those of women.

Women's networks were further affected by their discontinuous employment patterns, which were shaped by the sexual division of labour in the home and workplace, and by the labour market. The women had not experienced long stable employment within which to nurture wide and solid work networks. Their work networks were more limited – unlike, for example, those of many redundant steelmen in the Port Talbot study (Morris 1983, Harris, Lee, and Morris 1985). Whether employed or unemployed, women's informal networks were quantitatively and qualitatively different from men's and not as effective for getting a job.

The use of networks

There were two main ways the women gained from their informal networks, one moral and the other technical (Lee, Morris, and Harris 1983). The moral aspect was when someone was willing to exert influence with an employer on behalf of the job-seeker. The practice of 'speaking for' a relative is a well-engrained feature both of traditional working-class communities (Young and Wilmott 1957, Chaney 1981, Lee, Morris, and Harris 1983) and among some ethnic groups (Brooks and Singh 1979). Kin and close ties were more likely to 'put in a good word' than more distant acquaintances. It gave a competitive advantage to kin over other applicants while at the same time being used to discharge a moral obligation and social duty (Lee 1985). Karen's experience of how she gained her temporary job through her mother is indicative: 'My mother . . . had just got a job and she said, "Give me a couple of weeks and I'll get you in." So she'd been there a couple of months, then she asked about me, and of course I started work there.'

The technical feature of informal ties highlights an information channel with privileged access, as Deanne's experience demonstrates:

'My friend and I were just talking one day, well, when Prince Charles was getting married and she said, "They are starting them (new workers) like tenpenny pieces over with us, there's about twenty to thirty started." "Oh!" I said. "Bring us a form home." "Why?" she said. "Do you want a job?" "I wouldn't mind. I'll try, as long as I haven't got to go out hunting I wouldn't mind." . . . She brought the form for me. . . . I filled it in . . . and the next thing I know . . . I had an interview . . . and then a letter . . . to say I could start . . . It was knowing someone working there that could get a form because there's a lot of people that have phoned up for forms but they were not sent forms.'

Deanne's experiences show that people gain information about jobs when they are not 'searching'. Chaney (1981), examining women who had returned to work, shows how information about jobs was passed on in general conversation and that rarely was the initiative taken in asking about paid work. Granovetter has observed:

'Job information is deeply imbedded in social structural processes in a way that makes it difficult to assert that workers act as if they were conducting rational search. . . . Information . . . may often be acquired as a by-product of other activities. A prototype of such a situation is hearing about a new job at a party or in a tavern.'

(Granovetter 1981: 23–4)

Deanne's job demonstrates that people do obtain jobs without actively searching, unlike the claims of the literature. The mobilization of networks is a different activity, often engaged in once the formal and 'active' strategies have been abandoned. Although the use of informal networks looks inactive within officialdom, and also in economic terms, in reality it can be highly productive and efficient.

These findings are supported in other studies of women. Coyle observed that redundant women, 'whilst apparently doing nothing . . . had a very comprehensive knowledge of the local labour market, and jobs came *to* them on the local grapevines' (Coyle 1984b: 47). Martin and Roberts highlight a further point: 'Not all women who get a job look for it; some are offered a job without looking. This is more likely to happen to women wanting part-time work and is quite an important way in which women re-enter the labour market' (Martin and Roberts 1984: 167). Granovetter (1974) also showed how the best jobs people procured were those offered to them when they were employed and neither actively seeking work nor in the job market. White, when discussing long-term unemployed men and women, demonstrated how some unemployed 'were . . . presented with a job without making any prior applications' (White 1983: 104).

Why women use networks

Four main factors explain the popularity of informal social networks. Firstly, networks have advantages similar to direct applications to employers in that both are informal. There was little bureaucracy involved and there were no demands to fill in application forms or attend interviews. Indeed, when the women were recommended or offered a job such procedures were at times absent or an untaxing formality, for applicant and employer. Secondly, the mobilization of networks was relatively easy, did not demand a great deal of time, energy, or money, and could be used in a highly efficient but casual manner. Thirdly, informal networks were attractive because, in the case of an employee referral, the applicant could gain a range of 'inside' information about the workplace from the employee, information that would be unobtainable through formal sources or a job interview: for example, details of what it was like working for that particular employer, the kind of work, and more nebulous aspects like the workplace's atmosphere and friendliness – qualities that are traditionally especially important to women workers (Hunt 1968). In addition, if the woman gets the job, then she has a ready-made friend within the workplace who can help her integrate into that setting. Fourthly, as Chaney (1981) also has recorded, women's network contacts were seen as reliable sources of job information because they understood the problems associated with women's domestic responsibilities and their dual role.

The women who got jobs

All the women who gained new jobs did so either directly or indirectly through the use of informal social networks, including women who were offered jobs directly by their ex-employer at the clothing factory. The exception was the small minority who gained a job via the Jobcentre.

There was little to distinguish, on socio-economic criteria, between those women who were successful in gaining waged work and those who were unsuccessful. Given the strategy, the level and intensity of the women's job search had little relevance to the eventual outcome, again contradicting a major assumption of the job-search literature. Furthermore, there was no association between the apparent need for employment (as gauged by financial circumstances) and levels of activity and acquisition.

What determined whether or not a woman secured employment was the operation of her informal networks in the context of the overall demand for labour. According to Granovetter's thesis and his emphasis on 'the strength of weak ties', the redundant women's networks were of limited value because the ties were close and strong, and the networks were not extensive. However, Lee's (1985) work suggests that, contrary to Granovetter, what was most important for the re-employment of the Port Talbot steelworkers was the extent to which influence was exerted by the individual's contact. Yet these authors' arguments presuppose that the contacts are in employment, and both of their studies are gender blind. The women in my study were less likely to have networks connected with paid employment because they were female centred (Chaney 1981). Many of the women's contacts were not in paid work either because they were in full-time domestic and 'mothering' work or because they too were redundant/unemployed. Together with their social isolation, these women were cut off from the social networks of the employed and as a result did not have the same knowledge of vacancies or even access to that information. As Pahl and Wallace have shown, 'Employment tends to generate further employment; unemployment tends to generate further unemployment' (Pahl and Wallace 1985: 202).

Some contacts proved fruitless as an information channel because their jobs were so insecure: 'I do ask my friends, but they're in a bad way. . . . They're hanging by their skins in the factories . . . don't know if they're working from one day to the next.' The women's employed contacts were confined to a small number of occupations and to low-paid, unskilled work which was often temporary. The type and range of job information available to them through their contacts were correspondingly restricted.

The women had little opportunity to hear of alternative employment openings and were trapped into 'women's work'. The redundant women gained similar jobs to those of their contacts, which ensured the perpetuation of women doing 'women's work'.

Type of employment found

What kind of job did these redundant women find? There was sufficient diversity from the women's original preferences to show the women's flexibility in the employment they were prepared to accept. The type of job the women gained was predictably 'women's work'. About a third of the new jobs were in the service sector, and a considerable number of women experienced a downgrading of skill. All the jobs were unstable, temporary, and low paid. For example, Morphy got a job as a cleaner in an old people's home working shifts after the caretaker, a friend of hers, rushed up to her house telling her that additional replacement staff were urgently needed. Joan got a job serving at a local supermarket through a friend who worked there as a cashier, while Karen, after being recommended by her mother, was temporarily employed making Christmas decorations to meet the seasonal demand. Jill joined her mother and sister working at a car parts manufacturer for two and a half weeks but had to travel for an hour and a half and do night shifts. Of those women who had completed their spell of employment in their new jobs, many of them were hoping to be recalled to these temporary jobs. The women experienced recurrent unemployment and employment. Contrary to the research on this topic, job search was not some transient state prior to securing (permanent) employment but an ongoing process that was integrated into the women's daily lives. The nature and conditions of the new employment acquired echo Coyle's (1984a, 1984b) and Martin and Wallace's (1984) findings on redundant women. Together these findings point towards a trend in the 'casualization' of women in the labour market and the disenfranchisement of women's rights at work (Callender 1985a), resulting from changes in the industrial and occupational structure and a restructuring of capital.

Summary and conclusion

Through exploring women's activities, dominant ideas about job search and the unemployed are challenged. Firstly, even if the unemployed do not actively look for work it cannot be assumed that they do not want employment. Secondly, 'active' job search, as defined by social and economic research, will not necessarily lead to employment. The most effective strategy – the use of informal social networks – is different from that prescribed in the literature. Thirdly, the level and the intensity of such activity are neither indicative of the depth of interest in getting another job nor a gauge of perseverance. Fourthly, it cannot be assumed that those most committed to new work will hunt the hardest, or that those most motivated seek most actively and succeed in gaining paid work. Fifthly, getting a job is not the sole responsibility of the individual, an important qualification to the individualistic perspective in the literature. Those women who succeeded were highly reliant upon other people through their social networks for information about jobs and for recommendations. And the mobilization of informal social networks highlights the social processes and dynamics associated with recruitment and selection, issues that are ignored when job acquisition is understood primarily in economic terms. In reality the unemployed have limited 'choices' over jobs because of the way demand is structured. The nature of recruitment and strategies open to the unemployed are similarly restricted and limit employment opportunities.

The redundant women's ways of seeking jobs were derived from their subjective definitions of their employment status, which were in turn governed by the state of the economy and by male-dominated concepts of employment/unemployment. Getting a job was for these redundant women determined by their informal social networks, which were a product of the privatized nature of women's working lives, of the restrictive boundaries between home and paid work, and of the discontinuity of women's employment patterns. Their networks were closed, restricted, home centred, and female centred. And these social networks determined the type of jobs the women obtained and structured their employment opportunities. So, if they got jobs, the redundant women gained similar jobs to their female contacts, typically 'women's work'.

If one views informal networks and the grape-vine, or 'word-of-mouth' recruitment, as extending the scope of the internal labour market outside the formal boundaries of the organization (Jenkins 1985: 175), then the problems associated with the networks become even more apparent. The limitations of internal labour markets for women's employment opportunities, with their restricted 'ports' of entry, are well documented (Wilkinson 1981). The labour-market structures serve to limit opportunities presented to different groups of workers through segmentation. The labour market and the inequalities between men and women in that structure mean that men are likely to have better access to job information than women. The availability of information is often restricted and, due to vertical segregation, such workers are likely to be men.

This recruitment practice and strategy are discriminatory. The informal processes in this job search, which often go unrecorded, both allow scope for discrimination in recruitment and make it less visible, rendering intervention through the sex discrimination legislation ineffective. Despite this lack of visibility, there is evidence that this form of job acquisition and recruitment operates to the detriment of potential female applicants (Collinson and Knights 1985, Curran 1985).

One of the consequences of the recession has been to diminish managerial interest in introducing and pursuing equal opportunities policies. We can detect a rise in the use of potentially discriminatory recruitment policies and job-acquisition strategies at the same time as a reduction in the commitment to equal opportunity. All workers may use informal social networks, although this strategy clearly does not give all workers access to similar jobs. Women's disadvantage in the labour market is compounded by jobs found through informal social networks. The sexual division of labour is perpetuated, and the secondariness of women's labour-market position is reinforced by the use of these networks. Ultimately this, in turn, fortifies dominant conceptions of women's work and the durability of a male-dominated notion of employment and work. These notions undoubtedly affect and shape our perception of women's employment, unemployment, and job search, and permeate numerous aspects of social policy.

Notes

1. My thanks to my informal networks who read the first draft of this chapter, in particular Miriam David and Ray Lee.
2. The term 'work' is used for paid work. However, it is recognized that this use is inadequate when describing women's work activities.
3. The findings from these studies are not completely comparable because the women entered the labour market in different ways. Coyle's and Martin and Wallace's study were based on redundant women; Chaney examined only women returners; while Martin and Roberts adopted a broader definition of non-working. Women wanting a job cannot therefore be defined by one category. The comparisons between the author's findings and these studies must be considered with this caveat in mind.
4. The empirical work entailed interviewing in depth a small group of women who had been made redundant in December 1980 or May 1981. The women were picked randomly from a list of names supplied by the company. They were, or had been, married and were aged between 20 and 59. All the interviews were tape-recorded and transcribed, so the women are quoted verbatim.
5. At the time the fieldwork was conducted and until the 1982 Social Security and Housing Benefit Act, it was compulsory for all those claiming unemployment benefit to register for work at a Jobcentre. Registration is now voluntary.

References

Addison, J. and Siebert, W. (1979) *The Market for Labor: An Analytical Treatment.* California: Goodyear Publishing.

Beardsworth, A., Bryman, A., Ford, J., and Keil, T. (1985) Employers and Recruitment: Explorations in Labour Demand. *International Journal of Social Economics* 11: 2. Bradford: MCB University Press.

Bott, E. (1957) *Family and Social Networks.* London: Tavistock.

Brooks, D. and Singh, K. (1979) Pivots and Presents: Asian Brokers in British Factories. In S. Wallman (ed.) *Ethnicity at Work.* London: Macmillan.

Callender, C. (1985a) Gender Inequality and Social Policy: Women and the Redundancy Payments Scheme. *Journal of Social Policy* 14 (2): 189–213.

—— (1985b) Unemployment: The Case for Women. In C. Jones and M. Brenton (eds) *The Yearbook of Social Policy in Britain 1984–5.* London: Routledge and Kegan Paul.

—— (1986) Redundancy, Gender and Social Policy. In R. M. Lee (ed.) *Redundancy, Layoffs and Plant Closures: The Social Impact.* London: Croom Helm (forthcoming).

—— (1987) Redundancy, Unemployment and Poverty. In C. Glendinning and J. Millar (eds) *Women and Poverty in Britain.* Brighton: Wheatsheaf (forthcoming).

Campbell, B. (1984) *The Road to Wigan Pier Revisited: Poverty and Politics in the '80s.* London: Virago.

Chaney, J. (1981) *Social Networks and Job Information: The Situation of Women Who Return to Work.* Manchester: Equal Opportunities Commission/Social Science Research Council.

Clarke, J. (1983) Prejudice, Ignorance and Panic! Popular Politics in a Land Fit for Scroungers. In M. Loney, D. Boswell, and J. Clarke (eds) *Social Policy and Social Welfare.* Milton Keynes: Open University Press.

Collinson, D. and Knights, D. (1985) Jobs for the Boys: Recruitment into Life Insurance Sales. *Occupational Segregation by Sex.* EOC, Research Bulletin No. 9. Manchester: Equal Opportunities Commission: 24–43.

Coyle, A. (1984a) An Investigation into the Long Term Impact of Redundancy and Unemployment among Women. *Work and the Family.* EOC Research Bulletin No. 8. Manchester: Equal Opportunities Commission: 68–84.

—— (1984b) *Redundant Women.* London: Women's Press.

Cragg, A. and Dawson, T. (1984) Unemployed Women: A Study of Attitudes and Experiences. *Department of Employment Research Papers.* No. 47. London: Department of Employment.

Curran, M. (1985) *Stereotypes and Selection: Gender and the Family in the Recruitment Process.* London: Her Majesty's Stationery Office.

Daniel, W. W. (1974) *A National Survey of the Unemployed.* Political and Economic Planning Broadsheet No. 546. London: PEP.

—— (1981) *The Unemployment Flow: Stage 1. Interim Report.* London: Policy Studies Institute.

Department of Employment (1984) *Redundancy Payments*. London: Her Majesty's Stationery Office.

Department of Employment and Department of Health and Social Security (1981) *Payment of Benefits to Unemployed People*. London: Her Majesty's Stationery Office.

Granovetter, M. (1973) The Strength of Weak Ties. *American Journal of Sociology* 78: 1360–80.

—— (1974) *Getting a Job*. Cambridge, Mass.: Harvard University Press.

—— (1981) Towards a Sociological Theory of Income Distribution. In I. Berg (ed.) *Sociological Perspectives on Labor Markets*. New York: Academic Press.

Grieco, M. and Whipp, R. (1984) *Women and the Workplace: Gender and Control in the Labour Process*. Work Organization Research Centre Working Paper No. 8. Birmingham: University of Aston.

Harris, C. C., Lee, R. M., and Morris, L. (1985) Redundancy in Steel: Labour Market Behaviour, Local Social Networks and Domestic Organization. In B. Roberts, R. Finnegan, and D. Gallie (eds) *New Approaches to Economic Life*. Manchester: Manchester University Press.

Hill, M. (1981) Unemployment and Government Manpower Policies. In B. Showler and A. Sinfield (eds) *The Workless State*. Oxford: Martin Robertson.

—— (1983) Government Responses to Unemployment. In M. Loney, D. Boswell, and J. Clark *Social Policy and Social Welfare*. Milton Keynes: Open University Press.

Hill, M., Harrison, R., Sargeant, A., and Talbot, V. (1973) *Men Out of Work*. Cambridge: Cambridge University Press.

Hunt, A. (1968) *A Survey of Women's Employment*. London: Her Majesty's Stationery Office.

Jenkins, R. (1984) Classifying People/Peopling Classes: Recruitment into Employment and the Practical Production of Stratification. Paper presented at British Sociological Annual Conference, Bradford, April.

—— (1985) Black Workers in the Labour Market: The Price of Recession. In B. Roberts, R. Finnegan, and D. Gallie (eds) *New Approaches to Economic Life*. Manchester: Manchester University Press.

Jenkins, R., Bryman, A., Ford. J., Keil, J., and Beardsworth, A. (1983) Information in the Local Labour Market: The Impact of the Recession. *Sociology* 17: 260–67.

Lee, R. M. (1985) Redundancy, Labour Markets and Informal Relations. *Sociological Review* 33 (3): 469–94.

Lee, R. M., Morris, L., and Harris, C. C. (1983) Aspects of the Everyday Life of the Redundant: the Place of Informal Relations. Paper given at SSRC Conference on Urban Change and Conflict, Clacton, January.

Mackay, D., Broody, D., Brack, J., Diack, J., and Jones, N. (1971) *Labour Markets Under Different Employment Conditions*. London: Allen & Unwin.

Manpower Services Commission (1978) *The Employment Service in the 1980s*. Sheffield: MSC.

—— (1982) *The General Employment Service in Great Britain*. Report of the Employment Service Division Rayner Scrutiny. Sheffield: MSC.

—— (1984) *Labour Market Quarterly Report: Great Britain*. Sheffield: MSC.

Marsden, D. (1982) *Workless*. London: Croom Helm.

Martin, J. and Roberts, C. (1984) *Women and Employment: a Lifetime Perspective. The Report of the 1980 DE/OPCS Women and Employment Survey*. London: Her Majesty's Stationery Office.

Martin, R. and Fryer, R. H. (1973) *Redundancy and Paternalistic Capitalism*. London: Allen & Unwin.

Martin, R. and Wallace, J. (1984) *Working Women in Recession: Employment, Redundancy and Unemployment*. Oxford: Oxford University Press.

Morris, L. (1983) Responses to Redundancy: Labour-Market Experience, Domestic Organization and Male Social Networks. Unpublished paper. Swansea: University College.

Moylan, S., Millar, J., and Davies, B. (1984) *For Richer, For Poorer? DHSS Cohort Study of Unemployed Men*. Department of Health and Social Security, Social Research Branch, Research Report 11. London: Her Majesty's Stationery Office.

North Tyneside CDP (1978) *In and Out of Work: A Study of Unemployment, Low Pay and Income Maintenance Services*.

Pahl, R. and Wallace, C. (1985) Household Work Strategies in Economic Recession. In N. Redclift and E. Mingione (eds) *Beyond Employment: Households, Gender and Subsistence*. Oxford: Blackwell.

Purcell, K. (1982) Value Loaded: Women's Wages and Women's Worth. Paper presented at British Sociological Association Conference, Manchester, April.

Rees, A. and Shultz, G. (1970) *Workers and Wages in an Urban Labor Market*. Chicago: University of Chicago Press.

Reid, G. (1972) Job Search and the Effectiveness of Job-Finding Methods. *Industrial and Labour Relations Review* 25 (4): 479–95.

Salaman, G. (1974) *Community and Occupation*. Cambridge: Cambridge University Press.

Sheppard, H. and Belitsky, A. (1966) *The Job Hunt: Job Seeking Behavior of Unemployed Workers in a Local Economy*. Baltimore: Johns Hopkins University Press.

Siltanen, J. and Stanworth, M. (1984) *Women and the Public Sphere: A Critique of Sociology and Politics*. London: Hutchinson.

Stevenson, O. (1973) *Claimant or Client*. London: Allen & Unwin.

Walker, A., Noble, I., and Westergaard, J. (1985) From Secure Employment to Labour Market Insecurity: The Impact of Redundancy on Older Workers in the Steel Industry. In B. Roberts, R. Finnegan, and D. Gallie (eds) *New Approaches to Economic Life*. Manchester: Manchester University Press.

Wedderburn, D. (1965) *Redundancy and the Railwaymen*. Cambridge: Cambridge University Press.

Whipp, R. (n.d.) The Subjected or the Subject of History? Women and the Social Organization of Work in the Early Twentieth Century Pottery Industry. Unpublished paper. Birmingham: University of Aston.

Whipp, R. and Grieco, M. (1983) *Family and the Workplace: The Social Organization of Work*. Warwick Economic Research Papers, No. 239. University of Warwick.

White, M. (1983) *Long-Term Unemployed and Labour Markets*. London: Policy Studies Institute, No. 622.

Wilkinson, F. (1981) *The Dynamic of Labour Market Segmentation*. London: Academic Press.

Young, M. and Wilmott, P. (1957) *Family and Kinship in East London*. London: Routledge & Kegan Paul.

4. The laying off of hands – unemployment and the experience of time

David Fryer and Stephen McKenna

'Time doesn't matter now as much as it used to. . . . There's so much of it.'

(Redundant man, United Kingdom, 1980s)

How do people feel when they become unemployed? This is a difficult question about a complex issue. People, and the situations in which they find themselves, differ tremendously even in employment, and so too the experience of unemployment varies from person to person (Warr 1984a). However, we may assert with a confidence seldom enjoyed in social science that most people who experience unemployment find it distressing in at least some ways (Warr 1984b). Moreover, modern studies that follow individuals in and out of jobs over time have demonstrated beyond reasonable doubt that it is indeed the unemployment, or at least a combination of unemployment and relative poverty, that is responsible for the distress, rather than vice versa (Banks and Jackson 1982).

However, our descriptions remain woefully inadequate regarding the fine detail of unemployment experience. Most of the high-quality research of recent years has looked at undifferentiated indicators of psychological well-being (Fryer and Payne 1986), rather than scrutinizing in detail specific aspects of what it is to be unemployed. In this respect, classic studies of the 1930s (Bakke 1933, Jahoda, Lazarsfield, and Zeisel 1933, Jahoda 1938, Komarovsky 1940) are seldom rivalled today, although good-quality fine-textured work is continuing to emerge (Fagin and Little 1984, Fryer and Payne 1984, Ullah (forthcoming), and Bostyn and Wight, Chapter 8 in this volume). In this chapter we wish to contribute to this tradition by investigating in some detail how the passage of time is experienced by unemployed men.

Indeed, we wish to go beyond description and will attempt to contribute to the understanding of the *causes* of the distress so often found to be associated with unemployment. In this attempt we are indebted to Marie Jahoda, who has made a massive contribution to our understanding of the impact of unemployment. This contribution has taken the form of seminal empirical research (Jahoda, Lazarsfield, and Zeisel 1933, Jahoda 1938), influential synthesis, interpretation, and communication of evidence in both state-of-the-art (Jahoda and Rush 1980, Jahoda 1981 and 1982) and popular reviews of the field (Jahoda 1979a and b). In addition she has provided a valuable theoretical contribution. Her work in this area is not only the most dominant in the field; it is virtually the only explanation there is. Admittedly, other writers have offered accounts, but to all intents and purposes they are merely notational variants. It is for these reasons that it is so important to subject the account to detailed conceptual and empirical investigation.

Despite the foregoing, we have strong reservations about Jahoda's account for a range of reasons – pragmatic, methodological, theoretical, and ideological (Fryer 1986, but see Jahoda 1986). In this chapter we will focus on an empirical assessment of the account. Accordingly we describe, below, a field study based on a formulation of Jahoda's explanation derived from a careful reading of her accounts.

Some earlier evidence

In the 1930s a group of researchers lived for a period of months in the Austrian village of Marienthal, which had been plunged into mass unemployment by the demise of the textile industry (Jahoda, Lazarsfield, and Zeisel 1933). The researchers conducted an intensive sociographic study and reported that although the unemployed inhabitants had reduced the length of their day by spending extra time in bed, they were unable to account for the way the remaining time had been spent, were slower moving about the village and unpunctual for the few remaining fixed arrangements like meals. Weekends blended into weekdays and were no longer significant events. They lost their 'structuring meaning'. The phenomenon was later referred to by one of the researchers as loss, or disintegration, of the sense of time (Jahoda 1982).

Fifty years later it was found that the proportion of unstructured to structured time increased approximately twenty-fold with unemployment (Fagin and Little 1984). Since the researchers categorized time spent in preparation for, and travel to and from, employment as structured time, and watching television, sitting around, and chatting as unstructured time, this finding is perhaps not surprising; but it underlines the magnitude of changes in the way time is spent when one becomes unemployed.

These findings complement those of more quantitative studies. A recent investigation of nearly a thousand unemployed working-class men, drawn from forty-one unemployment benefit offices in the United Kingdom, found that around 30 per cent reported difficulties in each of the following areas: making a start on anything, concentrating on what they were doing, feeling 'rusty' at things they used to do well, and taking longer over the things they did do. The sample was structured to cover all durations of unemployment up to and beyond twelve months. All four difficulties became more common as the length of unemployment increased (Fryer and Warr 1984).

The implications for mental health are far reaching. It has been shown that whether a man felt he could occupy his time during unemployment was associated with his mental health as assessed by the General Health Questionnaire. The better the ability to occupy time, the better the mental health (Hepworth 1980).

What is Jahoda's explanation?

Jahoda claims that whilst the usual, intended reason for being employed is to earn an income, five unintentional consequences of employment turn out to be crucial for psychological well-being. Unemployment deprives the unemployed person of these consequences, leading to a deleterious psychological outcome. These unintended consequences are:

* compelled contact and shared experience outside the family;
* demonstrated goals and purposes beyond the scope of the individual;
* imposed status and identity;
* enforced activity; and
* a time structure imposed on the working day and week.

This last consequence is of particular relevance to the present chapter. Jahoda writes of 'the enforced destruction of a habitual time structure for the working day with the sudden onset of unemployment', with consequent 'heavy psychological burden'. She believes that only a few people are able to establish 'their own time structure for engaging in meaningful work outside the contractual arrangements of employment', whilst far more are not so able because of the 'compelling social norms under which we all live and which provide a supportive frame within which individuals shape their individual lives' (Jahoda 1982).

Towards a test of Jahoda's account

How could one begin to provide empirical evidence that would enable one to assess the validity of Jahoda's explanation? The account suggests that the negative experience of unemployment is a result of the deprivation of certain consequences of employment. The obvious strategy was to investigate individuals who were deprived of those consequences of employment identified by Jahoda as crucial, with particular attention to 'the enforced destruction of a habitual time structure for the working day with the sudden onset of unemployment'. However, we already know that many unemployed people report problems with time, so there was little additional theoretical advantage in simply investigating a sample of unemployed people. This would merely confirm that unemployment is associated with problems involving time sense, rather than evaluating a particular account of what it is about unemployment that produces these problems. Accordingly, we looked for people who were deprived of the consequences of employment claimed to be implicated by Jahoda, but who were not unemployed. We decided on a sample of laid-off men – that is, men on furlough from employment for a negotiated period of time but with an agreed date for returning to employment. During the time they were not employed the men concerned signed on, claimed unemployment benefit, and were arguably deprived of the consequences of employment identified by Jahoda as criterial for psychological well-being. Certainly they were 'deprived' of an employment-imposed day-to-day structure. Below, we call these men the 'laid-off' men.

The men were to be laid off for a seven-week period and then taken on again. We were interested in what would happen to their sense of time during lay-off. We thought in advance that, although they would, in Jahoda's terms, be deprived of certain identified consequences of employment over that time period, including a habitual, imposed time structure, they would not suffer a disintegration of sense of time.

However, we were aware that if we were to find no such disintegration, it would be justifiably open to critics to suggest that we had not investigated the relevant areas of experience in sufficient detail, or that the period of unemployment – seven weeks – was not sufficiently long for the deterioration to take place. Accordingly, we also investigated a second sample of men, who had been made redundant after a factory closure. They were interviewed after a similar period of time following the end of their employment. Below, we call these men the 'redundant men'. We used the same interview schedules with both groups of men. If we were to find a difference between the experience of time in each group, it could not plausibly be said to be due to differences in the extent to which they were deprived of Jahoda's relevant consequences, the length of time they had been non-employed, or to the detail into which we had gone in our interviewing.

The people who took part

Both groups of men came from engineering companies in an industrial town, heavily hit by unemployment, situated in the North of England. All the men were semi-skilled workers manufacturing transport components from steel. Each factory had a stable, predominantly middle-aged work-force. The average age of the laid-off men was forty-three; that of the redundant men was forty-eight. On average the laid-off men had been in service for seventeen years and the redundant men for twenty-four. Financially, the situation was complicated. The mean loss of income of the laid-off men at just over £62 was markedly less than that of the redundant men at nearly £75. However, the redundant men had also received moder-ate redundancy payments in the form of lump sums. All men who took part in the study did so voluntarily with the encouragement of their trade union conveners. In each case the interviews took place at the men's homes in the fifth week after the end of employment. The interviews were mainly semi-structured, in-depth and wide ranging, but we also collected information on perceived health using two instruments: the General Health Questionnaire (Goldberg 1972) and the Nottingham Health Profile (Hunt, McEwen, and McKenna 1985).

What the men told us

In this section we attempt to give a picture of the experienced time structure within which our laid-off and redundant informants perceived themselves to be living. We exhibit this under subheadings chosen to give an impression of daily temporal life outside the time structuring of employment: 'getting up', 'activity in the day', 'routine', 'clock-watching and time-checking', 'losing track of time', 'weekends', 'punctuality', and 'going to bed'. Under some of these headings differences between the groups were marked, while under others their experiences were similar. After this, we try to give a more integrated picture in the form of two pen portraits, of a laid-off and of a redundant man respectively.

Time structure in lay-off and redundancy

Getting up during lay-off

There was wide variation amongst the laid-off informants in the time they got up. Times ranged from six to ten o'clock, but most rose between eight and nine. Some reported getting up earlier during lay-off than when employed; others woke early but stayed in bed for a while. Most slept a little later than when at the factory. Many were prompted to get up when they did by external factors such as dogs barking or other noises. Families provided other prompts; wives getting up or needing to be taken to work, getting children up, making their breakfast, or sending them off to school.

However, many of the laid-off were getting up for their own personally chosen reasons. Sometimes this was for a special activity; to read the newspaper, to do paperwork, or to work in the garden. Where men did get up early for specific activities it was generally to get chores over with in order to liberate 'free' time later.

Some laid-off men were getting up early not to do anything in particular but because they thought it was good for them generally. This was not always precisely articulated: 'I just don't like lying in'; 'I just can't lie in bed if I can hear others downstairs.' Often it was more defined; one informant said he got up when he did to 'discipline' himself because he was 'frightened of getting into a slothful attitude'. A close relative of this man had been unemployed and stood as a gloomy example for him of what unemployment could be like. Another thought that 'early efforts are important' and said that if he started late it put him out for the whole day. He said that he felt tired if he sat down, even if it was first thing and he had just got up, whereas if he got going on things straight away the day was usually all right. Another laid-off informant said he was getting up every day specifically 'to get into a routine'; yet another said, 'I made up my mind to get up early. The more you lay in bed the more you want to.' Another said that he got up at a set time to 'keep the workaday situation going'. To set against this we must bear in mind that many informants specifically mentioned being able to choose when they got up as being among the redeeming features of lay-off. One mentioned how cruel and demoralizing it was to have to get up for a job at the crack of dawn in winter, another that it was good to get up at a 'nice pleasant time'.

Getting up during redundancy

The variation in the time at which the redundant informants rose, after five weeks without employment, was even greater than that of the laid-off informants, although there were about twice as many men in the laid-off sample. The mean time of rising was a quarter past seven, considerably earlier for the redundant than for the laid-off men.

Only two redundant men said they got up earlier than when in employment. One rose early to help family members get ready to leave the home, and the other said he woke up early because he was not tired by working on his job the day before and could not lie in bed once awake.

Just over a third of the redundant men were getting up at the same time as when in employment. Often this was accounted for by custom: 'I wake up through habit, get the wife up, and then can't go back to sleep'; 'It's built in over the years'; 'I'm used to it, conditioned. I never could sleep in, even at weekends.'

For some, guilt at lying in was a reason for getting up: 'My conscience gets me up.' For others, the day was too good to miss by lying in: 'I have a philosophy that I don't like wasting time – you've only got an allotted span'; 'Once awake I have to be up and doing something'; 'I like to get up early; it makes the day longer. I like long days.'

A majority of the redundant were getting up slightly later than when in employment. Some of these respondents were just enjoying a brief lie-in of half an hour or so, perhaps reading in bed after waking. For others, lie-ins were interrupted by domestic obligations; getting breakfast for the family, taking children to school, taking a dog for a walk. Some would have liked to have got up earlier than they actually did, but did not do so in order to avoid clashing with other family members in the bathroom or kitchen: 'I stay out of the wife's way in the morning'; 'The wife makes me stay in bed till the kids are off to school so I don't disrupt their routine.' Only one redundant man explicitly said that he stayed in bed because he was depressed, there being 'nothing to get up for'.

Compared to the laid-off men, fewer redundant men got up early because they thought it was 'good' for them, although on average they were getting up earlier than the laid-off men.

Activity in lay-off

Once up, what were the laid-off informants doing? There were two clearly distinguishable groups. The first were fairly inactive, could not find jobs to do or could not afford to do them. Many of this group had few interests outside their jobs or could not bring themselves to follow them. As one said, 'Sitting around is the way to get miserable.' However, some of the laid-off informants found it impossible to avoid sitting around. One said, 'I've just got nought to do. I can't be bothered to do things – I don't know why.' Another often sat around, 'unable to settle even to read', and even if he did start reading, he reported that 'Half an hour and I'm done.'

In fact the inactive laid-off informants were in the minority, with most strikingly active and busy. Nearly three-quarters said they had no spare time during the day, compared with about half of the redundant men. Many talked of never having the chance to sit around, of being too busy to make use of free facilities for sports, or of doing jobs they had never thought they would get round to.

Usually this activity was self-initiated: 'There are plenty of jobs to do. I don't like being bored so I look for something'; 'I've got a need to be active. I've got to do jobs even though they might not be urgent.' Occasionally the activity was initiated from beyond the person – a wife's request or list of jobs, ageing parents' needs, commitments or undertakings to the community or a club. Sometimes the activity was so compelling that they seemed to be working longer hours when laid off than when in employment. One man talked of having less time to read than when in employment, another of having only one day off from jobs per week, and one of working till ten o'clock each night. This extreme was not typical. Most had some activity and some inactivity, more or less in line with their personal needs and preferences. Some enjoyed a sit-down: 'not to mope but to enjoy sitting and reading', to think about an impending meeting, to have a rest, a cup of tea, or to have a smoke and a think (a 'Condor moment'). The activity level was apt to vary during the period of lay-off. Few generalizations seem warranted. Good weather was attributed as the cause of both more outside work and more outside recreation. Bad weather tended to be associated with just sitting around. In addition, as the lay-off period progressed, financial problems bit deeper, hampering the provision of materials for jobs. Also the jobs with most priority were completed early on, leading to lesser activity.

Sometimes laid-off men mentioned enjoying the better job they had been able to make of things because they were not limited by time. Outside jobs were meticulously prepared and carefully executed. As one said, 'I've been able to get on with things, take time, and enjoy the jobs. I had to change the car brake pads but instead of just shoving them on I cleaned the discs and cylinders. It took four hours instead of two', but provided the informant with the satisfaction of a job well done.

Activity in redundancy

Once up, what were the redundant men doing? Once again the sample divided into two clearly distinguishable groups; one active and one inactive. In the redundant sample these groups were approximately equal in size, whereas with the laid-off sample the active men formed a majority. The active redundant men made comments such as 'I very rarely sit down. I'm always doing something'; 'I feel a sense of elation, I've been so occupied'; 'There's always plenty to do'; 'I don't know how I found time for work. The only problem is lack of money'; 'I'm working harder at home than at work.'

Usually this high level of activity was self-initiated. Some mentioned wanting to keep their minds active: 'I don't want to vegetate. If you do nothing your mind gums up.' Others mentioned wanting to keep themselves active more generally: 'I don't like to be passive – I keep on the move.' Some liked to keep busy to avoid dwelling on depressing thoughts: 'If I keep busy, I tend not to start thinking about money later on'; 'If I sit around for a couple of hours I feel frustrated.'

Many of the inactive redundant men said they just sat around doing nothing. 'I get up, read the papers and walk round to [see a relative]. That's about the day', or 'I used to be a big reader. Now I get tired if I'm reading so I tend to do nothing' were typical statements. Generally, this inactivity was unpleasant: 'If it's fine I sit outside and brood. Things are getting a bit depressing and boring.' Sometimes the inactivity was attributed to habit: 'I suppose having been to work all those years it's hard to fill a day.' However, it was more common to put it down to depression itself: 'Sometimes I sit around 'cos I'm just fed up'; 'I sit around 'cos I've just lost interest in things.'

These statements raise an important issue. Time structure, activity, and purposefulness (or temporal disintegration, inactivity, and purposelessness) all tend to occur together, coalescing to contribute to the total experience of unemployment: 'I've lost interest in things. I've loads of jobs but I don't seem to have any interest in them; I just sit around'; 'I often sit around and get bored. I know simple jobs need doing but I just put them off.' Although this state of affairs is generally experienced negatively, this is not inevitably the case: 'I often sit around doing nothing but I enjoy it. I like to sit and watch the world go by. I often go to the park, sit, and drift quite happily'; 'I'm quite happy mooching around. Though I would much prefer a job, it's not breaking my heart.'

Routine during lay-off

Many of the laid-off informants were very active during the day. However, was this activity structured into a routine? Some of the laid-off informants totally rejected the idea that they had adopted a routine in lay-off. One said he tried to vary what happened each day; another talked of 'no fixed regularity, I just work until I've done the job'. Another said, 'There's no routine, I just do what I fancy'; and another, 'It varies as the fit takes me.' A couple of informants said there was no routine: 'It just depends on the job in hand.'

However, others said that they did have routines during their lay-off. Some found that preparing lunches or evening meals for their children, or taking children to school or play-groups, shaped their routines. Others had changed to routines that fitted in better with that of their family. Thus one had altered the timing of his meals to allow the family to sit down and eat together. Another found the later time he felt able to go to bed, because of having no early start for employment on the next day, enabled him to repair and develop a parental relationship that had been foundering.

Sometimes family responsibilities necessitated changes in routine during the lay-off. One laid-off informant had quite different routines on alternate days, taking turns with his wife to rise at seven and take their child to play-school. Another man went to his allotment on alternate days, and one described a fortnightly cycle – spending cycles of two weeks busy and then two weeks reading and sunbathing.

It became apparent that many of the laid-off informants were living in a routine during lay-off in some respects not very different from the employment routine; following the same pattern of a delayed breakfast, sandwich lunch, and tea-breaks at times not unlike those they were used to in employment: 'I have lunch and tea at the same time as at work because it seems normal then'; 'I stop for coffee just like normal working. It feels normal and natural'; 'I still have my meal at four p.m., because it's like when working.' Often this employment routine keeping was unconscious; it was just the way things felt natural and worked out. However, sometimes it was intentional: 'I try to keep in the same routine, to keep in contact with work'; 'I get up at the same time every day to get into a routine. . . . I want to try and keep a routine of keeping working.' The time structure of employment had permeated the lay-off experience of some in more subtle ways. One man commented, that when he started to get behind on jobs around the house he felt guilty if he took too long a break. Another had a strategy not unlike that he practised while working a piecework system; he worked very hard for the first few weeks so that he could take it easy later. He wanted to 'get it out of the way, then wind down and do what I want to'. Another used this strategy on a daily basis: 'I try to get a certain amount of work done each day and then rest on my laurels.'

One laid-off man had compressed a working day into the morning, doing all necessary jobs and housework. This left the afternoon free to do what he wanted. He got up early, did housework before breakfast and then jobs until lunchtime. He saw himself as having deliberately created a routine for himself. A major benefit of this personal routine was that it allowed him both the satisfaction and security of planned activities and achieved purposes, combined with the novelty of an unplanned period: 'It's developing a routine, and I rather like it. I can plan out what I want to do and the afternoon is a "surprise" period. I try to make it fall into a pattern.'

The experience of time, and the imposition on it of some routine structure, was an issue of marked variation in the laid-off men we talked to. Some definitely felt adrift and anchorless in an unstructured day of tea, minor household jobs, peeling potatoes, and waiting for the family to return. A majority lived in a highly structured day, fighting the clock to do all the jobs and other activities they had planned. Sometimes the employment routine was set aside and a radically different routine adopted. Sometimes no routine at all took its place – to the satisfaction of the informant. Learning to cope with no routine, or a different one, was a pleasant experience for some informants: 'If I'm laid off again I won't be bothered about abandoning routine. Before, it left a void, a mental void, but I've found it's not as bad as I thought.'

Routine during redundancy

What role did routine play in the activity or inactivity of the redundant men? A majority stated that they did not have much of a routine in their unemployed activities. About a quarter of the respondents did follow a routine and a further 20 per cent had some sort of variable routine within a non-routine week.

Those redundant men who did claim to follow a routine tended to give a rather sketchy account of it: 'I have breakfast at 8.45, have a look in the greenhouse, get the paper, look for jobs, write if there are any, have a sandwich lunch if I bother, and dinner at five'; 'Each day's the same. I eat to the clock.' It is interesting that most of those men with an admittedly limited daily routine were inactive. Only one man who described his day as, 'just routine, in a rut' was active; he 'never sat around' but always had something to do.

There were other redundant men who also had a routine of sorts, although not a daily one. One said that he did something different each day of the week – odd jobs one day, golf another, walking another, and so on – but that he repeated this routine week by week. Whereas he used to have meals very regularly when working, he had abandoned this habit in redundancy. He was a man who was so occupied that he felt 'a sense of elation'.

Other redundant men had purposely integrated elements of both routine and non-routine into their days. One had maintained his midday meal-time as a 'lifetime's habit'; but although he visited a dependent relative every day, he intentionally varied the time of the visit specifically to introduce variety into the relative's life. Another informant kept to a daily routine of fetching a newspaper, washing, and tidying up during the first half of the day, but did whatever he happened to feel like doing in the second half. Interestingly, these men were sometimes active and sometimes inactive. One said that he did sometimes tend to sit around for a couple of hours but would then feel frustrated and get busy doing something. All in all he could not think how he had 'had the time for' employment. It was quite common for some degree of routine or regularity to be maintained by most of the redundant men, if only listening to the news, eating meals at set times, or meeting recurring family obligations.

However, a majority of the redundant men said that they had very little routine in their redundancy; 'I take each day as it comes' and 'There's no regularity about it' were typical comments. Some openly missed the routine of employment: 'The problem is trying to get into one!' But this point of view was not often expressed. Not having a routine in redundancy was more often, though not inevitably, associated with a high perceived activity level. For example, one man who had no routine in his life whilst redundant, who ate his midday meal when he felt like it, and who sometimes missed the routine of his job, rarely sat around but was 'always doing something'. Another with no routine strove 'to keep as active as possible'. The man who found the main problem of redundancy not the routine nature of life but rather the difficulty of getting into a routine was too busy to watch television, liked to 'keep on the move', and 'didn't like to be passive'.

One man who denied any routine or regularity about his redundancy days stressed his efforts to plan ahead and how these efforts made routine less likely to occur. He said that he had 'done a lot' and that he 'never sat around doing nothing' – a viewpoint endorsed by his wife, who commented that, for her husband, finding something to do had become an obsession.

Clock-watching and time-checking in lay-off

Following a routine is largely a matter of the order of the things you do but it also has links with Greenwich Mean Time. Did the laid-off informants do much checking of time when laid off?

With regard to consulting watches or clocks, the laid-off men were divided. Many adamantly said they never checked the clock. 'I'm not ruled by the clock at all', said one man, pointing out that he didn't even bother to wear his watch at home during the lay-off. Another said that he ignored clocks altogether. One stated that he went through the motions of checking his watch, but seldom registered what time it was: 'You look at your watch, someone asks you what time it is, and you have to look again.' Some of these non-time-checkers admitted that under certain circumstances, when they were bored or lonely or when the weather was bad, they did clock-watch.

Another large number of laid-off informants did say they frequently checked the clock. 'I'm always conscious of time,' said one, 'I check the time whenever I walk past the clock.' 'I always know what time it is,' said another.

Apart from consulting a timepiece, there are many ways one might come to know what time it is. Radio regularly gives time checks, and a high proportion of informants had radios on during the day when they were laid off. However, there was a great variation even among the radio listeners as to the extent to which they noticed the time checks. One man, typical of many, said that the radio was always on, and he was often correcting the clock. Another said the radio was usually on and that 'the time checks come straight through'. On the other hand, there were a group for whom the following was typical: 'I've heard more of radio in the last few weeks than in the previous six months, especially news, but I don't notice the time checks unless I'm specifically listening out for them.'

Apart from radios, the regularity of family and local life very often played the same role as chiming clocks for the laid-off men. Some reported knowing the time by their wives arriving home or children coming home for lunch. Even where there were no children in the household, they were able to tell the time by the sound of children coming home past the house, by the noises at playtime in a nearby school, or by local tradesmen who came at regular times. One laid-off man could tell the time by the arrival of post, milk, and bread, and by local people leaving for and returning from work. These local comings and goings were quite insidious. One inform-ant explained how he had come to check the clock less and less often during lay-off and had got to the point where he no longer felt that time was important, claiming that he never checked the time at all now. Nevertheless, it later transpired that he knew the time that the breadman would arrive each day, to the minute.

Clock-watching and time-checking in redundancy

Nearly all the redundant men checked the time frequently. Sometimes this was put down to 'force of habit', sometimes it was in order not to miss specific programmes on radio or television. One said, 'I just check the clock though I'm not waiting for something to happen.' The redundant men looked at their watches and clocks, heard local church bells chiming and sometimes heard time checks on radio or television. There was more consciousness of the slowness of time passing among the redundant than among the laid-off men. As one man said, 'I check the clock more often than not – it's getting to be a bit of a habit. I never used to. It's because I've not got much to do.' One man was 'much more conscious of watching time go by'. Another often checked the time, thinking, 'Oh dear, it's another six or ten hours before I can go to bed.'

Whilst checking was frequent it was not universal amongst the redundant men. Sometimes this was because the sense of time was so ingrained that looking at timepieces was irrelevant: 'I'm aware of the time all day, without actually checking the clock'; 'I have a good sense of time ingrained after all those years at work.' It was uncommon to find that time-checking decreased among the redundant as a result of absorption in tasks.

Whilst clock-watching was more evident among the redundant than the laid-off groups, there was less awareness (or at least less reporting) of external time structuring. There was little mention of indiscriminate broadcasting attention – sport and news programmes being the most popular viewing and listening. Radio was more likely than television to be on; but again, whether men noticed the regularly given time checks seemed to be largely a matter of mood. Those who were inactive, bored, or depressed noticed them most. Little internal structuring of time was reported. Reading newspapers, attending to news broadcasts, and contacting relations were the main internally imposed daily events. The redundant men mentioned local life as a source of perceived regularity less than the laid-off men, an intriguing finding that our material does not allow us to explain. The comings and goings of neighbours and local tradesmen, and community regularities such as children being let out of school, were seldom mentioned. However, family members coming and going from school or work were frequently mentioned.

Losing track of time in lay-off

Given the different degrees to which lay-off days were structured by routine and to which reference was made to external time markers, it is not surprising that two-thirds of the laid-off group and only one-third of the redundant group reported losing track of time. It is interesting that generally, though not universally, losing track of time was associated with a positive state of mind. Men mentioned losing track of time when they became 'engrossed' or 'absorbed' in something enjoyable, interesting, worth while, or, best of all, all three – whether hobbies, jobs, entertainment, or exercise. Sometimes time was passing by so quickly that some started to wonder if 'there was going to be sufficient lay-off time to get it all done'. These men, appreciating lay-off in at least some ways, talked of how the day, whilst away from work, dragged less than employment days: 'Time passes quicker than at work.' They also talked of how lay-off was 'whizzing by' and of how they were 'surprised how quickly lay-off is going'. One man characteristic of this group said, 'I could do with another couple of hours on the day. I sometimes sit down at the end of the day and wonder where the time has gone.' Another said, 'I don't know how I ever got any time to do anything when I was working. I'm amazed where time has gone.' It was a characteristic of this group that there were 'not enough hours in the day'. It was common for men to comment that they had not been able to make use of sporting or leisure facilities (available free of charge to unemployed people) because they simply had not had enough spare time.

Whilst losing track of time was generally associated with high levels of activity, having spare time was generally associated with low levels of activity. Sometimes the period laid off felt like an awful 'prison sentence', which although known objectively to be seven weeks long seemed subjectively to stretch elastically on and on. Although a fixed term, for some laid-off informants time seemed to be passing more slowly than usual: 'Lay-off seems like an eternity. I have to keep asking my wife how long I've been off.' 'Crikey, is it only that time?' was a characteristic refrain for these men. However, time was reported to be dragging by less than a third of the laid-off men, compared with nearly two-thirds of the redundant men. The day was particularly likely to drag when, as one said, 'plans are frustrated'. This was most commonly brought about by bad weather disrupting plans for outdoor jobs, or financial difficulties precluding doing jobs or going out. If a man was used to certain activities at certain times, like going out for an evening beer, and this was curtailed by finances, time was very likely to drag: 'I'm restless at seven o'clock, when I used to go for a drink. I pace round the house, get bored, can't sit and watch TV.'

Indeed, the passing of time seems very sensitive to mood, which naturally varied. 'Time seems irregular,' said one man; 'sometimes you lose an hour, sometimes the day drags awfully.' This was true on a longer term too. For this same man, lay-off seemed to be passing slowly but then suddenly accelerated. Many people reported losing track of what day it was: 'In the week I often forget what day it is. Everything is so similar to the day before'; 'I've been that busy that I've had to stop and think what day it is.' This was particularly likely to happen when several days went by without any outside contacts.

Losing track of time in redundancy

Turning the focus of our attention to the redundant men, it was not surprising to find that those redundant men for whom the day dragged were typically those who were least active and most likely to describe their days as following a routine. In contrast, those men for whom the day did not drag were typically the active ones. There was an interesting subgroup who reported that the day dragged sometimes but not always and who specified some conditions: 'The day drags if I can't get out. If the day does drag, I sometimes get down and depressed but not for long'; 'The day drags if the weather's bad'; 'The day drags if I sit down and get a chance to start thinking'; 'The day drags whilst the wife's out' (at part-time work). What is interesting is that these were generally men who were moderately active and who made such comments as 'If I sit around I tend to go to sleep, so I find something to do'; 'I sometimes sit around but not often'; or, 'I do tend to sit around for a couple of hours – then I feel frustrated.'

Whilst within the day time often seemed to drag, on a longer time-scale it was striking that time was passing very quickly for the redundant men, unlike the relatively slower passage of time experienced by the laid-off men. 'Time flies when you're at home. It's passing very quickly', 'I'm really surprised by how time flies. I quite often can't believe it's so late', 'Time is passing quicker', and 'The days pass too quickly', were typical of the comments made by redundant men. To some extent the quick passage of time must be seen in relation to the men's gloomy expectations: 'Time's passing quicker than I expected'; 'Time's passing comparatively quickly – not as slow as I thought it would.' It was not only the very active and involved men who found that the days and weeks passed quickly. For example, a redundant man said that he was very depressed and bored and yet still asserted that time was passing too quickly. Another said that his day was 'just a matter of getting time over'. He was taking long bus rides and walking back on four-hour treks and still thought that time was passing quickly. A clue may be deduced from such comments as 'Time passes very quickly when you're looking for work, but otherwise not.' This period may be viewed as the time during which they had hoped to find new employment or during which their chances of finding employment were optimal, and this time was passing disturbingly quickly. Some support for this interpretation is provided by the finding that 90 per cent of the redundant men were 'looking forward to returning to employment', as opposed to 40 per cent of the laid-off men – although the meaning of 'returning to employment' was of course different in each case.

Weekends during lay-off

An interesting aspect of lay-off time structure was the extent to which weekend days would continue to have their own identity, separate from weekdays, when the latter were no longer distinguished by employment. Not unexpectedly two broad perceptions of weekends emerged. Some laid-off men felt that weekdays and weekends were no longer different in character, all the days being 'much the same now'. These men were generally those who were least happy in lay-off. One said, 'Weekends and weekdays are much the same now. I'm just sat here whatever it is. It's just like a weekend all week but not so much fun.' However, some who found all days similar felt that all the days of the week were special days. Two laid-off respondents remarked that they liked their laid-off days better than weekends when in employment because previously there had always been Monday morning lurking over the horizon to spoil things.

Other laid-off men maintained that weekends were still different from weekdays. They usually pointed to the fact that children and wives were about, as were people in the neighbourhood. The sounds of weekends – cars being tinkered with, lawns mowed, hedges clipped – were mentioned. Some were able to maintain their habits, when in employment, of Sunday lunchtime drinks, Sunday dinner, family visits, fishing, and cricket or football outings. No one mentioned church attendance as a distinguishing factor.

Weekends during redundancy

Some men in the redundant group also mentioned that weekends and weekdays were all the same now that they were redundant, but a majority felt that weekends were still different in character. Wives and children being around, traditional social events, Sunday pub visits, and going away regularly for the weekends still distinguished them for many redundant men. Some who were busy with do-it-yourself jobs did them only from Monday to Friday. Sometimes this was done intentionally to keep weekends as rest days; sometimes it was enforced. One man complained about not being able to do jobs on Sundays because he could not pop out and buy forgotten items needed to finish a job. There were some amongst the redundant who saw their lives as enhanced in some ways by the change in life-style: 'Weekends are still the same as they ever were, but now you've got more freedom on weekdays.'

Punctuality during lay-off

In the introduction we saw that earlier research claimed lack of punctuality as symptomatic of temporal disintegration. In this study no laid-off informant reported punctuality as being a problem. The occasions on which punctuality was required were naturally fewer, but meetings, benefit appointments, and family commitments, such as collecting wives from work or taking children to and from school, still arose. Several respondents commented that it was 'easier to be punctual now, as there's not so much rushing about'. Punctuality was something the laid-off continued to take a pride in: 'If I say, I'm coming for eleven, then I'm there for eleven. I try to be very punctual. If I say, I'll come when I can, I don't so much mind not going'; 'I'm always early. I'd be early for my own funeral in case I missed it.'

Punctuality during redundancy

As with the laid-off men, punctuality was not perceived by the redundant men to be a major problem, although compared to the laid-off men the redundant men seemed to perceive even fewer occasions when punctuality was required. Nevertheless, whilst none of the laid-off men reported punctuality as being a problem, two of the redundant men did. One man who usually prepared his daughter's meal commented that it was often late since he had been redundant even though he now had more time. Another reported punctuality as a problem and that it was a sign that he was 'getting lax'.

Going to bed when laid off

Many laid-off men said that they were going to bed later than when employed, although the actual time varied from night to night. The reasons people gave were largely to do with their freedom to please themselves: 'I'm not under any pressure. I stay up just as I want to'; 'You have the flexibility to do that [stay up] without the treadmill in the morning.' This general freedom was often exercised in one of two ways – in watching television or for social reasons – although other interests like reading were also mentioned. Laid-off men were particularly likely to stay up for late films on television, or occasionally video, or to go to bed when wives chose to, friends left, or other family members went to bed.

Going to bed when redundant

No pattern emerged in the times at which the redundant men went to bed. Some went earlier, some later, and some at the same time as when they were employed. The most general reason for retiring later was to watch television programmes they would otherwise not have seen. Those who went to bed at the same time as when in employment appealed to habit. Those going to bed earlier said that they did so because they became tired earlier. However, several redundant men spoke of difficulties sleeping when in bed. Thus time of going to bed is not necessarily as important an index as is time of getting to sleep.

Two pen portraits

The method of content analysis with examples presented in categories allows a detailed description and useful contrast between the experience of time during lay-off and redundancy and an appreciation of the variation from man to man both within and between these employment statuses. However, it necessarily fails to capture the seamlessness of the sense of time as it is experienced. We have so emphasized the range of experiences above that we hope the following pen portraits, one of a laid-off man and one of a redundant man, will not be taken as representative of their colleagues so much as illustrative of differing individuals' experiences, capturing a characteristic mood. Presenting integrated, individual portraits has the merit of bringing home the personal implications of such employment-status transitions in an immediate fashion.

George and lay-off

George was a skilled turner of crankshafts, working day and night shifts. He described his job as repetitive and boring but did get a satisfaction from 'turning the job over'. When on days, George regularly got up at 6.45 for a 7.40 start at the factory, giving himself just enough time to get up, wash, dress, and get to the job. He would have his first cup of tea at the factory and would make sure there was time for a cigarette, a look at the paper, and a chat with his mates before starting his lathe, dead on time. George considered his job to be a routine one. Admittedly, the routine was 'different for each particular job' but, when it came down to it, it was 'all basically the same . . . turning'. He broke up the time during the day to a certain extent for himself. The first interruption was for breakfast, and within limits George chose when to take it. He was hungry by then, but enjoyed the break primarily as a social occasion, with his group of friends all taking a break at the same time. Brews of tea, brief chats, walkabouts, and glances at a paper were all ways in which George structured his day for himself.

The basic time structure – clocking on, clocking off, and lunch break – was controlled by management, but George's personal time structure was not so much dictated by this as created by him and his mates to be consistent with it. George made crankshafts on a piece-rate system. However, it was a pooled, group system, and he was paid according to the output of his whole working group. This system, organized collectively by George and his mates through the union, appeared to be another way in which a degree of autonomy of time structure was woven around the official management time structure. If he felt off colour, he would slow down his work rate a little without his earnings slumping. Normally, a degree of pressure from his mates, or at any rate seen by George as coming from his mates, acted as an incentive for him to keep up his productivity, so as not to depress the earnings of the other group members. George said that he never watched the clock on the shop floor; he did not need to. He could tell from the number of cranks he had done near enough to the minute what time it was. He found it a continual struggle to complete his quota of cranks: 'The way things are, you are fighting the clock all the time. Time flies.'

George was tired when he got home after his day's work and yet he did not go to bed until about midnight, when the television went off and the rest of the family was in, or going to, bed. George claimed that he would not go to bed any later even if there were no job to go to next day, although if that were the case he would not mind a lie-in in the morning. Whilst still working George had not only made serious plans about a number of do-it-yourself jobs he would undertake during lay-off, but had also bought in the materials he needed to do the jobs, and had arranged to borrow the necessary tools.

We next meet George after five weeks of lay-off. The time, he says, is speeding past: 'When you're away from work, time flies.' George is now getting up regularly around half-past seven, giving himself a modest but promised lie-in. However, his lie-in is limited because he 'cannot lie awake in bed if I hear the others downstairs'. He brooks no suggestion that he has developed a routine within lay-off: 'It varies as the fit takes me.' He has lunch, snacks, and drinks of tea and coffee as and when he feels like them. He rarely has the radio on during the day, let alone the television. The only exception to this is the news at one o'clock.

George is very busy during lay-off. 'I'm never idle. I could do with another couple of hours on the day. I sometimes sit down at the end of the day and wonder where the time has gone.' He even 'dislike[s] going to bed at night. I often wish there was a bit more day. It seems such a waste!' George claims to be oblivious to the clock during the day, with two exceptions. Around lunchtime he checks the time so that he will not miss the television news, and towards evening he starts to look forward to his wife and daughter coming home. However, most of the time he is engrossed in his activities. As a result, he has no 'spare' time, almost never finds that the day is dragging, and discovers that the lay-off period is passing disconcertingly swiftly. The time when, compared to his paid job, 'I have the freedom to do what I want, when I want, how I want' is flying by.

Henry and redundancy

Although he worked for a different company, in a different factory, on the opposite side of town, Henry's job was similar to George's. Henry was a turner of engine parts, also working on a piece-rate system on alternating day and night shifts. His machinery admittedly left a little to be desired, and he had to use a fair amount of ingenuity to get 'a decent job done'. Henry too had found his job repetitive and boring and had found ways to break up the day with brief social events, snacks, and cups of tea.

When working days, Henry got up at six in order to get to his work on time, but in many respects his working life was similar to George's; for this reason, we do not go into as much detail here as we did for George. However, whilst George's bout of unemployment was negotiated and planned in a controlled fashion well in advance, Henry heard that his job was finishing in a different way. Rumours and hunches had been flying around for many months, and Henry was temporarily off work with a minor illness, often thought to be associated with anxiety, when he had a telephone call from a workmate telling him the factory was to shut down. That evening he read the news in the local paper and two days later received a letter from the firm confirming the closure and his redundancy.

Like George, Henry made some plans and arrangements for the future, but these plans were rather different in nature. Henry sent his television back to the rental company, and when his statutory redundancy lump-sum payment arrived he bought a set outright to avoid recurrent expenses he felt he would be unable to meet. Also, he bought generous Christmas gifts of bicycles for his grandchildren, months in advance. Christmas, normally a time of pleasure, was already assuming a threatening aspect.

When we meet Henry five weeks into his redundancy, he is still getting up regularly at six o'clock, the same time as when he was employed. He says that he wakes up then largely through habit and then wakes his wife so that she can start to get ready for her job. He could not go back to sleep then, though, because 'It's not nice to think that you are laying in bed and [your wife] is going to work.'

Henry does have some temporal reference-points in his day, but they are few and far between. He regularly eats his breakfast at 8.45 and his evening meal at five o'clock. His wife leaves and returns from her job at regular times, and Henry phones his daughter each and every day. However, in between these anchor points, Henry drifts. He may have a sandwich lunch, but is 'as likely as not' to miss it. He takes a desultory glance in the greenhouse, buys a newspaper, and checks the vacancy column for possible jobs. There is seldom anything appropriate. When there is, he writes off but seldom receives even an acknowledgement. Much of Henry's day is spent sitting around doing nothing, checking the time out of force of habit. He 'never' loses track of the time, which seems to drag by at a snail's pace, hanging heavy on his hands. The television is seldom on in Henry's house during the day, the exception being for the odd sporting programme. Weekends and weekdays blur into one another in Henry's mind; the only real focal point of the week being 'signing-on day'. However, he is strictly punctual – or rather he is 'always early'. He admits that he can now go to bed exactly when he feels like it, there being no early start in the morning for which he has to make sure he is adequately rested. Ironically, Henry goes to bed earlier in his redundancy then when he was in his job; he becomes exhausted much earlier.

Summary of the evidence

The most striking feature of these men's accounts of their experience of time during non-employment is the wide variation within each group. Both laid-off and redundant groups included men who had high levels of activity who perceived few problems with the passage of time, men who were inactive and dissatisfied with the way time seemed to them to be passing, and others between these extremes.

Nevertheless, there was evidence of more temporal problems in the redundant than in the laid-off group, in terms of both incidence and severity. The laid-off men as a group exhibited less variation in their time of rising and, on average, tended to get up later than the redundant men. Where the laid-off men were getting up earlier than their normal time, it was more likely to be self-initiated and in order to carry out pre-planned activities. The majority of the laid-off men were active, with nearly three-quarters saying that they did not have any spare time. About half the redundant men gave an impression of similar levels of activity, with only just over half saying that they had no spare time. There was more evidence of self-initiated and self-developed routines among the laid-off men than among the redundant men, who more frequently stated that they 'take it as it comes'. The redundant men were more likely to check the time repeatedly, were more likely to find that time was passing slowly, and were less likely to report noticing regular events in the neighbourhood than were the laid-off men. About two-thirds of the laid-off men said they often lost track of time, a state of mind that seemed to be associated with engrossed activity and absorption. Only one-third of the redundant men lost track of time. On the other hand, nearly two-thirds of the redundant men found that the day often dragged, compared with less than one-third of the laid-off. Both groups still felt that weekends were 'different' from weekdays. Whilst punctuality was not reported as a major problem in either group, two members of the redundant group did have difficulties being on time for appointments. More laid-off than redundant men went to bed later than they had when employed – generally for entertainment or family considerations.

These qualitative differences in time structure are reinforced by the quantitative data collected on perceived psychosocial and general health. As mentioned previously, our informants completed the Nottingham Health Profile (NHP) and the General Health Questionnaire (GHQ). The NHP assesses health perceptions in six domains: energy level, pain, emotional reactions, sleep, social isolation, and physical mobility. The GHQ is a screening instrument designed to indicate risk of minor psychiatric morbidity. Studies of large populations of employed workers have been carried out using the NHP, and it was possible to calculate the 'expected' scores to be obtained from *employed* samples matched by age, gender, and social class with our laid-off and redundant samples. Such normative data are not available for the GHQ, but a number of studies have used the instrument to assess morbid experience in unemployed samples. Thus it was possible to determine 'expected' scores on the GHQ of similarly matched *unemployed* groups.

The redundant workers showed evidence of more distress than either the employed comparison group or the laid-off men, on all six sections of the NHP. However, the laid-off workers were indistinguishable from the employed comparison group on all sections of the NHP except for pain and physical mobility, where they actually had fewer problems.

Turning to the GHQ scores, the redundant sample was indistinguishable from the unemployed comparison group, whilst the laid-off group showed evidence of less distress than the weighted comparison group.

Thus it seems that the experience of our unemployed sample was typical of that of other groups of unemployed men of similar demographic characteristics. In contrast, the experience of the laid-off group as a whole was as positive as for a comparable group of employed workers. This study therefore supports our claim that at a group level redundancy, but not lay-off, has a negative psychological impact generally, on sense of time in particular. However, there was considerable variation in experience within the samples.

Discussion

This investigation supports the *descriptive* claim that unemployment is associated with psychologically distressing experience of time. The redundant men, conventionally unemployed, suffered more of such problems than did the laid-off men. But what about the explanatory claim that 'the major psychological burden' is caused by the deprivation of the five unintentional consequences of employment, pinpointed as crucial by Jahoda (1982)? We argue that, in terms of Jahoda's explicit accounts, both our redundant and our laid-off men were being deprived of both the intended and unintended consequences referred to.

As regards the intended consequence – earning a living – none was receiving a weekly pay packet from an employer, and all were signing on at unemployment benefit offices, receiving unemployment benefit and, where means testing deemed appropriate, supplementary benefit. Men in both groups were applying for housing benefit and/or rate rebates, dealing with benefit office staff, and experiencing a sharp drop in disposable income. It was noted that the redundant men, who were as a group psychologically harder hit by the time out of employment, had suffered a greater drop in weekly disposable income than the laid-off men. We believe this aspect of relative poverty was instrumental in their greater distress, as indeed was the relative poverty of both groups in causing anxiety.

It is true that the redundant, but not the laid-off, men received modest statutory redundancy lump sums. Our observations were that this sum was not perceived by most of the redundant men we saw as a source of supplement to the weekly budget. Indeed some emphasis was placed on not 'frittering' it away.

In fact, neither the role of income deprivation nor that of redundancy lump sums is given *explanatory* prominence by ·Jahoda's account, although she acknowledges forcefully the *descriptive* fact that unemployed people are subjected to poverty: 'there is abundant evidence that, beyond financial problems, unemployment of more than a very short period is psychologically destructive because of the absence of the latent consequences of employment, even when adequate redundancy payments are available' (Jahoda and Rush 1980).

Turning now to the latent consequences of employment and their absence in unemployment: we claim that, according to Jahoda's account, the laid-off and the redundant are in her terms equally deprived of employment-imposed collective purpose, social contact, identity, activity, and time structure.

It might be argued that, as regards demonstration of goals and purposes beyond the scope of an individual but requiring a collectivity, the very state of being laid off rather than redundant was itself evidence of a collective goal achieved via employment. The lay-off cycle was negotiated by the men's trade union organization on their behalf equitably to distribute the reduced amount of employment available, to avoid compulsory redundancies, and to maximize income for its members over the lay-off period. The negotiation was the result of considerable struggle and collective solidarity over a long period of time. Lay-off, then, may have emphasized rather than deprived the men of the value and necessity of collective, employment-derived purpose.

However, reading Jahoda with care it is clear that it is *day-to-day* collective purpose that is held to be crucial: 'deprived of this daily demonstration, the unemployed suffer from lack of purpose' (Jahoda 1982: 24).

The same applies to social contacts. It would be misinterpreting the deprivation account to suggest that because employment 'sandwiches' lay-off it provides a continued source of imposed social contact. Again according to Jahoda (1982: 25), it is *regular, daily* contact of which one is deprived by unemployment with such negative effects: 'during unemployment such impoverishment of social experience follows necessarily from the change in the structure of daily life'. Again with activity, it is *imposed, regular* activity whose deprivation is responsible, according to the account, for the psychological repercussions.

Essentially the same point might be made about the 'foremost among these other consequences' (Jahoda 1982: 22), temporal distintegration. It would be stretching the point to suggest that the return to work after seven weeks might in itself constitute an employment-imposed time structure.

Once again, paying attention to the detail of Jahoda's claim undercuts this objection. It is the 'enforced destruction of a habitual time structure *for the waking day* which is critical' (Jahoda 1982: 22). The 'fixed time schedule' crucially involved in 'all employment' is often rigidly fixed by the requirement to clock in at the *beginning* and clock out at the *end* of the working day' (Jahoda 1982: 23).

Conclusions

This investigation reinforces the conviction that unemployment is associated with problems of time. However, in two respects the present study does not support the claim that the negative psychological impact of unemployment is due to deprivation of the allegedly supportive features of employment, identified as criterial by Jahoda. First, the laid-off men were apparently as deprived of the identified functions of employment as were the redundant men, yet as a group the laid off did not manifest as negative a response to non-employment. Secondly, even within each group there was a wide variation in the extent to which, and the ways in which, the experience of lack of employment was negative. We examined this in some detail in the case of time structure. All the informants were equally 'deprived' of an employment-imposed time structure, yet the extent to which they experienced problems of a temporal nature varied widely. We believe that this variation is due to differences in the self-directedness of the individuals, a feature of their agency.

The central and most obvious difference between lay-off and redundancy (which was noted by both informants and observers) was the temporary and circumscribed nature of the former and the uncontrolled and potentially limitless nature of the latter. It was uncertainty for the future – fears, forebodings, and the frustrations of being unable to plan realistically for, and develop contingencies to deal with, the unknown – that distinguished the two situations for the participants. Far more laid-off than redundant men had looked forward to and made plans for the period outside employment, even to the extent of making detailed preparations and buying equipment and materials in advance. The lay-off period was in many cases a race against time to fulfil all the plans made for it, with all the activity and commitment that implies. For the redundant men, the situation was dominated by the unknown. How long would unemployment last and how would it be resolved? Was it worth starting jobs when there might not be time to complete them? How far would resources have to stretch? Any such questions may obsess and depress. This chapter has sought to put these questions on to an agenda for future unemployment research.

We have been strict in our exposition of Jahoda's theory, with good reason. In so far as her theory is predictive of response to unemployment, it is very specific, and it would be an injustice to her to mould the theory to fit a relatively new (or at least now more commonly found) situation such as lay-off. Readers may well have become aware of Jahoda's account through the writings of others, who have tended to reinterpret what she said to fit their own beliefs. In Jahoda's terms, the laid-off men were all deprived of the latent functions of employment and consequently should have experienced levels of psychological morbidity similar to those experienced by the redundant men. This was not found to be the case.

We believe that Jahoda's account omits orientation towards the future and the role of planning. The laid-off group had a more clearly defined and predictable future, which had the effect of reducing their level of anxiety and of leaving them freer to plan for their period of non-employment. Having said this, it was equally clear that those laid-off men who coped best were the ones who either created a new, alternative time structure appropriate to their needs, or who maintained a time structure which imitated that experienced when in employment. Jahoda argues that few unemployed people can establish their own time structure for engaging in meaningful work outside employment. Our findings do not support this view.

Jahoda's account is essentially retrospective and rightly acknowledges that 'it stands to reason that the nature of the activity in which a person was engaged must have a bearing on the way in which he experiences its cessation' (Jahoda 1982: 27). We agree, but would argue that a complete understanding of the consequences of unemployment must also be prospective, taking into account the likely future activity in which a person might be engaged. All too often in the Britain of the 1980s this activity is likely to be without a contract of employment.

References

Bakke, E. W. (1933) *The Unemployed Man*. London: Nisbet.
Banks, M. H. and Jackson, P. R. (1982) Unemployment and Risk of Minor Psychiatric Disorder in Young People: Cross-Sectional and Longitudinal Evidence. *Psychological Medicine* 12: 789–98.

Fagin, L. and Little, M. (1984) *The Forsaken Families*. Harmondsworth: Penguin.

Fraser, C. (1981) The Social Psychology of Unemployment. In M. Jeeves (ed.) *Psychology Survey No. 3*. London: Alan & Unwin.

Fryer, D. M. (1986) Employment Deprivation and Personal Agency during Unemployment. *Social Behaviour: International Journal of Applied Social Psychology* 1.

Fryer, D. M. and Payne, R. L. (1984) Proactivity in Unemployment: Findings and Implications. *Leisure Studies* 3: 273–95.

—— and —— (1986) Being Unemployed: a Review of the Literature on the Psychological Experience of Unemployment. In C. L. Cooper and I. Robertson (eds) *Review of Industrial and Organizational Psychology*. Chichester: Wiley.

Fryer, D. M. and Warr, P. B. (1984) Unemployment and Cognitive Difficulties. *British Journal of Clinical Psychology* 23: 67–8.

Goldberg, D. (1972) *The Detection of Psychiatric Illness by Questionnaire*. London: Oxford University Press.

Hepworth, S. J. (1980) Moderating Factors of the Psychological Impact of Unemployment. *Journal of Occupational Psychology* 53: 139–46.

Hunt, S. M., McEwen, J., and McKenna, S. P. (1985). Measuring Health Status: A New Tool for Clinicians and Epidemiologists. *Journal of the Royal College of General Practitioners* 35: 185–88.

Jahoda, M. (1938; forthcoming) Unemployed Men at Work. In D. M. Fryer and P. Ullah (eds) *Unemployed People: Social and Psychological Perspectives*. Milton Keynes: Open University Press.

—— (1979a) The Psychological Meanings of Unemployment. *New Society*, 6 September: 492–95.

—— (1979b) The Impact of Unemployment in the 1930s and the 1970s. *Bulletin of the British Psychological Society* 32: 309–14.

—— (1981) Work, Employment, and Unemployment: Values, Theories, and Approaches in Social Research. *American Psychologist* 36 (2): 184–91.

—— (1982) *Employment and Unemployment*. Cambridge: Cambridge University Press.

—— (1986) In Defence of a Non-Reductionist Social Psychology. *Social Behaviour: International Journal of Applied Social Psychology* 1.

Jahoda, M., Lazarsfield, P. F., and Zeisel, H. (1933) *Marienthal: The Sociography of an Unemployed Community*. New York: Aldine Atherton.

Jahoda, M. and Rush, H. (1980) *Work, Employment, and Unemployment*. Science Policy Research Unit, Occasional Paper Series, No. 12. Brighton: University of Sussex.

Komarovsky, M. (1940) *The Unemployed Man and his Family*. New York: Dryden.

Ullah, P. (forthcoming) Unemployed Black Youths in a Northern City: An Ethnographic Study. In D. M. Fryer and P. Ullah (eds) *Unemployed People: Social and Psychological Perspectives*. Milton Keynes: Open University Press.

Warr, P. B. (1984a) Economic Recession and Mental Health: A Review of Research. *Tijdschrift voor Sociale Gezondheidzord* 62: 298–308.

—— (1984b) Job Loss, Unemployment and Psychological Well-Being. In V. Allen and E. Van de Vliert (eds) *Role Transitions*. New York: Plenum Press.

5. The middle class: unemployed and underemployed

Stephen Fineman

A common social category is 'middle class'. It is not one that immediately comes to mind when considering the unemployed because the majority of the jobless are not middle class. There are, however, over a quarter of a million professional and managerial people without jobs, and more than a million who have had, and are seeking, 'white-collar' work (Department of Employment 1983). Added to this are the swelling ranks of jobless, well-qualified newcomers to the job market – from the universities, poly-technics, and other institutions for advanced education. Overall, we have now fair reason to assume that the customary benefits of middle-class life cannot be taken for granted.

This chapter will examine some features of this phenomenon, in par-ticular what might be special about middle-class responses to unemploy-ment. More broadly, I will address some of the social consequences of an expanding pool of well-educated people, where some are without work and others are working at a level well below their desires or capacities – the underemployed.

The growth and surplus of the middle class

Since the 1950s there has been a steady decrease in manual occupations in favour of white-collar work. This has been a significant trend in all major industrialized countries. In the United States it is now estimated that for every new operative or craft job created there are nearly fifteen managerial, professional, administrative, or technical jobs (Levitan and Carlson 1984). In Britain there has been a sharp fall in the people employed in traditional blue-collar industries (such as manufacturing, transport, processing, agriculture, and construction) over the past ten to fifteen years. Yet, while employment in manufacturing and allied industries has fallen by around a quarter, professional and managerial workers have increased by a third (Department of Employment 1985).

The right to a middle-class job is now hard to separate from advanced education and training; it is one route to social mobility, the 'new' middle classes described by Goldthorpe (1978). So specialist knowledge and skills, often gleaned from years of study beyond school, are *de rigueur*, an essential prerequisite for an array of technical, professional, and administrative jobs. But there are now insufficient jobs to go round: higher education cannot ensure a passage to middle-class meadows. The statistics in this area present a sombre picture. The International Labour Office, reporting in 1985, records a quadrupling of newly qualified professionals without work in West Germany – 115,000 people. France and Switzerland have also been affected. In Britain unemployment amongst graduates rose from around 5 per cent in 1977 to a peak of nearly 14 per cent in 1982. A fall in 1984 to around 10 per cent still accounted for nearly 6,000 first-degree students without jobs (University Grants Committee 1985).

Behind these statistics lie marked variations between subject areas. For example, in Britain new graduates in botany, zoology, and geology entered a job market where over 20 per cent of their peers were unemployed. Arts graduates generally had a hard time finding jobs, as did sociologists. In contrast, few students of accountancy, dentistry, or law were left without work. Post-graduate education certainly does not guarantee employment – but it helps a lot. Unemployment of post-graduates averages a little under 4 per cent, with variations in subjects from 1 to 7 per cent. However, none of these figures takes account of those in temporary work, jobs that may not be considered by the incumbents as 'real' or matching their qualifications. Government figures for 1982–83 first-degree graduates, which include the temporarily employed, give some flavour of the often dramatically accentuated picture of those without permanent employment: such as 40 per cent for graduates in English, 36 per cent for historians, and 39 per cent for biologists (HMSO 1985).

The notion of temporary employment begins to get us closer to some of the personal realities of occupational constriction for the well educated. It gives us a first glimpse of people who may be underemployed. This is an area that is hard to get to grips with as there is little detailed information available. Temporary employment *per se* need not underemploy an individual, although any graduate seeking the scope and security of a career post is perhaps unlikely to feel a firm sense of engagement with a short-term temporary post. While some new graduates will choose to take up a job well below their capacities in order to delay what seems an irrevocable career decision, many others feel forced into working at whatever they can find. These people join the ranks of petrol-station attendants, clerks, waiters and waitresses, receptionists, and labourers. They fall into low-paid, low-skilled work, in effect taking positions away from the usual applicants for such jobs. Bath University's own records for 1984 indicate employment of this sort amongst graduates as diverse as economists, sociologists, architects, horticulturists, biologists, mathematicians, biochemists, and chemists (Bath University 1985). Such a pattern has been observed in the USA. Jones notes that about one-quarter of the total graduates (nearly 3 million) in the 1980s will have to accept the kind of job not taken by graduates in the 1960s: 'We can only guess at the amount of bitterness and resentment engendered by the collapse of the job market for college graduates' (Jones 1980: 24).

Underemployment is not confined to newcomers to the middle-class job market. The out-of-work manager, teacher, or engineer, in early or mid-career, may turn to any sort of temporary work to help prop an ailing bank balance and/or an ailing ego. Others may trade off a life of restricted opportunity within their own profession for better-paid underemployment elsewhere. For example, more than 1,500 teachers recently responded to an advertisement for photocopier salesmen. The advertisement was deliberately aimed to capture teachers and the like (it was placed in *The Times Educational Supplement* and the *Guardian*), offering promise of salary and fringe benefits well in excess of those normally available to teachers (Wilby 1985).

Surplus: specific professions

There is no comprehensive picture of unemployment as seen from within particular professions. To obtain an initial 'insider's' perspective I wrote (in April 1985) to the general secretary of each of eighteen different professional associations, ranging widely in form and type of expertise. I asked for their impressions about the employment position and prospects within their profession, the mood of their members, the position for new recruits, and what their unemployed did. I received ten replies (and three promises of reply). They were predictably idiosyncratic in form and content, but each appeared a concerned response from someone who was close to the political milieu of the profession: a sort of cultural representative. The professions closest to advanced technology and business administration were typically described in buoyant, optimistic terms, and with low or negligible unemployment. Such, for example, were the sentiments of electrical engineers and accountants. However, professions closely tied to government expenditure, and/or providing services that were not obviously related to the gross national product, were rather differently portrayed. Here are the pictures presented of four of these:

Nurses

'It is now estimated that there are approximately 15,000 nurses unemployed. We have become conscious that in areas of depression, such as Wales and the North West, many of our members have become the main bread-winners for their family and for them the threat of unemployment is very serious. Now 90 per cent of nurses are women and many of them provide second incomes. But many also are single as a high proportion of our members pass through the profession before they reach the age of thirty. Unemployment in the London area may be felt particularly by career nurses since many of the prestigious training schools are in London. Also, the opportunities for specialization are in London, so disruption to job opportunities there causes particular frustration. Generally, the mood is one of greater insecurity than ever before.'

Architects

'Architects have been affected by underemployment as well as by unemployment, and early retirement has increased, probably as a consequence of these factors. Older architects who are made redundant have the biggest problem in finding new jobs, while sole principals suffer most from underemployment due to lack of work. Opportunities for young architects (under thirty) have declined in the public sector and, although there have been new opportunities in the private sector, this has often meant lower pay. Unemployment has risen from almost *nil* ten years ago to nearly 2 per cent today. This figure may not look terribly large, but, together with declining satisfaction indicated in our own surveys, it has become much more of a problem.'

Probation officers

'The size of the Probation Service, despite growth over recent years, is unlikely to increase, and we anticipate a re-emergence of trainees completing courses with no jobs to go to. Our experience of those in this predicament is that they feel embittered. They have demonstrated commitment by training on a low salary (often having previously been in well-paid employment) to enter a specific occupation, and then been unable to. For some, unemployment has been a lengthy experience and a number have not found a job, despite qualifying up to four years ago. Once someone has been unemployed for a substantial period employers tend to disregard their applications. Some move into jobs within the service for which they have not been accorded the status, salary, and conditions of a probation officer. Others have had to move outside of the service for a job. Reduced employment prospects, less movement within to create vacancies, and fewer training places give us cause for concern. The numbers affected are perhaps lower than in other professions because we are a small service; but this does not diminish our concern.'

Town planners

'While we do not have any statistics available, it is clear that the employment prospect for planners is particularly poor at the moment. Over the last couple of years the increasing restrictions by central government on spending by local authorities have led to a general standstill in recruitment by planning and other departments. For the future the outlook is even bleaker, with government plans to further cut back on our resources. I fear that planners will fare particularly badly. I now see a considerable number of planners who are actively considering other careers within or outside local government.'

These brief accounts reveal, in an understandably partisan fashion, the sense of insecurity and futility that confronts those who have invested much in specializing, professionalizing, when they find that they cannot do what they expect to do. The signals they receive from educational and training establishments may sometimes be radically out of line with job-market opportunities; and political and economic shifts may render once valued services redundant, 'over-supplied'. We here confront one paradox of highly skilled occupations – which, on the one hand, are valued for their accumulated expertise and service, and (so goes the rhetoric) for the dedication of their members, but on the other hand are denied full expression. If the state is a major or monopoly employer (such as of probation officers or nurses) then those affected will feel the greatest helplessness when public spending is curtailed. If the professional skills are exclusive and inapplicable outside a limited range of activities or problems, then unemployment or underemployment seems inevitable.

Doctors

Highly specialized skills, combined with lengthy and expensive training, are epitomized by the medical profession. This group is an intriguing case to examine because it is one of our top professions in social prestige. The image of the unemployed or underemployed doctor in a country that is very conscious of its inadequacies in medical provision raises moral and practical issues about the use of expensively trained and highly qualified manpower. It also, of course, gives us food for thought about the position and role of the jobless doctor.

Internationally there are indications that medicine is no longer immune from the job difficulties experienced by other professions. One forecast suggests that the United States will have a surplus of 185,000 doctors by 1990 (Office of Technology Assessment 1980). There are also reports from France (Hermann 1980) and India (Thirugnanam 1977) of a significant proportion of doctors out of work. In Britain, soothing government figures on the robust health of the medical profession (low unemployment amongst new graduates) are inconsistent with a rather more troubled picture revealed from other sources. Each year some 3,500 newly qualified doctors leave medical school, but permanent career posts in consulting or general practice are available for no more than 2,000 (Brearley 1984). A recent survey concluded that one in five junior hospital doctors (who comprise the bulk of the profession) can expect to be unemployed in a given two-year period. On their typically short contracts, these doctors cannot take their next job for granted; and many, in their insecurity, seek posts in any medical specialism that has room for them, regardless of their own skills or inclinations (British Medical Association 1984). It is argued that this position has resulted in frustration and demoralization in the medical work-force, as well as the prospect of thousands of unemployed young doctors by the end of the decade (Parkhouse 1979, Poole 1984).

How doctors cope with and survive unemployment and the effects of job uncertainty and underemployment are unknown. It would be plausible to expect that vocational ideals would be eroded as job uncertainty increased, and notions about the status of the profession would be re-evaluated. Certainly, anecdotal evidence suggests that breaks in the doctor's employment and 'too much' locum work can substantially reduce the prospects of advancement. Perhaps more disturbing are the possible consequences of this situation to patients – where a vast proportion of care is delivered by doctors in training, concerned about the expedients of professional survival.

Dimensions of meaning

The dimensions of the meaning of work to the middle class have, in the main, been derived from studies of people at work (e.g. Kaufman 1982). Middle-class work is typically portrayed as:

* a key source of self-identity, self-respect, and social status;
* a central life activity, often more important than leisure;

* valued for its intrinsic rewards as much as, if not more than, for what it 'buys';
* hard to separate from other aspects of life;
* providing a career and security, predictable and increasing rewards for effort;
* an opportunity to develop (and acquire) discretion, power, and control over people, things, or processes.

These features, it is claimed, mark off professional workers from all others. While they provide a useful starting-point for considering the consequences of job loss, they require qualifying in a number of ways. Firstly, they are findings based, in the main, on surveys: asking people to express their feelings about themselves and their work on predetermined questions, to anonymous researchers. This reflects an old objectivist tradition in statistical social research, and is strongly represented in British and US work. Yet what work means to someone – the ebb and flow of encounter and experience, tension, frustrations, and joys – can be difficult, if not impossible, to express adequately in the naïve form and relationship of the classical questionnaire study. Thus the simple elegance of the research method and findings may do but slight justice to the often incoherent world of 'real experience' (e.g. Fox 1980, Fineman 1983a).

Such arguments are not new. In 1951 C. Wright Mills, writing about white-collar workers, was uneasy about the findings of job satisfaction surveys, which indicated higher satisfaction, interest, and enjoyment amongst professionals and executives: 'Such figures tell us very little, since we do not know what the questions mean to the people who answer them, or whether they mean the same thing to different strata' (Mills 1951: 229). Twenty-six years later Sarason (1977) revived this point even more trenchantly, arguing that the confession of private feelings about work, feelings that are at the quintessence of personal work meanings, required a candour that can rarely be gained from impersonal questionnaires or survey techniques. For the professional worker, in particular, it is very hard to admit to oneself, least of all publicly, that an 'important' job may have failed in its promise, is boring, lacks challenge, and most days feels like a stressful grind. When society ranks the doctor, academic, engineer, or lawyer as highly prestigious, it is hard for the disaffected to present a contrary image.

The importance of the self-projected image of an 'achieving', 'satisfied' middle-class worker should not be underestimated. This tells us something about the symbolic significance of maintaining 'proper' appearances in our culture; of indicating to others that our daily activity is one that deserves their attention, if not respect; that our career choice has been a sound one. Such a performance may indeed correspond to one's private belief, and in this sense be self-affirming; but what when it does not? What when work means nothing like it 'ought' to mean – when anxiety and tedium replace achievement and pleasure? Then the 'I' of the self, the often private part, splits off from the 'me', the public, respectable part. Many psychological processes come to bear to try to make this split tolerable, one being an image-honing one – keeping appearances in line with others' expectations. This is what our questionnaires are most likely to pick up. We need rather different approaches if we wish to penetrate beneath a carefully preserved veneer.

Studies that have a high degree of intimacy and involvement between the researcher and the researched move in this direction (e.g. Terkel 1974, Herzog 1980, Fineman 1985a) – where secret worlds can be safely divulged or shared; where the investigator can reflect with and maybe help the participant; most importantly, where people can disengage from their daily performed roles and examine those experiences that are normally taken for granted. Sometimes it is only after a substantial disturbance to the status quo, such as a personal crisis, that the taken-for-granted world is revealed. Ironically, unemployment can be one of these situations: job loss can reveal much about what employment has meant and provided, as well as about the impact of life without work.

Careful investigations of this type are important, but so are more vicarious data. By this I mean the fleeting revelations made when people are off-stage, or between acts (in dramaturgical jargon): what they say about their job when they put the questionnaire down, when they 'let go' at a party, when they confide to the stranger in the train, plane, or bar. Seymour Sarason's encounter with his doctor is a splendid example of this:

'I had just been examined by a locally well-known and highly respected surgeon to whom I went whenever I wrenched my vulnerable knee. He conducted his examination and prescribed a course of treatment. I started to leave his office and in a perfunctorily courteous manner I asked, "How has life been?" To my surprise he did not respond "routinely" but sighed and said: "I do not know why I allow myself to be so busy." His tone of voice suggested that he wanted to talk and so we did, in the course of which I told him about my current interests in the frequency with which people seem to be changing careers. He then said to me: "Surgery *is* interesting. For a period of years it did fascinate me. I *am* a good surgeon. In fact I'm a damn good one. So I'm good, so what? What I really want to do is to get into the history of medicine." He went on to relate how so many of his days were filled with uninteresting problems (like my knee), and only occasionally was he faced with a challenge which made his day.'   (Sarason 1977: 100)

This image of the effete, often underemployed, professional worker looks rather different in quality and emphasis to the generalistic dimensions of work meanings. It combines with a number of studies of the employed and unemployed (e.g. Pines, Aronson, and Kafry 1981, Frost, Mitchell, and Nord 1982, Greenhalgh and Rosenblatt 1984, Fineman 1980, 1983b and 1985a) to suggest, not surprisingly, that the closer we get to understanding the individual at work – his or her aspirations, disappointments, family and other life concerns, political pressures – the less neat and tidy the picture is. If any generalization is possible it is that middle-class work may have the potential for both greater frustration and greater reward than blue-collar work. Beyond this there are many shades of grey that contrast with the more colourful stereotypes of the working middle class. Their work can be chronically stressful and stultifying; boring and tedious; it can lead to burn-out quite early in career; it can provide the resources to seek achievements elsewhere; it can trap people in attractive conditions of work, but provide little else; it can exert many unwanted pressures, and demand a dedication that is neither appreciated nor desired.

Self and career

Against this backcloth, let us consider what job loss can mean to members of the middle class, and some of the consequences it can have for them. There are a number of factors to bear in mind. From the foregoing account it is clear that an individual's attachment, or relationship, to the job is a key one. Others issues relate less to the job *per se* than to the individual's stage of career and to significant people and events in his or her life. These are part of the essential social fabric surrounding unemployment, contributing, to a greater or lesser extent, to the impact of the event. Also to consider are the circumstances of job loss (e.g. a compulsory or voluntary affair), and the degree of support available for the individual. We can explore these areas by examining job loss at different career points.

Pre-career

There is, as has been argued, an expanding pool of people who move directly from higher education and training into unemployment or under-employment. What this does to them depends, in part, upon how strongly they have anticipated immediate, 'rewarding' work, and on how vocationally oriented was their subject of study. Evidence from those inspired to write to newspapers about their plight, and from my own work, reveals a sense of confusion, resignation, and waste. Far from experiencing the joys of a 'free ride' in society, or an extension of their student ways, a sense of bitter disenfranchisement prevails. Thus, for example, a new graduate in mathematics talks of his need to think of unemployment as a way of life now that his many job-seeking attempts have failed to realize a job that will utilize and develop his prime skills. And a recently qualified English teacher struggles with himself to retain some dignity:

> 'What does one write where the forms ask for "occupation"? Anything truthful looks about as dignified as a Chaplin custard pie! I see myself as a failure and I reckon others must think the same. I don't *think* this is paranoia. I see people around me on £7,000–£10,000 salaries, and I can't get in £1,000 a year. I'm sickened! Poison, anyone?'
>
> (Quoted in Fineman 1983b: 113–14)

It is helpful to view such reactions within a context of 'career making'. Restricted opportunities for work may be gradually assimilated into the mores of advanced educational establishments, but meanwhile those emerging from them will be inclined towards a certain set of pre-established professional attitudes and values. These are acquired from peers and teachers, as well as from a more diffuse sense of middle-class propriety. This much we learn from the literature on careers (e.g. Schein 1971, Hall 1976). But such literature fails to inform us what happens when the expectations stemming from this process are completely blocked at the outset, prevented from expression and from being tested out in a job. Typical expectations are those of challenge and responsibility, of intrinsic reward and increasing salary, and of opportunities for creative activity. Naïve these might be, but they constitute some of the material of youthful ideal and aspiration and the substance for an important stage of self-development in our career-oriented society. It is in a job that the new professional's competence begins to develop, and a firmer place in society is sought.

'Who am I?' is one early message from the graduate who fails to find an expected career post. The passage from higher education and training, often marked by ritual and by symbols of achievement and success (degree ceremonies, graduation certificates, congratulatory gestures), is jarringly contrasted with failure in the job market. Assumed personal worth is now open to question as old reference groups – fellow students, professors – give way to the judgements of potential employers, friends who have found work, and others unemployed. 'I am unemployed' is a position soon adopted as a sort of limbo identity as time without a job lengthens; but what on earth was the point of all that studying, all those hopes for the future? Relative poverty, combined with a less developed sense of moral indignation about 'taking something for nothing' (compared with unemployed established professionals) can lead to a heavy dependence on state benefit. Such individuals can feel desperately powerless, and very much cheated.

Early career

The early years of a career are often characterized as ones of apprenticeship and establishment. It is a period when the individual is being influenced by existing occupational practices, learning the 'rules of the game' about where he or she might exert influence (Dalton, Thompson, and Price 1980). This might involve some struggle between ideal self-image and the received realities: where fantasies are tested (Super 1957, Hall and Nougaim 1968). For some, survival in the job requires splitting off an 'inner self' from a more socially acceptable 'performing self' (Hochschild 1983, Fineman 1985b). It is a way of managing disappointments about the job through a degree of alienation and working at 'looking the part'. It is also a way of reducing the costs of change in career: the extrinsic benefits – salary, security, pension – seem worth hanging on to, especially when the labour market is tight.

Others may soon resolve any discrepancies between their pre-job expectations and their new encounters by readily taking on the professional and organizational mantle; identifying themselves with all that their new calling represents. There is no ready distinction between how they feel about their job and career and how they feel about themselves. They are the careerists, the achievers; devotion and commitment to work are paramount for 'getting on'.

New recruits can be particularly vulnerable to a 'shake-out' (see Sinfield 1981, and Roderick Martin, Chapter 12 in this volume). An early-career interruption can be the first blemish on the curriculum vitae, that symbol of worth and propriety. It immediately places the incumbent at a competitive disadvantage and at a focus for stigmatization – a process that makes few concessions to the reasons for unemployment (Fineman 1983b). But we might expect any sense of injury to the self to be more acutely felt by the careerists – 'Why me? What's wrong with me?'

All of those made unemployed in early career have potentially more freedom to seek alternative work than those made unemployed later. A small shift in specialism may do the trick. An extra qualification could increase employability. The more disaffected might consider a complete change of life-style. Youth and time are still on their side, even though it might not feel that way to them. Yet the potential for a new start cannot be separated from the legacy of the false start, which might be debilitating without appropriate emotional and practical help. Furthermore, the immediacy of a home and family to support can soon erode aspirations, and press the individual into any paid employment.

Mid-career

The literature on careers highlights the 'mid' period, spanning the ages from about 35 to 45. It is discussed as a time when careerists can lose their energy and sparkle, and maybe burn out; the alienated may become more reflective and clearer about what it is that alienates them. Other changes – ageing, health, family relationships – contribute to an increasing awareness of passing time, fallibility, and fading opportunities. Briers (1967) records three common patterns of mid-career attitudes and behaviour. Firstly, 'I see the company is not really interested in me or what I have to say; this is the way I am: I can't change; I do not want to change, so I'll continue to plough along and give them my best.' Secondly, 'If the company doesn't care any more, why should I? But I'm trained to make a contribution and I can't afford to go stale, so I'll do something else.' And thirdly, 'Nobody cares what I really do any more, so why should I knock myself out?'

The first reaction suggests acceptance of an important and central occupational identity: to grow and develop within existing organizational parameters; to entrench by maintaining a straight career path (see Raelin 1985). The second indicates a sharp shift in interests and energy away from the employing organization – such as towards a business 'on the side' – but still using the organization as a secure base (Fineman 1980). The third response reflects the ennui typical of deep disillusionment about work, and perhaps about life: a defensive withdrawal (Paine 1982).

These reflections indicate varying degrees of fragmentation of the self, but always positioning all or part of the self in relationship to the job. There develops an intimate association between self and job, the individual influencing the job and the job influencing the individual; they stand in complex relationship to one another. In Arthur Miller's words, 'The fish is in the water and the water is in the fish' (Miller 1958). Furthermore, by mid-career the employing organization, with all of its service and status trappings, becomes the taken-for-granted setting for most middle-class work. Indeed, the manager and administrator are direct products of the corporate enterprise, without which they are very much as fish out of water.

So, for some, mid-career adjustments are problematic enough without the added burden of unemployment. For others, job loss may provide unexpected opportunities. The impact is far from uniform, as indicated by the following synopses from my 1983 work on counselling the unemployed.

Finance manager, age 46: 'I was made redundant along with 360 others. I saw it coming, but was assured it wouldn't hit me. Nevertheless I was completely disillusioned with senior management. The managing director used to go out to the local pub at 12 noon and return at 3 p.m., absolutely paralytic. Another one washes his car, and the third would lock himself in his room. You begin to think you're wasting your time.

'So I resigned myself to redundancy and was happy to leave. I thought I'd get my house in order and then get a job. But it hasn't worked out like this. I've run into deep financial problems which have pushed me into tranquillizers. I've become very worried about spending my money with little coming in. I haven't told many people that I'm unemployed. Should I go back to finance? Or change my past completely? Self-employable? I'm beginning to think I've wasted my life up to date. Unless I do something now I'll never do anything.'

Managing director, age 43: 'Basically I had to close down my engineering business – there was nothing else I could do in the declining market. I don't feel too bad about it as I got a lot out of it. It had to happen. Nevertheless it is a failure, and I don't want to repeat it.

'What has come as a shock, however, is the realization that I don't know what job to seek. Also, I can find no niche at home. I've tried hard to help with things around the house that I couldn't do for my wife while I was at work – and I'm seen as a nuisance. I'm in the way. I feel rejected, and no one knows where they stand.'

Audit manager, age 36: 'Many operations hinged around my work – sales, workshops, production. I was being pressed very hard by other managers to get things straight. I was spending 14 to 15 hours at the office, working at home as well. It was all coming together when I was asked to resign. They wanted results in three months that needed a full financial year!

'I was sickened and disheartened. All that work for someone else to reap the benefit and cream. My sacrifice had been enormous, having also had to cope with a new baby at home.'

Rejection and failure are dominant themes in these accounts; personal recognition, security, and competence in the job were key to these individuals' self-esteem and proper place in the world. Unemployment was a dramatic vote of no confidence. There are also indications of personal loss, a feeling that preoccupied other respondents. Such people talked of unemployment less as a judgement on themselves than as the loss of something closely associated with themselves – such as time, energy, a business, a product, colleagues. To paraphrase their sentiments: 'The job was everything to me but it wasn't all me.' They frequently mourned their loss, and were depressed, but they were less threatened by their misfortune than those who could define themselves only through their jobs.

Misfortune, though, was not the primary experience of more than one-third of the 100 people in the study. This group talked gleefully of the 'release from a vacuum', 'escape' from the tedium, the 'enormous weight off my shoulders'. Their jobs (they were now free to admit) were stultifying, entrapping, or stressful. They now had a chance to do something different, something exciting. Some did; many did not. Often the initial euphoria waned as the realities of the market-place penetrated. After dozens, sometimes scores, of job refusals underemployment was viewed as an acceptable prospect. Even more soberly, usually after about six months, the full implications of being 'surplus' in mid-career struck home. The following lament, from a 43-year-old manager, encapsulates this:

> 'I've been rejected for being overqualified, underqualified, too old, not enough business experience, and too much experience! I've tried everything. I usually get on a short-list but there's always someone else. We have money crises. Everything that wears out and needs replacing becomes a major crisis. My young daughter can't understand why I can't get every job I apply for. My wife can't get used to me being at home under her feet. People who have highly paid jobs, husband and wife working, moan about being short of money. They used to amuse me. Now I go out of my way to avoid them. We don't entertain now and rarely go out to friends.'
>
> (Quoted in Fineman 1983b: 76)

The fact that much middle-class work is couched in an ethos of status, security, and self-determination complicated feelings and adjustment to job loss. Typically, there are no community values of unemployment that actively support the middle class. To fail to obtain a manual post as a steel-worker when much of the steel industry has collapsed is, perhaps, forgivable. But to fail to find a home for skills and expertise that seem, on the face of it, 'professional' and 'rare' looks dubious. Shame and humiliation were common reactions, regardless of the reasons for job loss. Those accustomed to managing their own destiny found their life gradually slipping out of control as they discovered that they were unable to put things right themselves. The sense of disintegration was exacerbated with each failure to get an interview for a job and as 'good friends' and old colleagues drifted away into the shadows. Support was at best idiosyncratic and fleeting, and the pressure on a marriage could be intense, a theme developed by Jean Hartley in Chapter 7 in this volume. Some relationships splintered or failed; others emerged strengthened from a crisis shared.

Thus job loss and prolonged unemployment in mid-career became a private, introverted affair, often mirroring the insularity of the middle-class estates where the people lived. Those who survived best would ritualize an imitation of 'real work' by adapting familiar routines of dressing, eating, commuting, contacting, to the job of finding work. This was a pale reflection of the work organization that had formerly defined and located other roles in their life of family and leisure. But it provided, in the terms of Budge and Janoff (1984: 27), 'a magical force for the individual, countering the spell of fatalism and immobility, itself a function of feeling lost and worthless.'

Late career

Career theorists (e.g. Super 1957, Fiske, Lowenthal, and Chiriboga 1975) characterize the years from around forty-five to retirement as a period of consolidating one's position and maintaining what is valued or has been achieved. It is also a time when the broken or delayed career of a spouse can become firmly re-established as children are leaving home. These general statements disguise many individual differences and particular circumstances, such as of those who continue to grow and develop in their profession while others mark time, awaiting their retirement. As before, these distinctions, and their implications for an individual's conception of self, are of considerable importance for appreciating responses to unemployment.

My own study (Fineman 1983b) reveals the conflict experienced by those who, on the one hand, were happy to be relieved of a job that provided little intrinsic pleasure but, on the other, were at a loss as to how to spend the last decade or two of their working life. Their age, which had once spelled status and respect, was now associated with liability in the job market. Younger people were a 'better investment': cheaper to employ, more flexible to train, and a likely longer life-span in the job. All the older unemployed faced the helpless feeling that, whatever their credentials, it was extremely difficult to counteract the negative image of their age; it seemed an immutable barrier. Exhortations to retrain appeared fatuous. They felt that their age would be a constant factor acting against their interests, whatever they trained for, so there was little incentive to expose themselves to the risks of failure in new learning settings.

There were those whose late career was marked by continued application and loyalty to their company. They had, in their own terms, little reason to believe that their dedication and hard-won seniority would not be rewarded by, at least, continued security. Consequently, they were totally unprepared for the sudden (as it often was) 'redundancy', 'contraction', 'advice to resign', 'let go', or 'retirement'. A number were victims of their unaffected and genuinely placed motives to work:

political manoeuvres had overtaken them. Others had not seen, or did not want to see, the signs of decline in the industry of which they were a part. Their late-career skills and life aspirations were, anyhow, ill-fitted to competition for other jobs.

For some, initial negative feelings were a little mollified by being able to negotiate terms of exit. This provided some sense of control and a tangible way of expressing resentment. Underlying passions were, however, difficult to suppress. They felt cheated, conned out of work after years of misplaced loyalty. They experienced deep insecurity and purposelessness in the face of shattered plans for retirement, especially when pension rights were curtailed. There were expressions of cynicism and stress, of feeling devalued, with little prospect of recovering their occupational value.

Legacy and change

For the middle class, unemployment highlights, and challenges, personal fantasies and societal myths about professional jobs and careers. The foundation institutions for many middle-class careers – the higher-education and advanced-training establishments – have been pushed and pulled into the centre of the commercial arena and been asked to account for themselves in cost-benefit terms. Those people who choose to study subjects of low currency by such criteria are likely to find themselves occupationally disenfranchised compared with those who take to more socially acceptable disciplines. Society, the argument runs, cannot afford to indulge freedom of occupational choice; there must be a rationing procedure. Choice is curtailed further by reducing government funds to the less 'viable' academic departments.

The values which underpin these directions are in part political, driven by the imperatives of a government that, to a lesser or greater extent, mirrors public opinion. What our study of the unemployed reveals, though, is that whatever formulas exist for the quality of life, they are often decidedly more complex than those applied to financial balance sheets. The expectations of those who are nudged by middle-class standards towards professionalized careers rarely include notions of likely redundancy or a nonstart to working life. If an occupation withers, so does the social fabric of which it is a part – job-holder, family, and community.

This can often be a one-way ratchet. Resetting the economic equation does not necessarily reset the social and psychological one (Estes 1973, Kaufman 1982, Fineman 1983b, Shamir 1985). For example, those unemployed who eventually find themselves a new job, which turns out not to be that change in direction that they so desired, can be more disturbed than their still unemployed counterparts. In addition, a family move for one member's job, in mid-career, away from a familiar community, can sow seeds of schism and resentment within the family. There are also indications that many of the re-employed feel far less sure of themselves, and less willing to take risks that might jeopardize their security. They work cautiously and with little commitment or careerist spirit (see also Fineman forthcoming).

The employment problems of the skilled and well educated raise difficulties that inevitably involve market-place considerations. But whether the market-place should determine policy and decisions on what is educationally worthy, what skills should be developed, and the nature of occupation in our society, must be open to serious debate. As the preceding account has shown, there are considerable social costs, and a certain psychological precariousness, when people become commodities of commercial exchange and pawns of political dogma.

Undoubtedly, there are practical issues to confront. In the face of what the International Labour Office (1985) has termed 'a multitude of exciting and rewarding new occupations ranging from ocean floor industry to moon mining', there are important strategic decisions to be made on resources for particular forms of training and education. Yet I sense a wistful sigh from the out-of-work ship designer, chemist, biologist, oil engineer, and town planner as they recall the early rhetoric of 'excitement and reward' associated with their own, now declining, professions.

How can we avoid educating and training for redundancy, and its attendant personal and social difficulties? Not, it would seem, by increasing emphasis on specialization in school and university (see Leo Hendry's discussion in Chapter 11, below). Not by encouraging early professionalization, locked in with a particular industry or firm (one route to disaffection and burn-out). And not by forcing career decisions through the economic flavour of the decade. All such moves, while perhaps expedient in the short term, work against a vision of a well-qualified work-force adapting to changing circumstances.

If we view a career in its more fundamental sense, a pathway through life, then *continuing* education, training, and guidance can support, generate, and capitalize upon change – a responsibility for governments, employers, and trade unions. Such an approach is more likely to produce 'change-wise' people who can, because of a combination of generalist and specialist skills and knowledge, shift their occupational talents around, as needs be, inside and outside conventional occupational settings and structures. Dependency on *the* organization and *the* profession is much reduced, while flexible expertise is enhanced. Such education and training would need to foster social and psychological insight alongside professional expertise if an individual is to understand and accommodate personal change and the vagaries of life. In this way choice for the individual may increase: choice in the use of time, choice about how and where to work, and choice of purpose. It could reduce the limitations experienced by many of the well qualified as they struggle for a niche in a society that deems them redundant, perhaps even before they start work.

A move in this direction requires a significant frame-shift in our values and practices about education and training. We currently fast limit an individual's options relatively early in the educational process; the educational dilettante is often regarded with some suspicion. Programmes of training and personal development at work tend to be accorded a low priority amongst British employers (Manpower Services Commission 1985). It is perhaps not surprising that we often lurch and stumble in the face of change.

References

Bath University (1985) *First Destination Return. Undergraduate Register by Course. 1984 Graduation Year.*

Brearley, S. (1984) *The Medical Manpower Crisis – Who Can Solve It?*. Unpublished paper. Hospital Junior Staff Committee, British Medical Association.

Briers, J. L. (1967) Older People as Wasted Resources. *Public Utilities Fortnightly* 80, 12 October: 45–50.

British Medical Association (1984) Hospital Junior Staff Unemployment Survey. *British Medical Journal* 289, October: 936.

Budge, S. and Janoff, R. (1984) How Managers Face Prolonged Job Loss. *Business*, April/June: 22–9.

Dalton, G. W., Thompson, P. H., and Price, R. L. (1980) The Four Stages of Professional Careers – New Look at Performance by Professionals. In M. A. Morgan (ed.) *Management Career Development*. New York: Van Nostrand.

Department of Employment (1983) *Labour Force Survey*. London: HMSO.

—— (1985) *Social Trends*. London: HMSO.

Estes, R. J. (1973) *The Unemployed Professional: The Social, Emotional and Political Consequences of Job Loss among Education Workers*. Unpublished doctoral dissertation. Berkeley, Calif.: University of California.

Fineman, S. (1980) Stress among Technical Support Staff in Research and Development. In C. L. Cooper and J. Marshall (eds) *White Collar and Professional Stress*. Chichester: Wiley.

—— (1983a) Work Meanings, Non-work and the Taken-for-Granted. *Journal of Management Studies* 20 (2): 143–57.

—— (1983b) *White Collar Unemployment: Impact and Stress*. Chichester: Wiley.

—— (1985a) *Social Work Stress and Intervention*. Aldershot: Gower.

—— (1985b) The Skills of Getting by. In A. Strati (ed.) *The Symbolics of Skill*. Trento: Dipartimento di Politica Sociale.

—— (forthcoming) Back to Employment: Wounds and Wisdoms. In D. Fryer and P. Ullah (eds) *Unemployed People: Social and Psychological Perspectives*. Milton Keynes: Open University Press.

Fiske, M., Lowenthal, M. T., and Chiriboga, D. (1975) *Four Shapes of Life: A Comparative Study of Women and Men Facing Transitions*. London: Jossey-Bass.

Fox, A. (1980) The Meaning of Work. In G. Esland and G. Salaman (eds) *The Politics of Work and Organizations*. Milton Keynes: Open University Press.

Frost, P. J., Mitchell, V. F., and Nord, W. R. (1982) *Organizational Reality*. Glenview, Ill.: Scott Foresman.

Goldthorpe, J. M. (1978) Comment on Structure, Consciousness and Action. *British Journal of Sociology* 29: 436–38.

Greenhalgh, L. and Rosenblatt, Z. (1984) Job Insecurity: Towards Conceptual Clarity. *Academy of Management Review* 9 (3): 438–48.

Hall, D. T. (1976) *Careers in Organizations*. Santa Monica, Calif.: Goodyear.

Hall, D. T. and Nougaim, K. E. (1968) An Examination of Maslow's Need Hierarchy in an Organizational Setting. *Organizational Behaviour and Human Performance* 3: 12–35.

Hermann, J. (1980) Unemployment among French Physicians. *Ther. d. Gegenw.* 119: 108–12.

Herzog, M. (1980) *From Hand to Mouth*. Harmondsworth: Penguin.

HMSO (1985) *The Development of Higher Education into the 1990s*. London.

Hochschild, A. R. (1983) *The Managed Heart*. Berkeley, Calif.: University of California.

International Labour Office (Advisory Committee on Salaried Employees and Professional Workers) (1985) *After Graduation – the Dole Queue?*. Geneva.

Jones, L. Y. (1980) My Son, the Doctor of Cab Driving. *American Demographics*, November/December.

Kaufman, H. G. (1982) *Professionals in Search of Work*. New York: Wiley.

Levitan, S. A. and Carlson, P. E. (1984) Middle Class Shrinkage?. *Across the Board*, October: 55–9.

Manpower Services Commission (1985) *Challenge to Complacency*. Sheffield: MSC.

Miller, A. (1958) The Shadow of the Gods. *Harpers Magazine*, August: 35–43.

Mills, C. W. (1951) *White Collar*. New York: Oxford University Press.

Office of Technology Assessment (1980) *Forecasts of Physician Supply and Requirements*. Washington, DC: US Government Printing Office.

Paine, W. S. (ed.) (1982) *Job Stress and Burnout*. Beverly Hills: Sage.

Parkhouse, J. (1979) *Medical Manpower in Britain*. Edinburgh: Churchill Livingstone.

Pines, A. M., Aronson, E., and Kafry, D. (1981) *Burnout*. New York: Free Press.

Poole, R. (1984) Letter to the *Guardian*, 22 August.

Raelin, J. A. (1985) Work Patterns in the Professional Life-Cycle. *Journal of Occupational Psychology* 58: 177–87.

Sarason, S. B. (1977) *Work, Aging and Social Change*. New York: Free Press.

Schein, E. H. (1971) Organizational Socialization and the Profession of Management. In D. Kolb, I. Rubin, and J. McIntyre (eds) *Organizational Psychology: A Book of Readings*. Englewood Cliffs, NJ: Prentice-Hall.

Shamir, B. (1985) *The Psychological Consequence of Re-employment*. Unpublished paper. Department of Sociology and Social Anthropology, The Hebrew University of Jerusalem.

Sinfield, A. (1981) *What Unemployment Means*. Oxford: Martin Robertson.

Super, D. E. (1957) *The Psychology of Careers*. New York: Harper & Row.

Terkel, S. (1974) *Working*. New York: Pantheon.

Thirugnanam, T. (1977) Unemployment among Doctors. *Journal of the Indian Medical Association* 69 (3): 64–6.

University Grants Committee (1985) *University Statistics 1983–84*. Cheltenham: Universities' Statistical Record.

Wilby, P. (1985) Teachers in Sales Drive. *Sunday Times*, 23 June.

Part 2
Families and communities

6. Families facing redundancy

David Y. Clark

Much attention has been paid to the plight of the unemployed and their families. Most of this has focused upon areas of heavy unemployment where there have been strong elements of community spirit and action (e.g. Sinfield 1970, Binns and Mars 1984, Morris 1984, Pahl 1984). At the other extreme research has focused on isolated individuals. This approach has either tended to over-emphasize the impersonal operations of the market economy or else has limited discussion to the problems of individual adjustment to the reality of unemployment (e.g. Kahn 1964, Martin and Fryer 1973, Hayes and Nutman 1981).

This chapter focuses on the middle ground, situated somewhere between the 'traditional' community – in which workmates are normally leisure-time companions, often neighbours, and not infrequently kinsmen (Lockwood 1966: 251) – and the postulated 'isolated' individual reacting to market forces and psychological stress. The main assumption here is that the response to redundancy cannot satisfactorily be understood in terms of a transitional cycle that affects only the redundant worker. Instead, I would argue that the response of the household as a whole, with its own priorities and own set of resources, has a crucial impact on individual reactions to redundancy. This study therefore focuses on the *household* as the unit of analysis.

Household organization

Ray Pahl (1980, 1984) has argued that there is an interrelationship between household decisions about labour-force participation and the domestic division of labour. I have suggested elsewhere that we need to place household decisions about work, whether paid or unpaid, in the context

97

of a wider theoretical framework for examining household organization (Clark 1984). In particular, I have favoured the use of a system model that would explicitly take into account the interrelationships between the different spheres of household activity, at work and in leisure. One means of analysing household organization in this way is through the application of an input/output model, as illustrated in *Figure 1*.

Figure 1 An input/output model of household organization

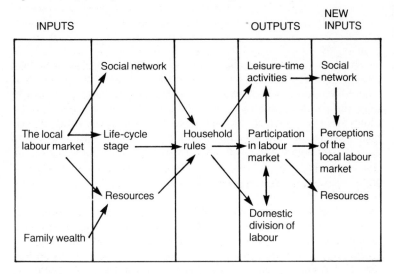

Inputs in this model consist of such factors as the state of the local labour market, stage in the life cycle, type of social networks maintained by the household, and the resources that each member brings into the household. These inputs interact with each other, so that stage in the life cycle influences to some extent the type of social network maintained by the household. Perceptions about the state of the local labour market, on the other hand, are partially filtered through the perceptions of other members of the social network and also partly distorted by factors connected with the stage in the life cycle.

Each household develops its own style in balancing the various demands and pressures generated by the different domains of household activity and the different external forces operating on these domains. The manner in which such a balance is struck is determined by the 'household rules' about household behaviour. Hence, while external inputs are fed into the household decision-making, this process is itself regulated by family codes about decision-making, about exchange and negotiation, about distributive justice and maximum joint profit, the use of power (whether non-legitimate power or authority), rules about communication within the household, and whether such communication takes place in an atmosphere of trust, conflict, hostility, or violence (Scanzoni 1979: 313).

The outputs in this model are choice outcomes in terms of decisions about the domestic division of labour, participation in the labour market, and leisure-time activities. These outputs also interact with each other, so that there is a close interrelationship between the domestic division of labour and participation in paid work, as Pahl (1980, 1984) has noted. Choices about leisure-time activities are constrained by the amount of time devoted to work, whether paid or unpaid, whilst the amount of financial resources available for leisure is generally dependent on the level of earnings.

Outputs also interact with inputs in a circular manner, as choices of leisure-time activities have implications for the type of social network maintained by the household, whilst the type of labour-market participation will influence the way in which the household perceives the local labour market. Thus, according to this model, household choices are determined partly by the inputs from the external environment and partly by the internal household system of rules, norms, and decision-making processes.

This chapter will explore the applicability of this model to the situation of households facing redundancy and will examine the extent to which factors such as the local labour market, family wealth, social networks, life cycle, and household rules affect household responses to unemployment. In particular, I will seek to apply this model to the pattern of responses of a sample of fifty-three households living in South London. These households were selected on the basis of the redundancy of one of their members.

Redundancies in South London

I had originally set out to undertake a study of shift-work in manufacturing industry in Wandsworth, an inner-city area in South London. This study was funded by a grant from the Social Science Research Council and was completed in 1983 (Clark 1983). However, during the course of my research project a large number of factories were either on short time or else in the process of being closed down altogether. In one case the process of closure was very dramatic. I had spent two weeks in November 1980 talking to shift-workers on the shop floor at Garton

Glucose (Tate & Lyle), in Battersea. The firm had more than five hundred employees, including 242 male workers engaged in shift-work at the time. There was some talk in the air of changes being introduced in the shift system, and there was unease amongst the work-force about these changes. Then, suddenly, came the bombshell. The firm announced that the plant would be closed down within three weeks. For the next week or so most of the employees went to work in a sort of daze, still not fully believing what was happening.

One-third of the shift-workers at Garton Glucose had previously agreed to take part in my survey on shift-work. Now they had to look elsewhere for jobs, whilst I had to look elsewhere for my sample of shift-workers. Nevertheless, I felt that it was important to monitor the effect of these redundancies on the workers concerned. I contacted twenty-seven redundant shift-workers and their households between February and May 1981, that is to say between three and six months after they were made redundant. I also interviewed the same respondents some six months later, between October and December 1981.

Elsewhere the process of plant closure was more gradual, and the workers were given more warning. At Keyswitch Varley, a light engineering firm, a decision had been taken to relocate from Wandsworth to new premises in Woolwich. The Wandsworth plant was closed down in June 1982; in the process of relocation some eighty employees were made redundant, sixty of whom were women who had worked on the shop floor.

In 1983 I obtained a grant from the Nuffield Foundation to conduct interviews with redundant workers in the South London area. In the course of this project twenty-six of the women who were made redundant from Keyswitch Varley were interviewed, some nine months after the redundancy (Clark 1985).

The local labour market

The most striking finding to emerge from the interviews with former employees of Garton Glucose and Keyswitch Varley was the very slow rate of re-employment. Only a third of those interviewed had obtained re-employment within six months of their redundancy.

The most important single reason for the low re-employment rate in the initial stages of redundancy was the acute shortage of employment opportunities in manufacturing industry. Wandsworth, like many other inner-city areas in Britain, had witnessed a long-term decline in manufacturing jobs, a process that had been speeded up even further by the recent economic recession. Many of the redundant workers were forced to seek employment in the service sector and generally to accept lower wage levels than those they had been used to in manufacturing industry. Only two former employees of Garton Glucose and two former employees of Keyswitch Varley had found jobs in manufacturing industry, whilst seventeen men and ten women in the sample had found new jobs in the service sector, within a year of their redundancy.

The wage drop incurred in the new jobs was particularly marked for the men, who had previously undertaken shift-work. Whereas they had been used to a take-home pay ranging from £105 to £150, many of them had to accept much lower wages in the service sector. A security guard working a sixty-hour week was able to take home £84 per week; a hospital porter took home £104 per week. Quite a few of the respondents were earning between £70 and £90 a week, after deductions.

In order to maximize their wages many of the male workers obtained jobs in the service sector that entailed shift-work. Eight out of the nineteen male respondents who had obtained jobs by December 1981, a year after their redundancy, were engaged in shift-work. Having once done shift-work meant that they were more likely to consider jobs that required shift-work. For those who had no special skills, willingness to work shift hours was perhaps their only marketable asset, and this was especially the case for older workers.

For the women, on the other hand, the switch to employment in the service industry was far less dramatic. Many of the women had previously undertaken work in the service sector at some stage in their working lives, and in any case the difference in female earnings between manufacturing and service industry was slight.

Women at Keyswitch Varley had generally been receiving between £50 and £55 per week in their wage packets. The average take-home pay for these women in service industry was £51.60 per week in the private sector and £71.50 in the public sector. Many women, however, stated that they had preferred working in factories, as working conditions in service industry were appalling, and this was especially so in the private sector. One woman, who had worked in a laundry firm for three months, said this about it: 'Too much work, watched all the time, no toilet-paper, cold, bad money, no tea-break.' Other women working for the same firm complained about the lack of facilities, the racism, and the fact that they had to stand all the time. Another woman, who had worked in a fast-food restaurant in Central London for one month, gave up her job due to the pressure under which she had been working, the long journey to work, and the fact that she took home only £36 per week for all her pains.

The shortage of employment opportunities in manufacturing industry and the unattractive nature of most service jobs probably accounted for the slow rate of re-employment in Wandsworth. By contrast, a study of redundancies in an outer London area found much faster rates of re-employment. A report on redundancies at Firestone Tyre & Rubber Company in Brentford, which closed down in February 1980, revealed that as many as 73 per cent of the redundant workers were in new employment within seven to eight months of their redundancy (Carmichael and Cook 1981).

Stage in the family cycle

The major factor pushing the redundant worker into work, however unattractive or poorly paid such work may be, is financial need. This is particularly noticeable amongst the men. All four male respondents who had taken on shift-work within six months of their redundancy were married with dependent children. These four men ranged from 28 to 48 years of age and were all semi-skilled. By contrast, those men who had obtained day-work within six months of their redundancy had no dependent children at all. They also spanned a wider age range, from 25 to 60, and included skilled as well as semi-skilled workers.

Amongst the female respondents, those who were quickest to take on new jobs were not necessarily those in most financial need, although some were the sole wage-earners. Thus, one widow had three dependent children under the age of thirteen, while another woman had five children to support.

While position in the family life cycle is by no means the only factor pushing redundant workers back into employment, the contrast between households that have reached different stages in the life cycle is revealing.

Households with dependent children

Case No. 1

This man, aged 41, had two dependent children, still at school, and a teenage son who had just left school and had gone through a series of jobs and a spell of unemployment. He also had an older daughter, aged 19, who had a steady job as a punch-card operator. His wife was not in regular paid work, although she occasionally did a cleaning job in the evenings.

Upon leaving Garton Glucose he obtained re-employment as a security guard. He had previously worked as a part-time security guard, as a second job, and this had enabled him to find a new job very quickly. The pay was relatively low, £1.44 an hour for the first forty-four hours in the week, £1.85 for any additional hours. He said that he had to work a sixty-hour week in order to make sufficient money. He was also dissatisfied that he had no weekends to himself, as he had to work at weekends as well (either on days or on nights) in order to make up the hours. During the week he generally worked on nights, which at least gave him time to do some shopping with his wife, to decorate the house, or to service his motor bike; but his wife did not like being on her own at night all the time.

Within three months, however, he was able to obtain a job elsewhere, still as a security guard, but this time with better pay and better hours. His older daughter had spotted a vacancy at her workplace and had obtained application forms for him. He now worked in the daytime only and on sixteen weekends out of fifty-two. He had better holiday provision and was now part of a pension scheme. He was far happier in this job and claimed he had merely taken on the previous job as a stopgap measure, in the hope of finding a better job later on.

As well as having few financial resources, the household had a very restricted social network. Both spouses came from Eire, and their parents still lived there. The respondent occasionally visited an aunt of his in another part of South London, but otherwise had few contacts with relatives in Britain. He had close contacts with a few neighbours and occasionally saw his ex-workmates from Garton Glucose or spoke to them on the telephone, but he had no friends he would see on a regular basis. Most of his leisure time was home centred, and when he was at home during the day he would take part in most of the household chores.

Case No. 2

An Indian widow, aged 34, with three children under 13, found another job within three months of her redundancy. She found work in a laundry, which she disliked. She would have preferred factory work and felt that her new job compared unfavourably with most jobs that were available in the area. The money was the most important reason she gave for working.

During her spell of unemployment she had relied mainly on her unemployment benefit. Her own parents lived in India, and she had not seen them for three years, but she maintained close contacts with her in-laws. She had a mother-in-law and two brothers-in-law who lived in the same neighbourhood and whom she saw twice a month. Her closest contacts were with a neighbour whom she saw daily and a former workmate, whom she saw once a week. She visited her Hindu temple about once a month and found the support she received from her own community very reassuring. Nevertheless, she had relatively few resources to fall back upon and felt compelled to accept whatever job she could get.

Case No. 3

One Ghanaian woman, aged 44, had five children living with her, ranging from 8 to 20 years old. Her husband was out of work at the time of the interview and had returned to Ghana to explore job opportunities there. None of the children was employed, and three of them were still attending school. They had been living in the same council flat for the past ten years and had fully expected to carry on living there.

The couple's joint experience of redundancy, however, had forced them to reconsider their plans. She had decided to find new employment in London, whilst her husband would explore the viability of returning to Ghana. Within two months she had found work in a factory, as a quality control inspector. This work was relatively well paid. Her take-home pay was £65 per week, but she had to work forty-two hours per week, on a two-shift system that included night-work and weekend working (on alternate weekends). She disliked working weekends and particularly disliked the night-shift, when she had to leave her children alone, in the care of her eldest daughter, aged 20. But she needed the money, as she had got into debt during her brief spell of unemployment, and hence she had taken on the job.

She had a number of relatives, mostly cousins and aunts, living in nearby Balham, whom she saw once a month. She also had friends on the same housing estate, whom she saw on a daily basis. She would often meet her workmates and former workmates when she went shopping, but had stopped seeing former workmates who lived further afield.

Households in the launching stage

Case No. 4

Another respondent, aged 45, had been unemployed for nine months after being made redundant. During that period he had taken on odd jobs and, all told, he reckoned he had done three weeks' work in the space of those nine months, mainly driving lorries and vans. He had seriously considered giving up his job even prior to his redundancy, as shift-work no longer suited him. His wife used to complain that she was often on her own in the evenings, now that their teenage children spent most of their leisure time outside the home. Moreover, financially he no longer needed to work quite as hard and he could afford to take a drop in wages by going on to day-work. Redundancy was for him a blessing in disguise, although he had spent some anxious months seeking work and at times had despaired of ever finding suitable employment again.

His wife had a full-time job throughout this period. By the time of the second interview, his 21-year-old son had managed to obtain a job he enjoyed. Nevertheless, his spell of unemployment had lasted longer than he had anticipated, and he had made strenuous efforts to find re-employment. He had even seriously considered moving in search of better job opportunities elsewhere.

He had spent three weeks in the North of England looking for work, as he had been advised by a friend that work was available there; but it turned out to be only seasonal work, so he had come back to London. He also had close friends who had moved to the United States and had suggested he join them. These friends undertook to arrange jobs and accommodation for the whole family, and so the entire household went to the USA during the Easter holidays to have a look. These friends found jobs for the respondent, his wife, and his son, and they were even shown round a number of houses that would have been suitable for them. At this stage, however, the respondent's children were reluctant to stay in the US, especially the younger daughter, who was about to leave school and did not want to leave her English boy-friend behind. They returned to London without making any final decision about whether to emigrate. Within the next few months the respondent was able to obtain the kind of job he had been looking for. It was a daytime job, as a truck driver for a chain store in London. It was the kind of work he enjoyed doing; the hours suited him, and it was local.

Childless couples

Households with no dependent children and with few ties to the locality were even more likely to contemplate drastic changes.

Case No. 5

One couple in the study was actively taking steps to emigrate. The husband had already found alternative employment abroad, and they were merely waiting for formal immigration procedures and visa applications to take their course. Admittedly the husband was in a better position to seek employment abroad than the other respondents in the sample: he was a skilled laboratory technician with some qualifications.

Nevertheless, the fact that the couple had no children and that they had few social attachments to people living in Britain made it significantly easier to contemplate emigrating. Both husband and wife were born in Poland, although the husband was brought up in Britain. The wife had only recently arrived here and although she had made a number of friends through her workplace, most of her close friends and relatives were still in Poland.

The decision to emigrate had not been an easy one, as the husband would be leaving his elderly mother behind, whilst the wife would be leaving her full-time job and the friendships she had recently established. It took at least six months before both spouses were fully committed to the idea of emigrating and began to regard it as a firm decision to leave.

It should by now be clear that it is not possible to explain household decisions merely in terms of a single factor. This last case, in particular, reveals the importance of such factors as position in the labour market (skilled work), position in the family cycle (childless couple), and the type of social network maintained by the household (loose-knit and cosmopolitan, with few ties to the neighbourhood). All these features interact in such a way as to make certain outcomes more likely: in this case, emigration.

The social network

Throughout this chapter I have pointed out the importance of social networks in providing a support mechanism for households facing redundancy and unemployment. Households that have more tenuous ties to the immediate neighbourhood are not likely to receive much support from the local community. In such cases, households in the child-rearing stage that feel the need for the comfort and reassurance of a locally based network of kin and friends might seek to return to areas in which they had previously established strong local ties.

If return migration was not a practical option, then re-employment as soon as possible was an economic necessity for such households. Respondents with few ties to the local area might take on the first offer of a job that comes their way, however unattractive such a job might be, in the hope of eventually finding a better one. This was the strategy adopted by the respondent in case No. 1, who took on a poorly paid job as a security guard. Within three months he had found himself a better job, with improved hours and pay. It is also worth noting that his daughter was instrumental in notifying him of the job vacancy.

The social network of respondents was vitally important in providing information about jobs. If respondents had few ties to the neighbourhood, they had to rely on other sources of information. Other household members were always good sources of information about job vacancies, especially if they were employed themselves. For example, the lorry driver in case No. 4 was able to rely on information from friends he had established in other parts of the country and he even extended his job search across the Atlantic on the advice of a friend who had emigrated there. For those seeking jobs more locally, former workmates were also good sources of information. Thus four of the women formerly employed at Keyswitch Varley ended up working in the same laundry; word had got round that there were vacancies at that establishment.

But social networks are important not only as sources of information about jobs; they also provide moral support and security in times of adversity. The Indian widow in case No. 2 visited her Hindu temple once a month, and this helped her to realize that she was not all alone in facing her problems. She also maintained close ties with her mother-in-law and her two brothers-in-law and their families. Her social network was an important source of continuity for her, providing a link with her traditions and customs, as well as maintaining the relationships she had established prior to her widowhood.

Another aspect of social networks is the extent to which they may provide well-established and long-term support mechanisms rooted in a particular locality, as illustrated by the following case.

Case No. 6

This household contained two school-age children. The wife carried on working full time while the husband was out of work for a year, doing occasional odd jobs. The wife had been born and brought up in Battersea, where they lived, and her parents still lived fairly close by. The husband had been born in the neighbouring borough of Lambeth and had moved to Battersea when he got married. Until he was made redundant, he had worked in Battersea and had made a number of close friends amongst his workmates. He had carried on seeing them regularly after their redundancy, usually meeting in a pub.

Although this household had contemplated emigrating because of the lack of job opportunities in Britain, this had never been regarded as a viable proposition. The wife was particularly keen to move out of their present accommodation to more desirable premises, but preferably still within Battersea; she did not want to move further afield. When I called upon the household a year after the closure of Garton Glucose, the husband was still unemployed and was helping one of his friends on a window-cleaning round.

The fact that both husband and wife had such close personal ties with people in the immediate locality probably acted as a restraining and at the same time supportive influence which helped the household in its decision not to move away. By contrast, the childless couple described in case No. 5 had few ties to the local neighbourhood and hence found the prospect of emigrating less daunting.

Wealth and family resources

Household responses to redundancy are likely to vary according to the particular financial circumstances of the household. Older workers with long-standing service in the firm might receive relatively generous redundancy payments and might be able to afford to take a break from work for a while. Households in which there are two or more wage-earners might be in a better position to cope with the unemployment of one of their members. The pressure to return to work as soon as possible is probably felt most directly by those with less financial resources to fall back upon.

It is particularly instructive to examine the responses of two households that were at the same stage in the family cycle but enjoyed different financial circumstances. Two women in their fifties, formerly employed at Keyswitch Varley, were both born and bred in Wandsworth, married with three grown-up children. Both women lived in council accommodation, which would suggest some similarity in economic circumstances, and yet there were interesting differences in their responses to redundancy, as revealed in the following accounts.

Case No. 7

This couple had developed particularly strong ties in the local community. The wife had three marrried brothers and one married sister who lived in Wandsworth, another sister living close by, a brother-in-law living in Wandsworth, and a cousin near by. She had a son, a daughter, and five grandchildren also living near by, as well as a married daughter living further afield in Basingstoke. She still maintained contact with one of her former school-friends and with another of her friends who had grown up together with her in the same area. She belonged to a local social club and went there once a week, together with her husband and married children. Her husband worked as a schoolkeeper in a local school and he too maintained strong ties in the locality.

She had been active in a trade union and had been a shop steward at Keyswitch Varley. Within three months of her redundancy she had found work as a calender hand in the laundry of a nearby hospital and had joined the union there. She reported that money was the most important reason for working, despite the fact that the household did not have any large financial commitments. During her spell of unemployment her family had been pleased that she was at home more, but she herself missed the spending money and the sense of independence. She had to manage during that time on what her husband gave her; she could not claim unemployment benefit because she had not paid any national insurance contributions.

This woman reported feeling bored and lonely at home. Her active involvement in the trade union movement had given her a sense of purpose, and she missed the contacts at work; hence her eagerness to return to paid work.

Case No. 8

This couple maintained fewer contacts in the area. They had one married son living locally, but their two daughters lived farther afield. One of the wife's sisters lived in the same neighbourhood, while the other sister lived farther away, in Great Yarmouth. The wife also had a number of cousins who lived in other parts of Britain. She had four sets of close friends, but only one of them lived locally.

At the time of the interview she had been unemployed for eight months. She said that she had been upset about her redundancy at first but had not been unduly worried, as she was not in particularly good health and was glad not to have to work. She felt that she had more time to relax and to do the things she wanted. Her family was delighted she was no longer working, and so were her friends. She had more time to visit her children, relatives, and friends who lived some distance away and she frequently went away on such visits.

Her husband was a company director and owned his own plastering business. The household could manage financially solely on her husband's earnings. After her redundancy, he had agreed to give her an increased allowance. Husband and wife jointly belonged to a social club, but, significantly, the club was in Battersea, which was at the other end of the borough from where they were living. They also frequently went out together for evening meals or to a dinner and dance at a club.

Clearly, this woman was under less financial pressure to seek work. She was also far less involved in social relationships within the neighbourhood, and she looked forward to more frequent contacts with friends and relatives who lived further afield and whom she might otherwise have seen less often.

In both these cases the household could have managed financially by relying exclusively on the income of the husband. In the former household the wife had gone back to work within three months of her redundancy, partly because she missed the financial independence and the extra spending money that she could obtain from paid work. In the latter household the wife was not in any particular hurry to return to work. Her husband was doing well in his plastering business, and they could easily afford to maintain a relatively high standard of living even without her returning to work. Thus they frequently went out to a dinner and dance at a club, and she had enough spending money to go on frequent trips to visit family and friends. Greater financial resources enabled this couple to maintain a standard of living after the redundancy similar to what they had been used to before.

Yet, in the second case, other factors also contributed to the wife's decision not to return to work as soon as possible. The couple's social network extended beyond the confines of the immediate locality. The redundancy provided the wife with an opportunity to travel and visit her various children, friends, and relatives living outside London. Her ill health provided an additional justification for not returning to work too soon.

Household rules

While material circumstances undoubtedly play their part in determining household responses to redundancy, there is another area involved in household decision-making, which I refer to as household rules. Household rules encompass all the established norms and tacit understandings that are particular to the household.

Whether the wife receives a household allowance, and whether this allowance is increased following the wife's redundancy (case No. 8), is something that is determined by pre-existing patterns of interaction and by the shared understandings within the household. Who is allowed to sit in the armchair in the lounge, whether children are allowed to play or watch television in the lounge when visitors are around, or indeed whether the television stays on throughout broadcasting time, regardless of other activities within the household – all these are determined by established household rules. The kinds of agreement reached, in particular by the marital couple, will have a determining impact on the way the household responds to redundancy.

The present study was unable to examine such household rules in any detail, as this would have required much more in-depth interviewing, long-term observation, and a greater degree of rapport than was possible to establish in the course of two interviews. Nevertheless, some of these rules can be discerned by examining some of the outcomes of household decision-making. This section will focus on two related issues: the domestic division of labour and enforced domesticity. The domestic division of labour is an area increasingly becoming a matter for negotiations between household members (Pahl 1982b: 14). In addition, I will examine the manner in which ethnicity may be a factor impinging on the development of household rules and so may influence the outcome of household decisions.

Domestic division of labour

The extent of male involvement in domestic tasks and responsibilities during spells of unemployment has received considerable attention from a number of researchers (Marsden and Duff 1975, Morris 1983, Binns and Mars 1984, McKee and Bell 1984, Pahl 1984). Marsden and Duff claim that unemployment reinforces traditional views of segregated male and female roles, with very little sharing of household tasks. McKee and Bell point out that, if anything, wives of unemployed men end up with even more restricted domestic lives, as the presence of their husbands in the home limits their control of the domestic use of space in the day without in any way reducing their domestic burdens. Furthermore, the social security regulations operate in such a way as to discourage the employment of women whose husbands are out of work; hence such women are forced to remain full-time housewives, thereby reinforcing female dependency.

Few researchers have examined the importance of household rules in determining the domestic division of labour, but a number of writers refer to the importance of such factors as incorporation in the labour market, the social network of the couple, and stage in the family cycle.

Binns and Mars suggest that older workers are much more likely to conform to traditional gender roles, whilst there is a greater shift towards joint conjugal relationships and responsibilities amongst the younger couples. They stress the importance of male incorporation into the labour market as the major mechanism for the perpetuation of male domination in the domestic sphere. The less secure the incorporation into the labour market, the more likely it is that the household will adopt less rigid definitions of gender.

Pahl, on the other hand, stresses the importance of the extent of female participation in the labour market. Pahl notes that households containing children under five years of age are more likely to have conventional patterns of domestic division of labour; in later stages of the family cycle women are more likely to be involved in paid work, and as a consequence men are more inclined to take on some of the domestic duties.

In addition, Binns and Mars refer to the importance of the social network in exerting pressure on the couple towards conformity to traditional gender roles, especially pressure coming from the parents of the couple. In a previous seminar paper, Binns also stressed the support for more egalitarian role relationships, which the younger couples received from their network of married friends in similar circumstances to themselves (Binns 1983).

One factor that I would add to the above list is the extent to which the household response to redundancy is influenced by already established patterns of household organization and household conventions. The couple described in case No. 6, for instance, was moving towards the model of the symmetrical conjugal family. When I arrived to interview the family, some six months after the redundancy, the husband had come back home from a day's casual work and was just finishing his evening meal. His wife, who worked full time in a junior managerial capacity, had cooked the meal that evening. The husband was complaining that he had not enjoyed the dinner; it had not been to his liking. His wife confirmed that she did not enjoy cooking and that her husband was the better cook. When he worked on shifts at Garton Glucose he used to cook the meal on his days off and now that he was at home most of the time he often cooked the family meal. The acceptance of shared domestic tasks had begun to take shape prior to the redundancy.

This gradual shift to more egalitarian role relationships is also described by Pahl for households on the Isle of Sheppey: 'Jim's day had not changed that much. He had always been at home a lot and he had always done work around the house. He had always collected the children from school but now he was getting up earlier – at 7.30 a.m. – and took them in the morning as well. He was also cooking more' (Pahl 1984: 298). Established patterns of interaction within the household and pre-existing household rules, then, play a large part in shaping household responses to redundancy.

Domesticity

As a result of redundancy a number of women found themselves drawn into increasing domesticity. This was particularly marked amongst women with five or more children and amongst women who were responsible for looking after an elderly relative in addition to their own children.

Case No. 9

One Pakistani woman, aged 42, had five children, ranging from 12 to 20 years old. Her husband worked as a company secretary, and the household relied solely on his income. She had been unemployed for nine months at the time of the interview. She was miserable about losing her job. She was bored at home and felt she was getting lazy. She had developed a number of health complaints since her redundancy; she had headaches and fits of giddiness and slept badly. She missed being busy at work and the opportunity of being away from the home and from her family. She no longer kept in touch with her former workmates, but she had been able to make new friends at the English language classes she attended during the day. Nevertheless, her social network was fairly limited. Her closest relatives still lived in Pakistan, and she had very few friends in Britain.

Case No. 10

A Jamaican woman, also aged 42, with five children, had found a job within three months of her redundancy, but then had left work on medical grounds. She had been unemployed for three months by the time she was interviewed. She reported that the worst thing about unemployment was having to stay at home all the time. Her family was not particularly worried about her lack of paid work. The household managed adequately as her husband and her eldest son were both employed. But she too complained that unemployment had affected her health, her blood pressure, and her sleeping pattern. She felt bored at home, but mostly she missed her wage packet and she felt more dependent on others.

Case No. 11

A Polish woman, aged 55, lived with her husband and three grown-up children (two other children had already left home). Her bedridden father-in-law, aged 93, also lived with them. Her husband and her three children were employed, and she felt that she needed to care for her father-in-law and so was not looking for work just then. She reported that whereas her husband used to help her in the home with domestic chores, since her redundancy he had ceased to help around the house. Her family was pleased about her unemployment, although she sometimes got bored. Her parents were no longer alive, and apart from her grown-up children she seemed to have few relatives in this country. She maintained close ties with one set of neighbours and as a practising Catholic she went to church every week, but otherwise had few contacts in the locality.

These three women held ambivalent attitudes towards their enforced domesticity. There were no financial pressures compelling them to seek work outside the home, whilst there were seemingly good reasons for them to stay at home. Domestic responsibilities, the need to care for young children or for elderly relatives, and ill health helped to legitimize their role as housewives; but they still longed for outside involvement. Undoubtedly, pre-established patterns of expectations about the caring role of women in the household contributed to such domestic arrangements, to the satisfaction of other members of the household.

Ethnicity

Household responses to redundancy were affected by the ethnic background of the households concerned. The sample was too small, however, to make any firm generalizations about the effect of ethnicity on household decisions. However, two areas stand out in which ethnicity does seem to make a difference. Household rules are likely to be influenced by cultural norms within the particular ethnic group to which the household belongs, while members of ethnic groups are also likely to have widely dispersed social networks and may not be closely tied into the immediate locality in which they live (unless they are living in an ethnic enclave). The following case illustrates these points.

Case No. 12

A Ghanaian woman, aged 36, had four children; the children, however, were being brought up in Ghana, where they lived with their aunt. The respondent lived with her husband in privately rented accommodation, and their life-style was perhaps more typical of earlier waves of migration, as they aimed to save as much as possible and then return to Ghana. In the meantime they would work, save, and keep consumption down to a minimum. Hence they had lived in a bedsit for five years before moving to their present accommodation, which was still fairly small.

The couple did very little entertaining in their own home and seldom went out. They had no close relatives in Britain and very few friends. The woman had two friends in the area whom she saw once a month and she kept in touch with one of her former workmates. Her husband had a full-time job as a machine operator, so she was able to prolong her job search until she found something suitable; she eventually found work as a full-time hospital orderly.

This couple had made clear choices about working in Britain and saving as much money as possible, even if this meant not looking after their own children. The children were being brought up by close relatives in Ghana, an arrangement that is quite common in West Africa (Goody and Muir 1973, Goody and Muir Groothues 1979). These household choices were based on shared understandings between spouses that were partly derived from the values and norms existing in the society of their country of origin.

However much such decisions may be influenced by particular cultural values, the household rules seem to operate in their own right and in their own particularistic fashion. The response of the above household contrasted markedly with the choices made by another Ghanaian household, described in case No. 3. This household contained five children, ranging in age from 8 to 20. The children lived in London with their parents, but when both parents became unemployed at roughly the same time, the father went back to Ghana to seek employment there, whilst the rest of the household remained in Britain. The mother found a new job in London within two months of her redundancy. As this job entailed shift- and weekend work, she had to entrust the day-to-day child care to her eldest daughter, aged 20, who was also unemployed at the time.

These two households responded to redundancy in very different ways, despite the fact that they shared certain common cultural values and expectations. It seems reasonable to conclude that long-established cultural norms and values are likely to influence the development of household rules, but that such rules are much more likely to be shaped by the particular circumstances and needs of the household, as well as by the ensuing negotiations within the household itself.

Conclusion

This chapter has outlined some of the responses to redundancy amongst a sample of households in South London. It has sought to demonstrate that the response to redundancy cannot satisfactorily be understood simply in terms of a transitional cycle that affects only the redundant worker. Instead I would argue that the response to redundancy must be understood in terms of the household work strategy already established prior to redundancy and in terms of other factors that also act upon the household's environment. We have examined the extent to which such factors as the local labour market, the stage in the family cycle, social networks, family wealth, and household rules *interact with each other* and contribute to the household's response to redundancy.

The local labour market determines the economic options available to the household, in terms of job vacancies, average rates of re-employment in the area, or job opportunities for other members of the household. The limits to choice are set by the state of the local labour market, which in turn is set within the context of a national and global market. Yet even within the limits imposed by the local labour market, the household has some choice as to how to respond to redundancy. The need to find immediate re-employment may depend on the financial pressures on the household. The stage reached in the family cycle and prior household arrangements are particularly important in this respect. Households with dependent children, especially with pre-school-age children, and where neither spouse is in paid employment, are likely to be particularly hard hit by redundancy. Households with no dependent children, and where one of the spouses is in full-time employment, are better able to cope.

The social network of the household has a mediating influence on the manner in which the household responds to redundancy. The redundant worker may use his or her social contacts to obtain casual work or to widen the scope of the job search, while locally based social networks provide positive sanctions and reinforcements to those households wishing to maintain a continuity of social relationships within the area. The social network may also reinforce some of the household arrangements and household rules established prior to redundancy, especially those rules concerning the domestic division of labour in the aftermath of redundancy.

This chapter has sought to contribute to the theoretical debate on household organization by demonstrating the interrelationship of a number of factors affecting household decision-making. It has focused exclusively on household responses to redundancy; nevertheless, I believe that the same model could be applied to examine household responses to other life events, such as a serious illness, divorce, separation, bereavement, a job change, or a house move.

On a more practical level, this model of household organization focuses attention on some of the factors that are often neglected by the statutory agencies dealing with redundant workers. Thus the social security system takes note of the financial circumstances of households applying for supplementary benefit. It also takes note of the family life cycle and takes into account the presence of dependent children within the household. Yet social workers and health workers may need to have a greater awareness of some of the other issues raised in this chapter. For instance, the chapter has consistently emphasized the supportive nature of social networks anchored in the local community. Such networks can help in the job search and in finding casual work. They also provide continuity of social relationships and social arrangements, thereby helping the household to maintain its established pattern of household organization. Yet, as Stuart Henry has noted, informal economies are not available to everyone (Henry 1982). Some households may have more tenuous ties to the immediate neighbourhood and so receive less support or no support at all from the local community. Such households are therefore likely to be much harder hit by redundancies than households that are more closely integrated into the local area; but the statutory agencies generally ignore this aspect altogether.

A further factor that needs to be taken into account in formulating a welfare policy for those households facing redundancy is the crucial role of household rules. For example, we are moving into an era in which there is a greater variety in household arrangements, with greater flexibility in gender roles and indeed a move towards more equality in conjugal role relationships, especially among younger couples. Yet much of present social policy assumes the primacy of the 'rule' that the male head of household should be the main bread-winner. Such legislation should seek to take into account the wishes of marital couples and should allow them to work out their own household rules. We therefore need to develop more flexible approaches in administering welfare policies.

References

Binns, D. (1983) Social Relations of Unemployment on a Glasgow Housing Estate. Seminar paper presented at the Centre for Occupational and Community Research, Middlesex Polytechnic.

Binns, D. and Mars, G. (1984) Family, Community and Unemployment: a Study in Change. *Sociological Review*, 32 (4): 662–95.

Carmichael, C. and Cook, L. (1981) Redundancy and Re-employment. *Employment Gazette*, May: 241–44.

Clark, D. (1983) *Social Consequences of Rotating Shift-work in Manufacturing Industry*. End-of-grant report to the SSRC (F/00/23/0046).

—— (1984) Types of Household Adjustment to Rotating Shift-Work: Employees in Manufacturing Industry. In A. Wedderburn and P. Smith (eds) *Psychological Approaches to Night - and Shift-Work*. Edinburgh: Heriot-Watt University.

—— (1985) *Metropolitan Families Facing Redundancy*. Report to the Social Sciences Small Grants Committee of the Nuffield Foundation, London.

Goody, E. and Muir, C. (1973), *Factors Relating to the Delegation of Parental Roles among West Africans in London*. London: SSRC.

Goody, E. and Muir Groothues, C. (1979), West African Couples in London. In V. Saifullah Kahn (ed.) *Minority Families in Britain*. London: Macmillan.

Hayes, J. and Nutman, P. (1981) *Understanding the Unemployed*. London: Tavistock.

Henry, S. (1982) The Working Unemployed: Perspectives on the Informal Economy and Unemployment. *Sociological Review*, 30: 460–77.

Kahn, H. R. (1964) *Repercussions of Redundancy*. London: Allen & Unwin.

Lockwood, D. (1966) Sources of Variation in Working-Class Images of Society. *Sociological Review* 14: 249–67.

Marsden, D. and Duff, E. (1975) *Workless: Some Unemployed Men and their Families*. Harmondsworth: Penguin.

Martin, R. and Fryer, R. H. (1973) *Redundancy and Paternalistic Capitalism*. Cambridge: Cambridge University Press.

McKee, L. and Bell, C. (1984) His Unemployment: Her Problem. The Domestic and Marital Consequences of Male Unemployment. Paper presented to the British Sociological Association annual conference, University of Bradford, April.

Morris, L. D. (1983) Renegotiation of Domestic Division of Labour in the Context of Male Redundancy. Paper presented to the British Sociological Association annual conference, University of Cardiff.

—— (1984) Patterns of Social Activity and Post-Redundancy Labour-Market Experience. *Sociology* 18 (3), August: 339–52.

Pahl, R. (1980) Employment, Work and the Domestic Division of Labour. *International Journal of Urban and Regional Research* 4 (1): 1–20.

—— (1982a) Family, Community and Unemployment. *New Society*, 21 January.

—— (1982b) The Pockmarked Road to a Private Life. *New Society*, 7 October.

—— (1984) *Divisions of Labour*. Oxford: Blackwell.

Scanzoni, J. (1979) Social Processes and Power in Families. In W. Burr, R. Hill, I. Nye, and I. Reiss (eds) *Contemporary Theories about the Family*, Vol. 1. New York: Free Press.

Sinfield, A. (1970) Poor and Out of Work in Shields. In P. Townsend (ed.) *The Concept of Poverty*. London: Heinemann.

7. Managerial unemployment: the wife's perspective and role

Jean Hartley

'The booklet suggested that families had to understand about the man's problems [in being unemployed] but it said nothing about the changes the family has to cope with too–that annoyed me.'
(Wife of unemployed manager)

Research has given us a reasonable picture of the psychological impact of unemployment on the former job-holder, but what is much less clear is the psychological impact on the family, and especially the spouse. This neglect springs from the tendency to view the unemployed solely as *workers* who are currently without work, rather than seeing unemployment as affecting the whole family unit. This chapter tries to fill part of this gap in our knowledge by examining the experience, role, and outlook of the unemployed person's wife. In focusing on wives, I do not wish to assume that only male unemployment is significant or worthy of study; it is simply that in my study the unemployed managers were predominantly men.

Studies of the family during unemployment have paid some attention to the relationship between marriage partners and to the degree of marital satisfaction (see, for example, Thornes and Collard 1979, Colledge and Bartholomew 1980, Stokes and Cochrane 1984); but these have tended to be concerned with outcome variables – such as divorce and strain – rather than with processes. Some studies interested in the partner as a social support still maintain a focus on the unemployed person (for example, Gore 1978). Understanding of the husband and wife's perspective comes from sociographic, descriptive accounts, largely of working-class communities or people (for example, Marsden and Duff 1975, Chappell 1982, Seabrook 1982, Fagin and Little 1984). The work of Binns and Mars (1984) and Morris (1983) is particularly interesting in examining the *interactions*

118

between husband and wife. In the working-class partnerships they studied, they noted that the effect of male unemployment has not led to a major change of roles between marriage partners; the division of labour in the home tended to remain gender based.

Middle-class marriage may, however, be different, although the dearth of studies prevents an accurate assessment. Fineman (1983) obtained fourteen written reports from wives about the recent or continuing unemployment of white-collar men. The descriptions indicate a wide variety of emotional and practical responses to unemployment by the wives. A number enjoyed the opportunity to spend more time with the husband, although the accounts also show a level of distress and frustration about how to cope with unemployment and help the husband. Fineman notes how 'in many senses it is [the family's] unemployment, not just the jobless person's (1983: 104). He also indicates that if the family was unable to provide support to the man, the chances of getting it elsewhere were slim. Kaufman (1982) spends a couple of pages discussing the role of the wife, principally in terms of whether she is able to provide financial support, and asserting that role reversal results in severe emotional disruption in the family. He also reported that thirty out of thirty-one unemployed professionals said their wives were generally supportive and understanding while they were unemployed. Burgoyne (1985) found that among her survey sample of 100 unemployed men, and their wives, those who reported an improvement in their marriage were more likely to be middle class.

Before turning to my study, it is useful briefly to summarize what is known about middle-class marriage. Given the relative lack of information about middle-class marriage during unemployment, we must turn to studies undertaken in more favourable economic circumstances. A number of psychologists and sociologists have described middle-class, and more specifically managerial, marriages (for example, Marshall 1976, Cooper 1981), and have especially explored the interface between home and employment for both husband and wife. A variety of patterns of marriage has been described, based on the degree to which each partner is home or employment centred, and the degree of sex-role segregation in the domestic sphere (for example, Bailyn 1970, Handy 1978). While potentially there is considerable choice for couples in how they pursue career and family goals, in practice, due to employment opportunities, sex-role socialization, and other factors, many couples adopt a more restricted range of options. Handy (1978) describes four patterns, but describes the commonest as being the 'thrusting husband–caring wife' pattern. This is similar to the conventional pattern described by Bailyn (1970) and Gowler and Legge (1978) and fits the dominant pattern described by Pahl and Pahl (1971). Gowler and Legge sum up the marriage

type as follows:

> 'The conventional marriage may be said to exist, when . . . the husband derives his greatest satisfaction from his job/career outside the home, while the wife derives hers, not from a job/career commitment, but from her activities within the home itself. In other words, a conventional marriage is one in which the career-centred husband with his home-centred wife engage in a high level of differentiation in their productive roles.'

(1978: 50)

This is not to suggest that the wife does not have employment outside the home. The marriage pattern simply describes the value and identity orientation of each partner.

Gowler and Legge (1978) suggest that a conventional marriage is supported by a 'hidden contract' – an implicit understanding that the wife will provide practical services and emotional support for the husband so that he can pursue his career goals single-mindedly, without too many distractions from the domestic front. Many husbands, and many organizations, rely on the wife's unpaid labour in running a house, looking after children, and even engaging in social functions on behalf of the organization. This behaviour pattern has been described by Papanek (1973) as the 'two-person single career', and by Finch (1983) as being 'married to the job'. The hidden contract is also implicit in the research data of Pahl and Pahl (1971). Some writers note that this pattern is supported by the social value that marital power should reside with the man (Edgell 1980, Finch 1983).

A major question arises when unemployment occurs. Gowler and Legge (1978) suggest that the hidden contract can be changed by crisis. Unemployment is likely to be a crisis for many people. Does unemployment, then, affect the hidden contract? Does the fact that the husband no longer has a job affect the implicit understanding of how roles should be enacted within the family? What do wives do when their activity and energy are no longer required by the organization and by the husband in his career? If unemployment is the loss of a job, then for a 'two-person single career' it means two people intimately affected by the change and not one being merely a bystander to the experience.

The issue of changed marital and domestic roles during unemployment has been discussed to some extent in the media. Some articles talk of 'role reversal' (for example, Kaufman 1982, Fagin and Little 1984). By this is meant a situation in the context of male unemployment, where the traditional roles in employment and domestic labour are exchanged between the partners, with the wife becoming principal bread-winner and the husband taking responsibility for domestic work and child care. There is frequently an implicit value that role reversal is undesirable, causing a disruptive change and an assault on male self-esteem. (There is rarely consideration of the benefits to women within the family.) However, the idea of total role reversal as the only shift may be extreme. It may be more useful to think of a continuum of role renegotiation, with differing degrees of change for different couples.

Our brief tour of the literature on unemployment and middle-class marriage raises a number of questions. As well as the queries about role behaviour and the hidden contract, there are large areas to be explored such as how the wife views unemployment, what her relationship with her husband is like, and whether it changes due to the experience of unemployment. There are also questions to ask about the degree of stress for the wife, given the prevalence of the 'two-person single career' among managers. Moreover, if unemployment causes strain for the wife, how does she *cope* with it? We know that social support for the male can play some buffering or moderating role in the experience of unemployment, but what is the situation for his wife? The current study addresses some of these issues.

Unemployed managers' wives: the study

My study was of the experience of unemployment by the wife – how she perceived and responded to unemployment and her unemployed husband. This was part of a larger study of managerial unemployment, which focused on the psychological impact of unemployment (Hartley 1978, 1980a, 1980b). Ninety unemployed middle and senior managers, unemployed for a median of 16.5 weeks (though with a quarter for over six months), took part. The managers came from a wide range of managerial functions. The majority had lost their jobs through redundancy. I gave everyone questionnaires and interviewed twenty-six about their reactions to and experience of unemployment. These interviews took place throughout the UK.

The eighteen wives, who are the focus of this chapter, were married to the interviewed managers. I spoke to fewer wives than managers because sometimes a manager did not wish his wife to be contacted, or else I interviewed the manager away from home.

Concerning their ages, ten wives were between 35 and 50. Five were older than 50, and three were under 35. All the wives were within five years of their husband's age, generally younger. In terms of their work outside the home two wives worked full-time (one as a clinical psychologist, the other as a secretary), six worked part-time (secretarial work, book-keeping, telephonist, other office work), one worked intermittently (helped with accounts of a friend's firm a couple of times a year). Nine were housewives, taking responsibility for domestic work and, in many cases, child care. Some of these did voluntary work; for example, with the Women's Royal Voluntary Service, hospital visiting, or church work. Most of the wives had responsibilities for child care: only five had no children or children no longer financially dependent. Two wives were married to divorced men, who had financial commitments to the previous wife.

The interviews were semi-structured and covered certain topic areas, often in considerable depth. With some areas I left the wife to determine how intensively. I used this approach, mainly because I wanted to explore previously uncharted areas, but also because I was unsure initially how far the wife would be willing to discuss sensitive issues. As it turned out, almost all the wives appeared willing to discuss most topics, however painful. I interviewed the manager and wife separately and tape-recorded most interviews. Interviews with wives lasted from forty minutes to two hours. In addition, I was often invited to stay for a meal with the family and could then be involved in more informal interaction.

The research sample is small: eighteen wives. So the study is exploratory rather than hypothesis-testing, and should be read in that light. The interview material will be used to illustrate the issues, problems, and opportunities of unemployment as perceived by wives. To do this, I will present a composite picture of the experience of the women. The sample is too small to make any meaningful distinctions on the basis of husband's or wife's occupation, background, number of children, or so forth. In describing views, I use terms such as 'most', 'several', 'the majority'. The interviews took place between May 1976 and February 1977; the rate of registered unemployment, although then on the increase, has risen sharply since. Despite these changes in unemployment rates, the study is still useful given the lack of alternative data sources about the experience of managers' wives during unemployment.

View of roles prior to unemployment

I asked wives about their perceptions of the husband's job prior to unemployment, and about their own work, both inside and outside the home. All wives except one described the husband as having a strong interest in his job. The self-image of the men concurred with the views of the wives, who described the men's desire for challenge in a job, their strong sense of ambition, competitive spirit, commitment, and involvement in their jobs. The commitment to work was exhibited behaviourally in long hours at work, and in travelling.

Most wives reported that they felt the husband had been overworking in his last job. This view coincided with that held by the managers themselves, although more women than men reported overwork. Although working hard for many years, in the last six months (longer for some) the pressures of business had risen to an uncomfortable level. Take-overs and reorganizations, office politics and financial stringency often accompanied the lead-up to redundancy. The stress for the manager became manifest in different ways: bad-temperedness at home, sleeplessness, high blood pressure, the use of tranquillizers, bringing a lot of work home, never switching off, being constantly tired. However, other wives reported the husband had less to do at work, although they were aware that this spelled the likelihood of job termination. A small number of wives did not report anything unusual or different about the job towards the end. Wives, with two exceptions, saw their major occupation, whether employed outside the home or not, as providing a comfortable and supportive home environment for husband and children. The exceptions were the full-time professional psychologist and the wife who had a part-time job as a telephonist but who was contemplating divorce. For the majority, however, shopping, cooking, cleaning, making things for the home, child care, arranging children's activities, buying the family's clothes, arranging appointments for the family (e.g. dentist), financial arrangements (e.g. household bills), and a host of other family and house-maintenance activities fell to their lot.

Eight wives worked in employment as well, and both full- and part-timers reported enjoying their work since it gave them a chance to get out of the home, use their skills, and meet people. Part-timers found that they were still able to run the house in the way they wanted, without feeling overworked. Those without jobs tended to be either the younger wives with pre-school children, or older wives who had given up employment upon marriage according to the social norms of their day. Two women would have liked full-time jobs, but had found it difficult to have a career since the husband's geographical mobility in the past had been disruptive to their own job aspirations.

This description of the managerial marriage prior to job termination is so far a familiar one adequately described and analysed by social scientists such as Pahl and Pahl (1971) and Gowler and Legge (1978). With hardly any exception, we see here the traditional middle-class marriage with employment-centred husband and home-centred wife, and the acceptance of the hidden contract. However, there are two additional features of the pre-unemployment relationship that are significant, particularly since they influence reactions to unemployment.

Firstly, wives tended to be ambivalent in their attitudes to the husband's career and their own home-centredness. On the one hand, there was an acceptance and enjoyment of a supportive role: 'My main job is to give the baby a secure home and help my husband be successful.' However, for half the wives the support and acceptance of the husband's needs as primary were tinged with resentment or resignation, which surfaced from time to time. Being supportive meant denying their own needs and wishes on occasions: 'I'm last on the list so far as I'm concerned – and sometimes I get quite cross about it, but somehow I never quite get around to me.' Resentment was expressed about the inability to pursue a career due to the mobility required by the husband's job. Some felt resentful occasionally, especially if they had young children, of the travel and excitement the husband had. Many saw and resented the incursions of the organization into their own family life – through the husband's stress symptoms, through the time and emotional pressures on the marriage, through having to bring up the children virtually single handed. Several wives saw one of their principal functions as protecting the family from too many organizational pressures.

Secondly, the majority reported favourably on the autonomy and independence they experienced in the marriage. Most wives had learned to spend a lot of time on their own, while the husband worked long hours or was away for days at a time. Although some expressed resentment, many enjoyed being or having become independent. They had time for their own activities, and took pride in coping with events or even crises on their own. A number were expert decorators; two mentioned being handy at electrical and plumbing problems. In some cases the husband's frequent absence meant the wife really held the family together: 'I feel that I've brought the children up, though I like to involve him as much as possible. Things about the family get done a lot my way.'

Reactions to the job termination

Just over half of the managers had lost their jobs through redundancy, with resignation being the next largest category (although boundaries between types of job termination are often blurred: Sinfield 1970). Less than half the wives had been expecting the job termination. Even for them the news still came as a shock: 'Obviously, I was a bit shaken. I'd thought about it and more or less accepted the fact but when it came to the point it was a bit of a shock. It shouldn't have been, but in a way in your mind you think perhaps everything will work out.' Wives who had not anticipated the event described it as a shock or even as devastating.

Several wives also felt angry at the way the organization had treated the husband. They felt it had been unjust in dismissing him or making him resign, particularly in view of the long hours, sacrifice, and worry he had undergone for the organization's benefit: 'I feel he flogged himself to death in that firm – for what? They had no right to accept all that from him, and then just pay him off.' This anger indicates the loyalty and support wives tended to show towards their husbands and also their resentment that their sacrifices for the husband's career had been nullified. In this reaction of anger, particularly, we can see that unemployment happens not simply to the unemployed manager, but also to the person providing the hidden services necessary in the two-person single career.

Relief was another dominant reaction. A couple of wives even felt happy. Relief occurred because an indecisive situation was resolved after months of uncertainty, or because the job loss meant the end of a period of considerable stress:

'I feel it's the best thing that has ever happened to him health-wise. If he'd gone on like he was he would have had a breakdown or a heart attack or something.'

'It was a bit of a rat-race brigade, and I wasn't sorry that he left, although I wish it could have been in other circumstances.'

Several wives mentioned concern or worry about the job termination and impending unemployment. Concern centred upon money, uncertainty about the future, the effect on the marriage, and having no family or friends close by for support. Several wives mentioned feeling helpless on hearing of the job loss.

In general, reactions of wives appeared to be similar to those of the managers (although not matched by couple) in being a mixture, in different combinations for different people, of shock, anger, relief, and anxiety. The women overall expressed less confidence and optimism about the future than their husbands did, and were perhaps more aware of, or at least more prepared to talk about, the practical problems and issues that might arise.

Positive and negative aspects of unemployment

'It's difficult to describe all the variety of reactions I've experienced. It changes so much.'

Wives generally expressed more positive aspects of unemployment than husbands did. Many wives enjoyed having the husband out of work, and some would have liked unemployment to continue if only the husband would enjoy it as much as they did, and if money was not such a worry. We have seen that a number of wives viewed job loss as providing relief from the stresses of the last job. This was reinforced by seeing the husband take advantage of the long-overdue opportunities for improved health and relaxation. Such a benefit made some wives anxious about re-employment.

Popular belief asserts that having an unemployed man about the house leads to friction between the partners. However, contrary to this view, many wives positively enjoyed having the husband at home. Although at times this increased contact did result in tensions, many felt that relative to the pleasure of having the husband at home this was a small and occasional price to pay. This was particularly so if the family was new to the area (lived there under a year) and the wife had not yet established a strong routine or many friends. The husband was available to go shopping with, to have morning coffee with, and to talk to – 'silly little things, like getting him to walk up to the baker's or the bank with me'.

Some couples rediscovered a relationship that had been besieged by the day-to-day pressures of managerial life:

> 'I *love* having him at home. We get on better now than when he was working.

> 'Senior executives live under high pressure and it inevitably affects their marriage after a while. It would be easy to be stable if you could just get off for a bit and calm down – but you can't because you're both bound up in it. So there are tensions. We've had six months' break from that now.'

Not all wives described an improvement in the marriage and enjoyment of daily routines, but it is striking how many did.

Several wives felt that unemployment had led to improved (and increased) family contact:

> 'I don't think it's a bad thing, because for the last five months we've all sat down to tea together. The children began to realize what Daddy looks like again. We've never ever done that before anywhere, except maybe at weekends.'

> 'Although our standard of living has dropped, we've gained enormously as a family.'

Wives who reported less satisfaction and few benefits from unemployment tended to be those whose husbands took little interest in or placed little value on home-based and family activities.

Although a number of wives enjoyed extra contact with the husband at home, this is not to suggest there were no 'bad times' during unemployment. Wives were generally more open about discussing these than husbands. Relationship difficulties featured prominently in the descriptions of negative aspects of unemployment. Pressures, tensions, and frustrations could flare up, with partners getting angry, expressing frustration and resentment, quarrelling, crying, and getting on each other's nerves. Many wives also reported more enduring consequences of tension and difficulty, resulting in either the husband or the wife (or both) becoming depressed for periods, and in simmering resentment, guilt, and blame between the partners.

The problems seemed largest, and the slough of despond infinite, when both partners felt moody, irritable, or depressed at the same time. Most wives felt that if only one partner was affected the situation was much easier to cope with. But one person's moods often acted on the other, and this was the worst time:

'. . . like when he's frustrated and he's lost his temper and you've lost your temper.'

'When we're on our good times, we get on very well together, but if the situation changes him it changes me. I don't have the capacity to ride through it.'

This could frequently be disorientating, resulting in a merged identity, making resolution of the difficulties harder: 'Sometimes I feel frustrated. I don't know if they're mine or his frustrations coming out in me.' For a few wives, the emotional problems were causing considerable strain:

'I feel as if I've aged fifteen years. I feel I've grown up and yet in some ways I haven't. I can't see much good has come out of it, and we've lost a lot of what we had.'

'I hoped we would ride through unemployment with greater resilience. That was a great myth – we've ridden through it very badly.'

In addition to the wife who was already considering divorce, another was anxious that she might be divorced.

Other negative aspects of unemployment existed, although these were generally not seen to be as important as relationship difficulties. Waiting for the post in the morning and waiting for job decisions could be very frustrating. Unemployment could also delay decisions about family life. As well as holidays, and the uncertainty and anxiety about raising the money for children's school trips, there were longer-term decisions that could not be taken until the husband's job and work location had been decided. For example, one couple had a child who was unhappy in school, and they were unsure whether to move her now, with the prospect of a second change later if the family had to move for work, or whether to let her continue feeling unhappy until the future was clearer. Another couple wished to divorce, but had neither the money nor the certainty about the future to be able to plan future living arrangements and access to children (again, in case the man had to move for his job).

Some wives reported irritation about extra washing-up, and extra (especially midday) meals to cook, which could upset routines, but these were minor difficulties. Most wives adapted their domestic and social routines to fit in with the husband's changed life-style. A couple of wives commented that they had had to 'learn' to become less competent domestically: 'The vacuum cleaner broke down, so I grabbed a screw-driver and was just fixing it, when I realized my husband was quite upset that I hadn't turned to him for help.' A few wives said that the husband interfered with well-established routines for the children (for example, bedtimes and homework), of which he had previously been unaware.

Several wives mentioned financial worries. Explaining financial restric-tions to teenagers was difficult. Children of other ages seemed to adapt well, although some wives felt guilty at being unable to provide generously for them. In addition, small events could reach larger proportions: 'He'd phone and say he wouldn't be in for tea and then not come in till midnight or one in the morning. I used to get really worried about him. He's too stable to do anything serious, but you begin to get your doubts.'

Summing up this section on positive and negative aspects of un-employment, we can see that the experience is mixed for many wives. Many were, in fact, surprised by how unemployment had turned out for them – in that it provided stronger positive experiences than they had anticipated. On the other hand, for a few wives the negative features were much worse than they had imagined. In terms of both ups and downs, the centrality of relationships stands out: unemployment had good features because of greater opportunities for interaction with the husband and for the whole family to be together; but also the build-up of negative emotions between husband and wife formed the principal features of the nightmarish quality of unemployment.

The wife's role during unemployment

All the wives went to considerable lengths to help the husband cope with the experience of unemployment and help his job search. Explicitly or not, wives provided several means of support, both practical and emotional.

In practical terms, most wives felt that running the house was an important aspect of support. This occurred whatever the employment status of the wife (with one exception where domestic and career roles had been extensively exchanged compared with a traditional marriage). While occasionally resentful about the extra work, none of the women felt they should 'use' the husband while he was at home. It would be degrading for the husband to have to partake in housework; it would be 'rubbing it in'.

The only variations to this outlook were when the wife was ill or when some wives enlisted the husband in *companionable* activities such as shopping. Most husbands continued to do domestic chores they had undertaken before – for example, washing-up, tidying up, or some weekend meals (now extended into the week) – but they did not, apart from a couple, take on new chores. Husbands 'helped' with housework (Oakley 1974). Responsibility for children was handled similarly, with pre-existing duties continuing into unemployment.

Although the division of domestic labour was essentially stable, several wives mentioned that they had changed their routines to spend more time with the husband or to make life more comfortable for him. Most wives tried to be available when they could for the husband. Two concealed some manual skills, so as not to undermine the husband. Those with jobs also adapted their schedules: 'I felt a bit rotten going out to work and leaving him at home, so I didn't stay out any longer than I had to.'

Practical, intertwined with moral, support was also given in help with job-seeking. About half the wives typed letters and helped with the wording of application forms and curricula vitae. Most wives wanted to help by discussing jobs plans, although some husbands did not wish to discuss these matters. Some wives felt they could not be much help in decision-making on technical matters, but wished to provide a listening ear for the husband.

Emotional support was given in a variety of ways. It was conspicuous, firstly, in the fact that most had considerable confidence in and admiration for the husband: 'I suppose I didn't worry too much because I've got this faith in him and his abilities'; 'If it had happened to me, I wouldn't be able to *apply* for another job, let alone sell myself.' This admiration was not constructed on an unrealistically favourable opinion of the husband, or on a desire to present him as faultless, since the majority of wives were able to comment on the husband's shortcomings too.

Secondly, several wives showed considerable acceptance of the husband as he was. One wife recognized that, however frustrating she personally found it, her husband did not like to talk about his unemployment. Some wives wanted more help around the house but felt it was 'just not him'. A few wives talked of 'having to come to terms with things' and accepting the situation, however much they would like the situation or the husband to be different.

Thirdly, a related but separate factor was the patience that several wives showed towards the husband. It was important not to interfere too much. One wife likened the situation to having another child about the house: 'It's something he's got to do for himself. I can't do it for him unfortunately, even though you feel you might want to. . . . You feel protective – but you've got to stand by and watch them get on with it.' Several wives mentioned feeling helpless while they watched the husband cope with unemployment.

Fourthly, many wives felt that not complaining was an important contribution they could make: 'The only thing you can do is be as cheerful as you can, even though you feel terrible inside.'

Fifthly, support was given though a strong sense that selflessness was necessary if the husband was to be protected from emotional damage by unemployment. One wife, with children having started school, was herself eager to return to employment, but decided to postpone such plans until the husband was well settled into a new job. Several wives mentioned that they would feel guilty doing what they wanted to do. These feelings related to the loyalty that most wives showed: 'There have been times in the last twelve months when I could cheerfully have walked out. But you know why this is happening and so you don't do it. You grin and bear it.'

Even where support was tinged with bitterness and frustration it was still given in large measure: 'It's got to be give and take, and at times like this you feel you're doing all the giving.' Most wives did everything in their power to deny their own needs if this would aid the husband's job search and ease the strains and tensions he experienced while out of work. Their attitude was often self-sacrificing and is epitomized in the comment 'If I could have got him another job I would have.'

Wives' evaluation of their role

Despite the considerable contribution to helping the husband, the majority of wives were self-depreciating when talking of the support they gave: 'I'm not sure I help him that much when we discuss things'; 'I tried in my own stupid way to suggest a few ideas, which probably didn't go down very well'; 'I do whatever I can, though it's not a great deal'. In one case self-denigration was severe: 'I wanted to have more tact, more understanding. I've let him down and I've let myself down.'

These comments are at variance with the details wives gave about their perceptions of where and how help was needed, and about the varieties of support they freely gave. Their own assessment of their role suggests that they have high standards about appropriate behaviour as the wife of an unemployed manager. Their comments also differ from those of the husbands. Most husbands were ready to acknowledge the help, practical and emotional, they received from the wife. (Some managers indicated that their wife's evaluation of them was of little personal value, however, their source of validation and satisfaction deriving from their career and job identity rather than from the home.) The overall picture is of wives struggling to achieve even more to ease the burden of unemployment for the husband, while failing to recognize the full benefit and extent of the help they were already giving. For some wives this resulted in considerable despair and guilt.

How wives coped with unemployment

All the wives felt pressures due to the husband being out of work. Some found it an acutely distressing experience; others found it 'got on top' of them only from time to time. Although their circumstances differed, many wives adopted a cautiously optimistic outlook towards the future and, in spite of being aware of shortcomings in the spouse, generally showed considerable support for the husband. It therefore seems pertinent to enquire about the sources from which the wives derived their often considerable emotional stamina.

The traditional role as a manager's wife may have facilitated coping with unemployment. Acceptance of the 'hidden contract' was an integral part of the wives' role. Their supportive role in relation to husband and family had helped them cope with problems in the past. Many wives had learnt to cope on their own, and their independence may mean that they were fairly well equipped in terms of personal resources.

Part of the traditional marriage pattern is the acceptance of the husband's needs and goals. All wives, except two, approved of the husband's needs and desires taking priority in any decisions made about jobs, and hence also about marriage and family life. The wife generally saw her principal responsibility as fitting herself and the family into those decisions. While prepared to accept virtually any managerial job, wives hoped that the new job, whatever and wherever it turned out to be, would not affect the husband's health or the family too much or 'let him get hurt again'. Acceptance of the husband's work as priority may have facilitated the wife's ability to cope.

The positive features of unemployment may also have been contributory. We have seen that a number of wives saw unemployment as providing relief from the stresses of the last job. Unemployment partly represented to them less pressure on the husband and less pressure on the marriage and family. Additionally many wives, as we saw, enjoyed the husband's companionship, having previously spent less time than they would have liked with the husband.

Another aspect of the wife and her role that may have helped her cope and maintain support for the husband was a certain acceptance of events, which may be part of the traditional role: 'I tend to be rather fatalistic. He believes you can make things happen. I believe you can influence them only slightly.' It also helped to have an understanding that arguments and difficulties were caused by pressures and therefore should not be taken too seriously or personally: 'Obviously a husband will take things out on his wife because she's the closest person.' However, as we have seen, not all wives were able to have such an overview of arguments; some became quite disoriented by them.

Other people were important as support for the wife. While for some the husband was important as a companion with whom to share the trials and tribulations of unemployment, most wives had someone else – relatives and/or friends were important in helping them. A couple of wives had parents, siblings, or other relatives living within twenty miles or so, and drew on them for sympathy and support. However, much more important were personal, female friends, who were contacted either by telephone, if they were far away, or in person: 'No one knew how I felt except my friend across the road. I used to cry on her shoulder occasionally. If it wasn't for her I think we would have had more rows at home. She was someone to talk to; she didn't really have to answer.'

Many wives were well embedded in their local community. Others were less fortunate, because of either the husband's recent or his past job mobility, which meant that the wife had not developed close friends: 'All my friends know – but in fact we don't know many people round here. Only two or three neighbours.' In addition, two wives reported that they saw their own friends much less as a result of the husband's unemployment, either because they did not wish to leave the husband on his own while they were out with friends, or else because they found it difficult to invite their friends round to the house for coffee, which might embarrass the husband.

Conclusions

Much of the preceding description requires little additional comment, but I would like to draw together the principal findings and conclusions of this small study. What have we learnt about unemployment from the perspective of the wife?

The wives overwhelmingly described their marriages in terms suggesting that prior to unemployment they were of the traditional pattern – i.e. employment- or career-centred husband and home-centred wife, with the needs and goals of the husband taking precedence over those of the wife. This pattern was discussed earlier, and I suggested that it is a common pattern found by a number of writers who have researched middle-class and/or managerial marriages. This study adds to that picture the features of some resentment about the effect of the husband's job on the marriage, and the independence wives had developed. All these features influence the wife's experience of and feelings about unemployment.

When unemployment occurs for couples in traditional marriages we have not seen, in the main, the dramatic role reversal sometimes predicted (or implicitly feared) by many researchers. On the contrary, with only two exceptions the couples in this study maintained the relationship they had prior to unemployment.

Some husbands, we saw, did relax more and become more family centred, although it was clear that their primary goal was to gain re-employment. In terms of domestic labour in the home, there is little indication of a dramatic role reversal (except in one family where considerable role renegotiation took place). In some cases the husband 'helped' more in the home, especially where the couple were able to join in the task together, or where it was a small extension of work the husband already did in the home. To the extent that it occurred at all, such change can be more validly described as role renegotiation than as role reversal.

For wives, whether employed or not, their role also remained essentially unchanged: to take care of the home and the emotional relationships within it. Indeed, such roles intensified with the physical presence of the husband in the home and the added psychological support he required given the assaults on his self-esteem due to unemployment. The dynamic of the traditional relationship is continued and developed in unemployment, with the wife providing, in the majority of cases, a variety of practical and emotional support. We noted resentment, irritation, and frustration in the provision of support, perhaps unsurprising given the stresses of unemployment. However, loyalty and selflessness are very much in evidence.

The study also shows that wives are intimately involved in the experience of unemployment. Reactions to the news of job termination indicate that the wife was not a passive witness to her husband's unemployment; she was directly involved. The wife is a key person in understanding the experience of unemployment. In adopting a supportive role she tends to be deferential where there is a potential clash of interests (between their needs), which preserves the existing marital relationship.

The joint (but hidden) contribution to the job also helps us to understand the positive and negative aspects of unemployment as experienced by the wife. Given the emphasis in a traditional marriage on the hidden contract, the wife has to accept little leisure time with the husband, and an emphasis on the importance of his needs. In a situation where the job has effectively starved the wife of much of her husband's company and energy, it is perhaps not surprising that so many wives should report the pleasure of having extra time with the husband, who is also more relaxed. This was a feature of white-collar unemployment that Fineman (1983), in his study of written reports of wives, remarked on. This may be a particular feature of middle-class (as opposed to working-class) marriage, with its great emphasis on the hidden contract, although further research is necessary here. In terms of both positive and negative aspects of marriage, wives focus on relationships, which again is consistent with a traditional middle-class marriage pattern.

For some researchers and policy-makers the conclusions reached so far may appear adequate. These couples have chosen a particular life-style and way of relating to each other and they maintain it in spite of the pressures and tensions of unemployment. The couple remain committed to work and to each other. The wife is, in many cases, a tower of support to her husband. By both practical and moral support she sustains and encourages him in his search for a managerial job again. However, the description and evaluation so far open up a host of other questions. Most importantly, if the wives are such a powerful form of social support for the husband, who supports the supporters?

There has been little interest in the effects of providing support. Supporters, especially within the context of marriage, are expected to absorb the pressures and tensions of the person who relies on them for help. As the wife who provided the opening quotation to the chapter so aptly noted, little concern has been expressed about how spouses of the unemployed cope with the experience.

This is a crucial area to explore. My study suggests that wives both gave plenty of support and also tended not to recognize how helpful they had been. Their own evaluation of their role was self-depreciating. A number believed that their help had been too little or badly timed, or inadequate in other ways. While some were able to see tensions in the family as due to unemployment, others blamed themselves – for failing to perceive, anticipate, or intervene in ways to prevent the problem occurring or to resolve it. This study did not try to assess the stress effects of unemployment on wives, but various details are indicative of strain. For example, self-depreciation is often a sign of low self-esteem and depression. A few wives reported considerable despair and strain, and there were two reports of feeling constantly ill or having aged considerably with unemployment. The difficulties of maintaining a separate identity when partners' moods acted on each other may also indicate some degree of strain. The high standards wives expected of themselves may have further contributed to strain. All these are indications that the mental health and psychological well-being of wives deserve to be explored in greater detail.

In answering the question of how wives are themselves supported during unemployment, this study noted the difficulties some wives experienced in finding a friend to confide in within the neighbourhood. Some women were without close friends due either to having recently moved or else to having moved so often in the past that no close friends had been developed in the current location. One might expect such women to be particularly vulnerable to the stress effects of unemployment. Even for those women who have their own network or forms of social support, the lack of knowledge of, interest in, or value placed on the wife's experience of unemployment means that the type and degree of support available to wives may be limited, however well intentioned the sympathy.

It is already well established statistically that marriage is frequently 'bad' for women (for example, Hinkle and Wolf 1957, Gove and Tudor 1972): women's mental health tends to be impaired by marriage, while men's improves. It has been suggested by some psychologists that the mental health of women, especially within marriage, is more vulnerable, because cultural norms in society encourage women to absorb and attend to the husband's and other family members' needs while ignoring or suppressing their own (Eichenbaum and Orbach 1982). The ideology of male dominance in marriage reinforces this dynamic. Certainly, in this study, the suppression or minimizing of the wives' own wants and desires was widely found.

If, then, within a patriarchal framework of marriage wives are susceptible to poorer mental health, then one may have cause for concern when this situation is exacerbated by the stresses and strains of unemployment. If the physical and mental health of the male breadwinner who becomes unemployed is worthy of widespread research, surely then there is a strong and compelling argument for considerable further studies of wives of unemployed men.

In practical terms, the study underscores a need for support for the unemployed to allow for opportunities to include the marriage partner in many cases. This point has already been made by Fineman, on the basis of his work, but warrants repetition. Self-help groups, management courses, and unemployment centres could perhaps consider including partners in schemes for support and job search, since unemployment is a difficult experience for both partners.

References

Bailyn, L. (1970) Career and Family Orientations of Husbands and Wives in Relation to Marital Happiness. *Human Relations* 23: 97–113.

Binns, D. and Mars, G. (1984) Family, Community and Unemployment: a Study in Change. *Sociological Review* 32: 662–95.

Burgoyne, J. (1985) Unemployment and Married Life. *Unemployment Unit Bulletin*, November, 18: 7–10.

Chappell, H. (1982) The Family Life of the Unemployed. *New Society* 62 (1039): 76–9.

Colledge, M. and Bartholomew, R. (1980) The Long-Term Unemployed: Some New Evidence. *Employment Gazette* 88: 9–12.

Cooper, C. L. (1981) *Executive Families under Stress*. Englewood Cliffs, NJ: Prentice-Hall.

Edgell, S. (1980) *Middle-Class Couples*. London: Allen & Unwin.

Eichenbaum, L. and Orbach, S. (1982) *Outside In . . . Inside Out. Women's Psychology: A Feminist Psychoanalytic Approach*. Harmondsworth: Penguin.

Fagin, L. and Little, M. (1984) *The Forsaken Families*. Harmondsworth: Penguin.

Finch, J. (1983) *Married to the Job: Wives' Incorporation in Men's Work*. London: Allen & Unwin.

Fineman, S. (1983) *White-Collar Unemployment: Impact and Stress*. Chichester: Wiley.

Gore, S. (1978) The Effect of Social Support in Moderating the Health Consequences of Unemployment. *Journal of Health and Social Behaviour* 19: 157–65.

Gove, W. R. and Tudor, J. F. (1972) Adult Sex Roles and Mental Illness. *American Journal of Sociology* 78: 812–35.

Gowler, D. and Legge, K. (1978) Hidden and Open Contracts in Marriage. In R. Rapoport and R. Rapoport (eds) *Working Couples*. London: Routledge & Kegan Paul.

Handy, C. (1978) The Family: Help or Hindrance? In C. L. Cooper and R. Payne (eds) *Stress at Work*. Chichester: Wiley.

Hartley, J. (1978) An Investigation of Psychological Aspects of Unemployment. Unpublished Ph.D. thesis, University of Manchester.

—— (1980a) The Impact of Unemployment upon the Self-Esteem of Managers. *Journal of Occupational Psychology* 53: 147–55.

—— (1980b) The Personality of Unemployed Managers: Myths and Measurement. *Personnel Review* 9: 12–18.

Hinkle, L. and Wolf, H. (1957) Health and Social Environment. In A. H. Leighton, J. A. Clausen, and R. N. Wilson (eds) *Explorations in Social Psychiatry*. New York: Basic Books.

Kaufman, H. (1982) *Professionals in Search of Work*. New York: Wiley.

Marsden, D. and Duff, E. (1975) *Workless: Some Unemployed Men and their Families*. Harmondsworth: Penguin.

Marshall, J. (1976) *The Mobile Manager and his Wife*. Bradford: MCB Monographs.

Morris, L. (1983) Renegotiation of the Domestic Division of Labour in the Context of Male Redundancy. Paper to the British Sociological Association annual conference, Cardiff.

Oakley, A. (1974) *The Sociology of Housework*. London: Martin Robertson.

Pahl, J. M. and Pahl, R. E. (1971) *Managers and their Wives*. London: Allen Lane.

Papanek, H. (1973) Men, Women and Work: Reflections on the Two-Person Career. *American Journal of Sociology* 78: 852–72.

Seabrook, J. (1982) *Unemployment*. London: Quartet.

Sinfield, A. (1970) Poor and Out of Work in Shields. In P. Townsend (ed.) *The Concept of Poverty.* London: Heinemann.

Stokes, G. and Cochrane, R. (1984) A Study of the Psychological Effects of Redundancy and Unemployment. *Journal of Occupational Psychology* 57: 307–22.

Thornes, B. and Collard, J. (1979) *Who Divorces?.* London: Routledge & Kegan Paul.

8. Inside a community: values associated with money and time

Anne-Marie Bostyn and Daniel Wight

This chapter concentrates on two themes arising from a study of an ex-coal-mining village in the central industrial belt of Scotland. We gathered the information over two years while living in a council flat in 'Cauldmoss', by participating in village life and conducting interviews and a questionnaire. (See Turner, Bostyn, and Wight 1984 for a more detailed discussion.)

The village is seven miles from the nearest town. Most of the 1,800 population live on a local authority housing 'scheme'. The inhabitants often refer to Cauldmoss's mining past, and the village shares the traditions of areas of Britain dominated by heavy industry. These include highly differentiated gender roles, the work ethic (the moral imperative to be industrious), and support for the Labour Party, although in Cauldmoss political issues are rarely discussed. This community (a word often used by the inhabitants themselves to describe Cauldmoss) is seen by locals as highly interrelated and close knit.

The majority of the work-force are manual workers (a quarter being skilled). Most of those employed today work in service industries or in distribution and catering, in manufacturing, transport, or construction, mainly in the nearby towns. The only businesses in Cauldmoss are shops and small haulage, scrap-metal, and construction firms. Work is usually found through personal contacts.

Our questionnaire in 1982 showed that at least 30 per cent of men in Cauldmoss were unemployed. The figure today is probably nearer 40 per cent. (Unemployment in the local authority area as a whole is about 20 per cent.) Over the last decade there has, however, continued to be an increase in the proportion of Cauldmoss women in employment. In 1982 approximately 40 per cent of women had jobs outside the home, many part-time. There are usually clear differences in the roles and consumption patterns of women and men; like Claire Callender (Chapter 3, above) we found that women questioned rarely described themselves as 'un-employed'. Lack of space means we focus primarily on men, particularly in Section 1, although we refer to women's experiences.

Our questionnaire also revealed that 'work' is defined in Cauldmoss as having one or more of the following characteristics: something that is done for money, that involves effort (usually manual), that is unenjoy-able, that is necessary. Here we will use the word 'work' in the way it is normally understood in Cauldmoss, to mean paid employment, unless otherwise indicated.

Whereas the social obligations to work and to consume normally complement each other, there are some in Cauldmoss who can command only a wage that is lower than the welfare benefits to which they and their families are entitled. This is the so-called 'unemployment trap'. In such cases individuals have conflicting desires and can suffer much confusion, particularly since many in Cauldmoss believe that the level of a man's wage is evidence of his inner worth; a man can be in the dilemma of either making a 'mug' of himself or of not working at all. Section 1, while mainly being about the unemployed, is also applicable to those who *do* choose to work for very low wages.

The key themes of this chapter, money and time, will be dealt with separately (by Daniel Wight and Anne-Marie Bostyn respectively). In the two sections the consumption or time-use patterns of the *employed* are considered before those of the unemployed. The former demonstrate the social norms in Cauldmoss; employment is experienced by most men older than about twenty-five, and is constantly presented by the media as normal. In this very conservative community there is consistent informal pressure, through gossip and public opinion, to conform to the norms of 'full employment'; we consider the consequences of the unemployed's inability to match up to this consensus.

Section 1: Values associated with money

Personal identity expressed through commodities

The overwhelming majority of men in Cauldmoss expect paid work to be arduous, monotonous, and routine, offering no intrinsic satisfaction. Their conscious motive to be employed is, above all, the remuneration, which implies a high value attached to consumer power. Here we explore the importance of consumption in people's personal identities, and the consequences of this for those with severely restricted incomes, taking personal identity to be an individual's synthesis of the various social roles expected of him/her. This will suggest why the unemployed find it so difficult to develop new ways of living to cope with their circumstances.

In order to make the world intelligible we have to impose on it some kind of order, principally through establishing categories that have meaning in relation to each other. Such abstract concepts have far greater force in defining one's world if expressed physically in symbols. Consumer goods provide materials with which to represent one's self-identity, create or confirm particular social relationships, and provide the medium for the ritual marking of time (as discussed in Section 2). The goods people choose to buy are a physical expression (often not conscious) of their characters, or at least what they want to project as such, otherwise presented principally in words.

It is crucial to be able to confirm one's personal identity, which is more secure the wider one's social network extends. This supports the view that poverty is the inability to participate socially, recognized long ago by Adam Smith (1776: 691) and more recently by the Department of Health and Social Security (Donnison 1982: 8). It seems common sense to assume there is an absolute biological poverty level, but culture assimilates biological factors in its system of values, and these cultural values determine the interpretation of need. To understand what it means to exist on an income considerably lower than that of most people at work, it is necessary first to study the consumption patterns of the employed with respect to different aspects of identity.

A 'respectable' level of consumption

In nearly all areas of consumption there is what might be called a 'respectable level', below which people are ashamed to fall. A good housewife in Cauldmoss always has a fully stocked kitchen, and meat of some kind is considered essential for an adequate main meal. Warmth is the hallmark of Cauldmoss living-rooms, achieved with wall-to-wall carpets, net curtains distancing one from the weather, and a deep, soft three-piece suite facing the open fire, where plenty of coal is burnt (probably three or four sacks a week in winter). Essential furnishings include a dresser or cabinet with miscellaneous family mementoes, a coffee-table, a thick hearth-rug, and a colour television; outside, the imputed cost of one's car is a manifestation of one's general status. The moral obligation to maintain a respectable standard of living is intimately bound up with the qualities still attributed to being 'a good worker'; uninterest in consumer goods is interpreted, and criticized, as an implicit preference for idleness. Physical objects have become visible symbols of inner worth, but the connection with hard work is now less essential, 'big spenders' having prestige in their own right, whether or not the money is earned.

The clearest example of how self-esteem as a worker is expressed through consumption is in drinking. Although many people have savings accounts, increased earnings are often spent on alcohol, a mining tradition that avoids temporary wage differentials becoming embedded in differential ownership of capital goods (Douglas and Isherwood 1979: 168). However, it also means the heavy drinker often earns the prestige accorded to a good worker. One of the few remaining miners in Cauldmoss talked of how he enjoyed the reputation of being 'the top machine worker in Scotland . . . you know, when you stand at the bar and say, "I'll buy yous a round" '. There is also a physiological link here, since what constitutes 'real' work is in general 'thirsty' manual labour.

Seeing unemployed men enjoying their pints undermines the traditional connection between hard work and rightful access to alcohol as its reward. Although such attitudes are changing, an unemployed man was made to feel 'no entitled to a pint of beer' by his own working brother when they met in the pub. For the most part the unemployed feel 'it's ignorant' to go into a pub unless they have got enough money for several drinks.

Restricted eating habits are one of the most immediate effects of unemployment. Women usually get most of the week's 'messages' (shopping) on Thursday as soon as their giro (welfare cheque) is cashed, so that resources cannot be diverted from this priority, although by the following Wednesday supplies are often running short. Savings are made by substitution and doing without. Tea replaces coffee; powdered soup, bread, and rice pudding instead of fish and chips; 'beans on toast for *dinners*, not suppers' ('supper' being a late-night snack), and 'not much steak going!'. Unemployed men often keep their cars as long as possible but eventually sell them or replace them with an inferior one. This is a very public manifestation of their impoverishment. As a woman said when her husband got a different car, 'You've reduced your style. . . . You're going down.' In the living-room furnishings are replaced far less frequently than before, while the main daily economy is on fuel burnt. .

Constant renewal

Keeping up with fashions and ahead of the obsolescence of goods also demonstrates a continuous application to work. At the Senior Youth Club the teenagers in employment wear something new to the discos every three weeks, while their parents replace their three-piece suite after a couple of years. For those without work the inability to renew their clothes (probably the most public form of consumption), or being reduced to cheap wear, is a constant source of frustration. They often inherit the furniture thrown out by their more affluent relatives, which at least means a change of décor, however second best. The power of fashion, the regular redecoration of interiors (however worn), and the replacement of goods suggest a desire for renewal in itself, existing independently of work values. Could this be a sort of ritual regeneration to maintain one's purity? The symbolic importance of redecorating a new home was illustrated when an unemployed couple immediately repainted the council house they were 'flitting' to, although they were already in debt and the interior decorations showed no visible signs of wear.

Growing up and gaining 'an independence'

Leaving school in order to go to work is essential in the process of becoming a 'real adult' in society, largely because it means establishing 'an independence' from one's parents, the hallmark of which is paying 'dig money' to one's mother. Wages are the passport to the adult world with one's own belongings, and eventually marriage and one's own home. Furthermore certain commodities confer adult status in themselves, for instance (with lads) the use and, if possible, acquisition of motor bikes and, later, cars; while drinking demonstrates involvement in adult life or an independent (adult and masculine) rejection of the law.

Given this significance of alcohol it becomes understandable why un-employed teenagers in Cauldmoss often spend a large part of their 'bru' (welfare benefit) on one or two evenings' drinking, and why their self-respect is at risk when they have not got 'money in their pocket'. Without the transition conferred by earning a wage they are growing up more slowly, according to their parents, lacking the self-confidence of financial autonomy as they supplement their 'bru money' with free food, ciga-rettes, and 'subs' (loans) from their family. As Willis speculates (1984: 476), the young are in 'a new social state' of extended dependency.

Providing for the family

Marriage and parenthood bring a man enormous responsibilities to pro-vide his wife and children with the means to consume, and their standard of living reflects on him. While mothers face the daily pressures from their children to have as many sweets, toys, or clothes as their friends, ultimately the entire family's style of living is an extension of the man's identity. Occasions such as an evening out at the club illustrate how women are more constrained to dress up than men, supporting Veblen's idea that men exhibit their income through the fineries of their wives (Veblen 1899).

Maintaining a respectable standard of consumption for their children is one of the highest priorities for unemployed fathers, so that at least the 'young-uns' maintain their self-esteem. They are proud to be able to provide meat in their diet, will retain the colour television for them, and one of the commoner reasons for going into debt is 'clothes for kids. You *had* to take them on credit.' Few parents can withstand the whingeing of their children for money when their playmates have just rushed off to the ice-cream van for sweets, and Christmas is rarely a joyous season for impoverished fathers: 'There'll be an awfie lot o' men in Cauldmoss sore-hearted because they've nothing for their wains [children] at Christmas.'

Money and masculinity

The association between hard work, masculinity, and big earnings has already been mentioned and is epitomized in the use of alcohol, but gender identity pervades almost every area of consumption. Some commodities, such as meat and powerful, sophisticated machinery, have intrinsic masculine attributes. Even in households that have a car the woman usually cannot drive, and where she can she will almost never do so when travelling with her husband, unless he is drunk. This reflects and reinforces the general differentials in society as to who takes the initiative, who provides materially for whom, and who has the power, between the sexes. However cheap they are, most cars in Cauldmoss have fairly powerful engines, giving men more control over time.

It was previously noted how men are loath to sell their cars on becoming unemployed. Despite the traditional association of physical labour and masculinity, it seems that access to labour-saving technology gives an impression of greater manliness through having extended physical capabilities. Men reduced to cycling are somehow emasculated by this old-fashioned dependence on physical exertion. The manly qualities of eating meat suggest another reason, apart from the hallmark of solvency, why it remains a high priority in spending for the unemployed, despite its expense.

The rituals of consumption (particularly of alcohol) are so established in courting women that lack of money means a diminution of masculine self-esteem. Sex is thoroughly embedded in the culture of purchased commodities. When it was suggested to three unemployed lads that a girl who is herself on the dole (welfare benefits) might understand that they have no money and be attracted without it, they laughed: 'So she'll no want you. She'll be looking for someone with money.' The young unemployed often talk bitterly about the problem of chatting up girls: 'They say, "What do you do?" and you say "Fuck all", that's it.' One lad described how at a disco they soon 'suss you out' – whether you have a car and what job you are doing – and when you go back to their place their parents 'suss you out even deeper'. Without a car or a good job it does not matter 'if you look like Robert Redford'.

Reciprocal exchange

Social interaction in Cauldmoss is largely determined by the universal principle of reciprocity. A gift is never free, and unless reciprocated it involves a loss of prestige. Thus a network of relationships is established through shared consumption. In everyday life alcohol is the main medium of exchange for men, while for women it is tea or coffee and biscuits. Exchanging pints among a small number of men is fairly typical and establishes the participants as equals – as men, as workers, and as earners. It should be possible for a group to conform to a low level of consumption as much as a high one, but as with cigarettes (the third main item of exchange) a ratchet effect leads everyone to consume at the rate of the fastest drinker or smoker, since one can always precipitate the next round but not (within the conventions) delay it.

Reciprocity leads to the division of drinkers according to their purchasing power, since few would be prepared to accept drinks continually or tolerate scroungers for long. An unemployed man said of his old mates (still in work) that he 'still had them as friends, but couldnie afford to run aboot wi' them'. Consequently unemployed men enter the pubs only around the weekend after they have cashed their giros, and for much of the rest of the week stand outside at the crossroads. This avoids their feeling of inadequacy at sitting in the pub without a pint or the inferior role of a recipient, while on the other hand it maintains contact with friends and is a second best to participating in the world of the pubs. This is the main social nexus for men in Cauldmoss, and, since most jobs are found through personal contacts, alcohol is important for economic as well as for social involvement. This drug is at the centre of Cauldmoss culture. Exclusion from drinking is one of the greatest social deprivations for the unemployed, and as a result most of the pubs and clubs maintain a steady trade by allowing people to buy 'on tick' (credit).

For housewives the obligation to provide a satisfactory amount of food also means being able to offer visitors a snack and tea or coffee at any time of the day. Although this hospitality is largely symbolic, since there is no suggestion that the guest needs to be fed, the unemployed feel inferior if they cannot offer the normal wrapped chocolate biscuits or have only tea and no coffee left by Wednesday. The obligations of reciprocity extend to furnishings as well; a couple are likely to feel belittled if they have only a worn old couch and 1930s fireplace when more affluent friends drop in. Although they might economize on fuel when alone, as soon as visitors arrive they will get a good fire blazing.

The tenacity of full-employment values

The unemployed suffer from an impoverished personal identity not only because they are not workers, but also because they still subscribe to values associated with 'full employment'. Despite being unable to participate fully in the culture of purchased consumption, they cannot establish a new culture in which they can instead construct their identities through productive or recreational activities, although a few talk about it. Recently writers have speculated that, with more time and less income, those losing their jobs would become more self-sufficient, thus saving money and using their extra time productively (e.g. Gershuny and Pahl 1980, Dauncey 1983). This simple logic underestimated the basic equipment needed in order to carry out do-it-yourself activities efficiently and, more importantly, it ignored the cultural values of that group most vulnerable to unemployment.

In Cauldmoss the only areas where self-provisioning has significantly increased are with the substitution of certain previously bought services – such as window-cleaning, car maintenance, and 'carry-out' food – and in the collection of fuel, a practice well known during the 1930s. There are several other areas where the unemployed could save money, but very few do so. Most folk have large gardens, yet the few who grow vegetables are mainly in employment. There is no do-it-yourself entertainment organized in response to unemployment; and although beer is so important and the technique of brewing is familiar, very few brew their own on a regular basis. Few in Cauldmoss accord intrinsic value to articles because they are self-made.

Although collecting fuel is close to 'real' work for a man, many other activities of self-provisioning would be seen as part of the woman's sphere. The unemployed cannot abandon their industrial culture, in which prestige is related to involvement in the cash economy. Without a substantial moral shift, labour and time will remain something to be exchanged for money, and thence goods. In the absence of a radical response to unemployment, any 'liberation from wage slavery' can all too easily appear like a regression to a peasant-like past. The social imperatives for money dominate, and many of the unemployed in Cauldmoss resort to alternative means of gaining income (see Jeremy Seabrook's accounts in Chapter 2 of this volume).

Conclusions and possible political implications

To summarize, personal identity in Cauldmoss is sustained by appropriate symbolic consumption. One's identity as an adult, a father, and a man are subsumed in that of a hard worker, and people's roles as workers and as consumers are largely entwined. A man's wage is taken as a measure of his worth and masculinity, and these values are extended to a person's spending capacity, however it is earned. In establishing his son's credentials a man said in the same breath, 'He's a *worker* . . . a big earner, can't stand idle.' The boast of being one of 'the big earners' also means being one of 'the big money men . . . askin' what ye're drinkin''. Weber observed that whereas riches might once have been prestigious as a sign of the owner's devoted work and (by implication) his or her position as one of the elect, today they are esteemed in themselves: 'the care for external goods . . . [has] become an iron cage' (Weber 1930: 181).

'Working on the side' when unemployed, 'fiddling' (defrauding) the authorities (in particular the 'electric meter', but occasionally the Department of Health and Social Security), and stealing all provide cash (or save it) and perpetuate the consumer ethos. They affirm people's identities not only by conferring the esteem of a worker or the respectability of solvency, but also by allowing the unemployed to feel able to act on their environment again. It seems likely that these responses to unemployment also have significant political implications, and they suggest reasons why (to many people's bewilderment) mass unemployment has neither 'destroyed the fabric of society' nor even lost the incumbent party a general election.

These illegal activities exacerbate the isolation of the unemployed, since however much they are condoned they make one vulnerable to 'grassers' (informers). This reduces the scope for solidarity, while the financial (and sometimes emotional) shock-absorber provided by the hidden economy probably makes people less prone to militancy. Furthermore, the moral outrage people might feel when deprived of their jobs is compromised when they are themselves bending the rules. To take the argument further – as Seabrook does (1985) – it seems that the active poor are more ready to take private action to better themselves, in keeping with the predominant consumer ethos, than to seek a long-term solution for their poverty through collective political action, which would challenge the existing order.

The foregoing may be seen as evidence that the government has in practice a benign view towards the hidden economy, whatever its rhetoric. To businesses mass unemployment and wide-scale work on the side are doubly advantageous, in that they mean an increasingly subservient legal work-force and also access to a cheap, unprotected source of labour that can be used or ignored at will. The significance of work on the side to different firms varies considerably and is difficult to assess; certainly several employers around Cauldmoss employ people who they know are 'signing on'.

Section 2: Values associated with time

Work structures time

People in Cauldmoss, like most in our society, do not often consider time in the abstract. However, time is a useful focus for investigating ideas about work and unemployment. It is a concept that provides a means of structuring change. As we suggested earlier, structure is introduced into the world by separating and demarcating. In terms of time, human activities are made meaningful and can be regulated by setting limits on their duration (limits sometimes marked by ritual).

As E. P. Thompson (1967) describes, the standardization of time measurement throughout our society, facilitated as clocks became wide-spread, went hand in hand with the idea of 'time thrift' promulgated by educators, moralists, and employers. Mass consciousness has gradually absorbed an ethic that one's time should be spent in clearly purposive action, and this is still in general held to mean being engaged in, preparing for, or supporting those in paid employment. Those whose life has no such purpose, notably the unemployed (but also the sick and the retired) today tend to be condemned and/or accorded low social status. As with money, the use of time is constrained by cultural dictates. These determine how one's day and night, one's week, and one's life should be organized.

The need for some kind of regularity and order is fundamental to humankind. In more 'traditional' societies, structure is provided through various kinds of ritual (often religious) activity. In our own society this need has come to be associated with the desire for a forty-hour working week and a working life often spanning fifty years. When asked, most informants said that if they earned the same pay for working only twenty hours a week they would seek a second job to occupy their time. They believe that, on a national scale, the only feasible solution to unemployment is early retirement, which is seen as a legitimate reward after many years of work. As for job-sharing, 'I think you've either got to *have* a job or you've *not* got to have a job' is the typical response. Government employment schemes are condemned in Cauldmoss partly because of the time scale of the work involved. One teenager did not want work on a Youth Opportunities scheme but 'a *right* job, a proper job, not just being there and just getting used to the job and then having to leave'.

People in Cauldmoss concentrate on the financial rewards when asked why they work or want to work, although they also frequently mention wanting to avoid being seen as lazy, and a desire to 'get out of the house'. Employed men rarely speak of valuing the discipline and regularity work imposes, but it is clear from what is said about the effects of joblessness that the time structuring involved in paid employment is important.

Older people especially bemoan the fact that the young cannot get jobs and therefore forget how to get up 'in good time' each day. Many who lose jobs describe how they have become conscious of time passing more slowly than it did before.

Jahoda states that 'time experiences are structured in industrialised societies through the ubiquity of employment conditions' (1982: 59–60). Formal employment provides a basic grid against which a man's life is charted out. It defines 'free time', and pay-day (often the cause for a celebratory night out) marks the passage of one week, or one month, to the next. One's first job, then promotion, and retirement all signal transition to a new stage in life.

Work and leisure

The preoccupation with very regular hours of work emphasizes the feeling that the employee is selling his time rather than his labour (which contributes to the common alienation from work). Time-served tradesmen in Cauldmoss are proud of their skills, but lay stress on the hours worked and the rate of pay, rather than on how long a specific task takes. One is thus constantly made aware of the value of one's time, including one's 'free time'. This is a notion that is meaningful only when juxtaposed with that of 'working time', so that work and leisure cannot substitute for one another. This distinction is important in understanding the experience of the unemployed in Cauldmoss, for whom time no longer seems such a limited resource.

Although a man's autonomy is normally sacrificed during working hours, this does not mean that he will necessarily take *active* charge of his leisure time, organizing it to achieve a definite aim. The difference between these two categories of experience (work and leisure) is not necessarily due to the nature of the activities involved, nor to the extent to which either is internally structured. It depends on the fact that a man feels he can *choose* what to do with his leisure hours, although the range of socially acceptable leisure activities is not an open-ended one. Often a wife has her husband's evening meal ready when he comes in from work, and he then sits down to watch television for a couple of hours, if not all evening. Most men go out drinking only on certain nights of the week, and other common leisure activities are similarly regulated; for instance, day trips, Sunday afternoon walks round about the village, and church, community centre, or sports club meetings.

Although some of a man's 'free time' may be taken up with activities that he would not describe as 'leisure' ('helping' with the kids, for example), it is generally accepted that a working man deserves a night out, or a rest at the weekend.

Reactions to unemployment

We lack space here to consider the extent to which the unemployed of Cauldmoss go through the various psychological phases identified by different writers on unemployment. However, some described their experience in terms of a series of stages; one man, for example, said, 'At the start you enjoy it; then get bored of it; then get depressed; then get lazy.' This was the kind of pattern found among the unemployed Marsden interviewed in the early 1970s (Marsden and Duff 1975: Chapter 9). One of the unemployed told us that those on the 'bru'

> 'get to a stage and say, "I'll need to get a job." . . . You actually begin to hate living. [But then] you just begin to *accept* it . . . to make the best of "Well, I'm not employed and I can't get a job." A lot of folk get into a rut, and don't even want to go out and look for a job . . . 'cos they know there's nothing there.'

We suggest that the depression and apathy joblessness often produces are due to the unemployed's sense of having little control over their lives. This results from an absence both of money and of structure, the latter arising from their inability to differentiate one period of time clearly from another, from the lack of variety in the activities that 'occupy' them.

Most people expect to direct only a certain amount of their time, the rest being under the control of those they work for. To have too little of one's 'own time' is seen as unsatisfactory. Occasionally a man in Cauldmoss is criticized for being 'a workaholic', while women (around whose 'house-working hours' there are no firm temporal boundaries) sometimes complain that they have 'no time to just be myself', rather than a wife and mother.

The unemployed, however, face *too much* time of their own. One fifty-year-old redundant man with several hobbies pointed out that 'When you get fed up with a hobby you can just stop. At work, you get an awful lot of routine work . . . day in and day out . . . you're not choosing to do it.' Yet he said many times how much he would prefer to have a job, not just for the money and for renewed self-respect, but because time passes 'very slowly' now that he is unemployed and is continually forced to decide for himself how to spend his time. In theory the unemployed could choose to do many different things with their days. In practice, without work other activities often lose their appeal. As one person conceded, the redundant man who is 'quite happy to relax to his hobby – quite enjoy[s] life' is the exception to the rule.

The way a person passes his time and experiences unemployment depends on his position in the life cycle, as well as on the length of time he has been out of work (as is demonstrated by Fryer and McKenna and by

Fineman in Chapters 4 and 5 in this volume). For example, it is important to distinguish between those who have never been employed, and those laid off in their twenties or at forty-five. In general middle-aged men seem the most disturbed by their unemployment and most pessimistic about getting another job. However, members of all age groups suffer from the loss of the temporal structure they are used to, whether this was dominated by school or by work routines (the former being, after all, supposedly a preparation for the latter).

When first laid off, many men try to divide up their day as it was when they were working. In the early months of unemployment, looking for work – trips to the Jobcentre in the town, reading newspapers, writing letters to, or calling at, firms – occupies a lot of time, and there are also often jobs around the house waiting to be done. After this, however, many face long periods of featureless time, where days, punctuated only by meals, merge into one another. Young people frequently complain that 'Every day's the same.' One unemployed woman described a typical day: '[I] get up in the morning and moan about. . . . There's nothing to get up for. . . . I'll maybe take a walk up to [a neighbour's]. . . . She's as fed up as me. So I'll walk back. . . . You're just trailing about.' The house needed cleaning, she admitted, 'but I just can't be bothered! You just say, "Well, what's the good of it?" I don't know!' She wanted the level of welfare benefits raised to allow recipients to go out just one night each week, which she felt was impossible without getting into financial difficulties. 'Aye, to break the monotony. . . . It's all right sitting in for a wee while, but *every* day and *every* night? It's not right.'

When asked if there was any day of the week that was different from the rest, almost all the unemployed questioned said no. Even 'bru day' (when welfare payment is received) 'comes and goes; nothing special'; 'I don't really look forward to it because I know as soon as I get it, it's spent' – on 'the messages', bills, and often on repaying loans, usually to kin. Some do look forward to a weekly football match or shopping trip, but apart from that, life lacks variety.

Alternatives to a job

The range of activities that can substitute for a job is very limited, for a variety of reasons. Full-time leisure is a contradiction in terms (several informants pointed out that the unemployed 'don't get time off'), and the concept of 'education for leisure' was rejected by many informants. (See Leo Hendry, Chapter 11, below.) Even attendance at club or church meetings tends to be cut back. For most of the unemployed, only those pastimes requiring little or no cash can be used 'to kill time – kill boredom', as one man put it. Some young unemployed lads spend a lot of time on fishing or ferreting expeditions; their failure to keep to the basic guidelines of these activities (which *they* describe) suggests that they are more concerned to pass the day than actually to catch anything. The division of domestic labour is in general still too rigid to allow a man to assume substantial 'female' duties. Further education is regarded as suitable only for young people ('students'), while only women and retired folk should do voluntary work.

Men of course work for money, but the fact that emphasis is laid on the hourly rate of pay, rather than on the value of 'a job well done', means that consideration is seldom given to new *kinds* of work or to new patterns of working. Because work is seen as a relinquishing of one's time as well as one's actions to an employer, those who lose their jobs usually have little inclination to start organizing their own 'working day' on a formal self-employed basis. (Of the small number in Cauldmoss who tried this, few were successful.) Some arrange 'wee jobs on the side' for themselves, such as mowing lawns or repairing cars, but even when a man can get informal employment, say on a building site, it is rarely an adequate substitute for a formal job because it lacks regularity and security.

Obtaining cash is the prime motive for most of the illicit activities in Cauldmoss, such as fiddling the Department of Health and Social Security or stealing. But, as we said, they often have the additional benefit of allowing a feeling of control over one's life. In some cases they provide something to look forward to and give some sense of being able to determine future events. However, of the few (mainly young lads) who break into buildings, most do it with little advance planning. Such acts, like vandalism, are often a spontaneous response to boredom and an expression of frustration.

In a conservative community like Cauldmoss, it is hard enough for those who *can* satisfy society's requirements to be innovative, let alone for those who lack the legitimation and self-respect gained from employment. In fact, we would suggest that many of the unemployed do not really want to fill their days with 'purposeful' activity. Carefully to plug the gap meant for a job is almost to acknowledge that one will never have employment again. The dichotomy of work and leisure in Cauldmoss means that any alternative to 'real' work tends to be seen as a devalued form of leisure. Activities 'replacing' work, therefore, are taken less seriously than the search for 'a proper job', and most do not believe that experience gained from such endeavours can be of help in this search. Moreover, it is important to display poor adaptation to unemployment since, when jobs are scarce, only those doing so are believed really to deserve work.

Attitudes towards the future

Although time passes so slowly, many seem prepared to wait passively for a long time for a job. And while many in Cauldmoss believe that 'full employment' is not likely to be achieved in the foreseeable future, most hope their children or grandchildren will have 'proper jobs'. Many have a cyclical view of the economy, believing that the current recession will eventually end and then many more jobs will be created. There is talk of 'new technology', but few seem to have considered its implications in detail (which may be a further reason why the unemployed do not protest more strongly about their situation).

In terms of his own short-term future, one informant described the changes unemployment had brought: 'Your full way of living is changed. . . . [In the past] you could plan ahead and do things . . . [now] it's sort of week to week.' Another complained that 'You can't really *plan*. I couldn't say, "I'll go with you next Wednesday somewhere", because I wouldn't have the money to go.'

The problem of trying to save money for future use is demonstrated by the fact that many unemployed in Cauldmoss ask for their benefit to be paid weekly, rather than fortnightly, as is the usual procedure. It is also reflected in the way many have their standard electricity meter replaced by coin meters. The wives of unemployed men (as well as unemployed women) often prefer to get an item now, from a friend's 'book' (mail-order catalogue), and then pay for it in instalments. For some, this means juggling various debts. Of course, the families of those *with* jobs can also get into debt, and they also use catalogues, although this practice is probably more common among the unemployed, to whom other forms of credit are barred.

Occasions that mark the progress of time from year to year (birthdays, holidays, etc.) and through one's life (weddings and house-warming parties, for example) can no longer be planned and celebrated in the same way without a wage-earner in the house. Such events give people a clear sense of the difference between one period and another, something many of the unemployed are lacking, even in their daily lives. Because each day, each week, and even each year becomes, to an extent, indistinguishable from any other, the jobless often 'lose track' of time. The result is that many unemployed, and their families, tend to focus attention on the present rather than on the future. 'People are just grasping at life at the moment,' said one woman, describing how many are now using their savings to enjoy themselves while they can, rather than keeping them for 'feelings of security'. Many of those without jobs spoke of taking 'each day as it comes'.

Conclusions on time

Entailed in the crucial role of worker in this community are clear ideas about how individuals should spend their time: if not actually engaged in regular paid employment, then in preparation for it, in retirement from it, or in supporting those involved in this process. The structure of employment provides a temporal framework for life, on both an everyday and a longer-term basis. It governs the way time is experienced, which is in terms of differentiated units of activities. The loss of the status and financial rewards of being a worker is often accompanied by changes not only in the way the individual uses his or her time, but in the way he or she experiences time; a feeling of lack of purpose is frequently combined with a sense of timelessness. Depression and boredom are almost inevitable, in some cases temporarily alleviated by 'leisure' pursuits or, for a few, by more blatantly illegitimate activities, such as theft or vandalism. Apathy often predominates, with many of the unemployed concentrating what interest they can muster on the present, not wanting to plan for a future without work.

The tenacity of traditional notions of work, particularly regular hours of employment, prevents the unemployed from taking up new kinds and patterns of 'work' (in its broadest sense). We believe that a revision of ideas about 'work' can come about only through a restructuring of the format of employment, with much greater flexibility regarding both working hours and the sorts of activities that are recognized and rewarded as legitimate forms of work. This requires a rethinking of the tax and benefits system (see Leach and Wagstaff 1986: Chapter 12).

Our findings suggest that attempts at 'education for leisure' and special (temporary) job schemes can counter the unemployed's feelings of timelessness and aimlessness to only a limited extent. Unlike older unemployed men, young people who have never had a job cannot mourn its loss. But the prospect of life stretching out before them without the kind of goals currently provided and made possible by employment is a very bleak one.

Summary

The lack of both money and a clear time structure means that many of the unemployed are deprived of meaning in their lives. The first section of this chapter emphasized that shortage of money is in itself perhaps the greatest hardship for the unemployed. Low income undermines one's personal identity since one cannot establish or confirm one's status through symbolic consumption. In the same way, when men lose the temporal pattern provided by regular employment, the significance that

154 *Unemployment*

different periods of time had for them (as work time, leisure time, week and weekend, holidays, or retirement) is lost. One's sense of purpose and the extent to which one feels in control of events tend to diminish; both what one is and what one does are no longer as important as they were when one had a job. The values accorded to consumption and time in our society are so entrenched, and the unemployed are so passive in the face of this orthodoxy, that such people's experience of life is severely impoverished.

References

Dauncey, G. (1983) *Nice Work If You Can Get It: How to Be Positive About Unemployment.* Cambridge: National Extension College.
Donnison, D. (1982) *The Politics of Poverty.* Oxford: Martin Robertson.
Douglas, M. and Isherwood, B. (1979) *The World of Goods: Towards an Anthropology of Consumption.* London: Allen Lane.
Gershuny, J. I. and Pahl, R. E. (1980) Britain in the Decade of the Three Economies. *New Society* 51 (900): 7–9.
Jahoda, M. (1982) *Employment and Unemployment: A Socio-Psychological Analysis.* Cambridge: Cambridge University Press.
Leach, D. and Wagstaff, H. (1986) *Future Employment and Technological Change.* London: Kogan Page.
Marsden, D. and Duff, E. (1975) *Workless.* Harmondsworth: Penguin.
Seabrook, J. (1985) The Society which Offers Hope on the Underworld Lottery. *Guardian,* 25 March.
Smith, A. (1776) *An Inquiry into the Nature and Causes of the Wealth of Nations* (1892 edn). London: Routledge.
Thompson, E. P. (1967) Time, Work-Discipline and Industrial Capitalism. In M. W. Flynn and T. C. Smout (eds) (1974) *Essays in Social History.* London: Oxford University Press.
Turner, R., Bostyn, A. M., and Wight, D. (1984) *Work and Non-work in a Small Scottish Lowlands Town.* SSRC final report (HR7700/F00230066).
Veblen, T. (1899) *The Theory of the Leisure Class.* London: Macmillan.
Weber, M. (1930) *The Protestant Ethic and the Spirit of Capitalism.* London: Allen & Unwin.
Willis, P. (1984) Youth Unemployment. *New Society* 67 (1114): 475–77.

Part 3
Social responses and structures

9. Social services and unemployment: impact and responses[1]

Yvonne Dhooge and Jennie Popay

As the previous chapters have vividly described, unemployment affects individuals, families, and communities in many different ways, and people develop various strategies to cope with or adapt to their situation. In this they often draw upon informal systems of support, involving relatives, friends, and neighbours. However, people's ability to cope with unemployment and the informal support systems they can call on will vary enormously. There is good reason to suppose that a significant number of people experiencing unemployment may require support from elsewhere.

First, unemployment is distributed extremely unequally and is concentrated amongst the most disadvantaged groups in our society, whose resources – material and non-material – are already very limited, even in the best of times. Second, an increasing number of people are now experiencing long-term unemployment. In July 1985 around 40 per cent of all those officially unemployed had been out of work for more than one year; people's ability to rely on their own resources and those of relatives and friends may diminish as the period of unemployment lengthens. Third, as some of the case studies in this chapter will show, unemployment can create such crises that individuals or families can themselves no longer deal with them. For these reasons, statutory and non-statutory organizations have an important role to play in providing advice and support.

This chapter focuses on only one part of one statutory service, social work. There are two distinct dimensions to a possible social work role in relation to unemployment. At one level there is the question of whether social workers are responding to the needs of existing clients experiencing unemployment.[2] It is however also important to note that the vast majority of people experiencing unemployment never approach the social services. Clearly, many factors are at play, one of which may be people's lack of information about the kind of services provided and perceptions of social services as difficult to approach and stigmatizing (Strathclyde Regional Council 1983). At another level, then, there is the question of whether social workers can and should develop ways of working that destigmatize the services and make them more accessible. It is beyond the scope of this chapter to discuss both issues fully. Here we will primarily limit the discussion to the implications of unemployment for social work with existing clients, although brief mention will be made of the latter issue.

Whilst a great deal of social work activity is determined by legislation, the kind of work individual social workers do varies enormously. Social workers may have specialist responsibility for work with young people who have offended, or for work with the elderly or mentally handicapped. Conversely, they may have mixed or generic case-loads, although a large proportion of such case-loads are families with children. The vast majority of people social workers see involve short-term work. Indeed, research suggests that between a quarter and two-fifths of all referrals are completed within a day (Barclay Report 1982). Short-term work may be undertaken by all the social workers in a department on a rota basis or may be the responsibility of a special team – the intake team – with other teams dealing only with long-term work. Many intake teams set a limit of around three months before transferring people to long-term teams. Although only about 8 per cent of people who have contact with social services departments become long-term clients, they do take up a great deal of social work time. These people tend to fall into two categories: those suffering from chronic physical or mental conditions, and families where children are considered to be at risk.

Not only the work social workers do but also the setting in which they work may vary. Social workers may work out of a central office or sub-office as part of an area team; they may be patch-based with responsibility for a small geographical area and work out of a community centre, for example; or they may be based in a hospital, residential home, or health centre. These variations in the type of work and the work setting will influence what social workers perceive to be the impact of unemployment on the people they work with and on their day-to-day practice. Whatever the work or work setting, however, it has been demonstrated that people receiving social work support are disproportionately drawn from the most disadvantaged groups in society and therefore from those groups most likely to experience unemployment (Goldberg and Warburton 1979).

In the next section case studies are used to describe, through the eyes of social workers, how some of the individuals and families they work with are affected by unemployment and how social workers feel able to respond. It is then argued that social workers in general respond to unemployment in an *ad hoc* way. By this we mean that social workers tend to respond only in those situations where unemployment is an immediate and obvious factor. It is not a factor that is regularly considered in social workers' assessment of people's problems. Social workers or their managers rarely step back and consider whether the way they respond in these crisis situations is the most effective way of doing so and whether unemployment has a more general relevance to their work. The existing responses to the crises unemployment causes therefore create serious dilemmas for social workers. In addition, traditional social work strategies for dealing with the employment problems of some client groups – the young and the mentally ill, for instance – continue to be seen as the only option, albeit one that is increasingly considered inappropriate in the face of large-scale long-term unemployment.

Alternatives nevertheless exist. Whilst much of what social workers can do in relation to unemployment is limited, the support and advice already given to people experiencing unemployment can be improved, and some more imaginative responses are being developed that provide pointers for other ways of working. After considering some of the professional and organizational constraints on the development of social work responses to unemployment, we describe in the final section of this chapter some elements of an alternative strategy.

Unemployment in the social work context: some case studies

As we have briefly noted, unemployment is not a new phenomenon in the context of social work. For a variety of reasons many of the people receiving social work support have difficulties obtaining or keeping paid employment. Similarly, poverty and complex family situations are familiar problems for social workers and clients. However, the present high levels of unemployment have increased the scale and complexity of these problems. The impact of this on short-term social work – intake work – appears to be threefold: an increase in the number of people contacting the social services, a change in the type of people coming for advice, and the emergence of some new types of problem, in particular homelessness amongst young people. The increase in unemployment has also affected social workers' ability to close cases. Unemployment not only creates new long-term cases, where previously individuals and families may have received social work support for only a short period of time; it also hinders successful rehabilitation work with certain groups of clients.

The case studies presented here have to be interpreted against this background. The case studies are social workers' accounts of the experience of unemployment. They have been selected to illustrate what social workers see to be the main effects and are intended to give a qualitative rather than a quantitative picture.

One of the main consequences of unemployment documented in much research is the growing poverty in the community. Unemployment still implies a considerable loss of income (Moylan, Miller, and Davies 1984). For some people a reduction in income might mean cutting back on luxuries and may cause financial difficulties only if unexpected expenses occur. But, as various studies have demonstrated, it more often means problems in meeting essential expenses such as rent, mortgage, fuel, food, and clothing (Berthoud 1981 and 1984, CAB 1983, CPAG 1985). Financial problems are certainly one of the main reasons why people seek help from the social services. As two of the social workers in our study stated:

'A lot of people are coming through the door because they can't make ends meet.'

'People who some years ago would have associated social work departments with being "bad", in trouble, are now coming in looking for financial help, clothing, or information about organizations which might be able to help.'

Unemployment can create acute family crises, which in extreme cases might result in violence. In such instances the help of the social services may be called in by other service providers, as happened in the case of the following family.

Mary and Reg Williams were referred to the social services by the health visitor after a serious fight in which the police were involved. They had never been in contact with the social services department, and the social worker went into the home expecting the problem to be marital. However, he found that the core of the problem was unemployment.

Mary and Reg are in their twenties and have three children. Reg, a highly skilled craftsman, was made redundant a year earlier. Reg felt that Mary was making demands on him that he could not fulfil. On the one hand she wanted him to do the housework, but on the other she didn't want him to take over her 'job'. She also felt that she couldn't get on with her work because he was around all the time. Whilst sympathetic to his situation, Mary admitted that deep down she felt that if he really tried he could get a job, and Reg agreed that some part of him thought she was right.

Reg had become very depressed. He found it hard to get to bed because he had started to have nightmares; he also found it difficult to get up. He didn't want to go to the doctor as he felt this was a sign of weakness and he was afraid that he would be diagnosed as mentally ill.

The family also had heavy debts – electricity bills and hire-purchase commitments – and this was an additional cause of stress. They had begun to have violent arguments, which were affecting the children. The youngest child had started to wet the bed, which increased Mary's housework even more, and to make matters worse they had stopped taking her to the nursery, so they had lost the nursery place. Now not only Reg but also Rosie was at home all day.

Family dynamics are complex. It is very difficult, indeed probably inappropriate, to look for a single explanation for violence within families. However, the social workers we interviewed and other commentators feel that unemployment can be an important contributory factor in marital violence and in some instances of child abuse (Cater and Easton 1980, Crighton 1984).

According to the social worker, unemployment was the main reason for child abuse in the case of Peter Johnson, a forty-year-old lorry driver. Like Reg he was made redundant. His unemployment seriously affected the stability of his family, and the mounting tension resulted in a one-off incident of child abuse involving his thirteen-year-old daughter. Although Peter is still unemployed, the family seem to be managing well now. The girl is doing fine at school.

Many individuals or families find themselves, at one time or another, in a situation where other family members need either short-term or long-term nursing care. In contrast to the many public statements about the failure of present-day families to take on these caring responsibilities, in reality it is predominantly relatives, mostly women, who look after the elderly, the handicapped, the sick, and those with psychological problems, with only occasional help from statutory and voluntary services (Finch and Groves 1983). Some people would argue that because of unemployment more people are now available to take on a caring role. However, as the following case study shows, unemployment can seriously undermine people's ability to care for family members.

Liz and Bob Stevenson are looking after Liz's elderly father. Although Liz's health is not very good, they have coped very well. Since Bob became unemployed, this situation has changed. According to the social worker Liz is most affected by Bob's unemployment. She is increasingly worried about her own health, and about her husband and her father, who is getting older and needs more and more care. Unemployment has meant a substantial drop in their standard of living. It is also creating emotional stress, and Liz's health is deteriorating. Although she wants to continue to care for her father, she expresses more openly the difficulties she has in looking after him.

With unemployment, the problems of caring for people who may normally receive social work support for only a short period of time can compound to create what social workers call 'a case'. George Adams's situation is a clear illustration of how this process may operate:

George Adams gave up his job more than a year ago to support Ann, his wife, who had been mugged. The experience had made her anxious and nervous and had affected her ability to deal with the children and with routine household tasks. George had intended to stay at home just for a short time to help Ann through this crisis. However, he has been unable to find another job. The family are now experiencing acute difficulties. They have serious debts, and George has started to gamble. He and Ann have lots of arguments, and this is also affecting the children.

The social worker became involved when Ann was close to a nervous breakdown. The social worker concluded: 'As long as there is no chance of George finding employment, the future doesn't look very bright. They are just coping, really.'

The examples given so far constitute only a small proportion of the kind of people who might need the support of the social services because of unemployment. The social workers we interviewed identified young people on probation or leaving care, older ex-prisoners, and people with a history of mental illness as other groups where unemployment can have a particularly serious impact. Employment has always been central to the social services' involvement with these groups. As indicated at various places in this book, in our society employment performs a number of functions that most people need to manage their everyday life successfully; it provides an income, gives structure to time, enables people to widen their social contacts and experiences, and gives people self-esteem, status, and identity (Jahoda 1982). With the present high levels of unemployment it has become very difficult for these particular groups to find employment, and this can have serious consequences for successful 're-habilitation' work.

For young people leaving care, for instance, unemployment can make the transition to an independent life problematic:

Gail is eighteen years old. Since leaving school after obtaining a number of Ordinary-level certificates of education, she has had a variety of jobs, ranging from secretarial work to catering. She presently lives in a residential home, but the plan is to move her into a flat of her own. Although Gail wants to live on her own, her attitude towards the move to a flat changed once she became unemployed. She was very motivated to set up an independent life when she worked. Now, being unemployed, Gail finds it difficult to motivate herself to carry out tasks set by her social worker to help her prepare for living on her own.

David has already made the first step in this transition. He is seventeen and has been in care since being an infant. He now lives in a flat alone. He left school with no qualifications. Despite considerable effort from his social worker to help him find work, David eventually took a place with Community Industry. However, he complained about the small amount of money he was being paid, and his time-keeping was poor. He was asked to leave because of this. He then got a job with a firm delivering lemonade. According to the social worker, 'They exploited him. They offered a twelve-hour day for relatively little money. He was there for a week and was almost physically worn out.'

At present David has a temporary job in a social services department's old people's home, which the social worker managed to arrange for him. Whilst there are hopes that this job might become permanent, this is still uncertain. The social worker feels that unemployment will have serious implications for David's ability to manage an independent life successfully.

When David was unemployed he tried to steal a car. 'He was terribly frustrated. He had no job of any kind. He was very resentful . . . couldn't see himself ever owning anything much. If he loses his job, I don't know how he will cope. He has no family, and a flat to maintain. If he gets bills he can't pay there is nobody to underwrite him. He wouldn't have needed social work help if he'd had a job.'

For ex-prisoners unemployment can have profound effects on reintegration into the family and the community as a whole. Norman Gray's situation illustrates some of these problems:

Norman has completed ten years of a life sentence and is now on parole. His wife Shirley kept in contact with him throughout his time in prison. They are living together with their eleven-year-old daughter.

Shirley works full time, twenty miles away from home. She is very low-paid, and there are no chances of promotion. Because she worked, Norman couldn't get supplementary benefit, and he was unable to find work. In the words of the social worker, 'He was introduced to society after ten years with little prospect of a job, no income that he could call his own, dependent on his wife. He feels he's very much in the situation he was in prison with no control over his life, totally dependent on somebody else. She doesn't resent it but he does.'

During the first nine months he was unemployed Norman and Shirley had serious problems with their relationship. This has now lessened, and they are able to talk about it. However, they are in real financial hardship because Shirley's earnings are so low.

For people with a history of mental illness unemployment can add to the stigma they already experience because of their illness, and it can result in a worsening of their condition:

Bill Stewart is in his early fifties. He has a history of mental illness but in the past he has managed to maintain himself with a variety of casual work. He used to live alone, but since losing his job he has gone back to live with his mother – though not entirely because of unemployment, since he always found it difficult to live alone. Being out of work has made the relationship with his mother difficult. The social worker involved with him commented: 'There is little I can do with this case.'

Alex Gates is of a similar age to Bill but married. He has three children, two at school and one in work after a spell of unemployment. Alex has had social work support for a number of years because of his mental illness, but he was able to maintain himself between hospital stays with unskilled jobs. He has been unemployed for about a year now, and there has been a drastic change in him, causing much extra pressure on May, his wife. Alex feels more and more incapable and is becoming increasingly unstable. In addition the family is experiencing real financial hardship, with May also unemployed. This situation has started to affect the children.

Alex has been for a number of interviews without success but he continues to look for work. He is trying to decide whether to be honest about his mental illness when applying for work. If he got a job by lying, he might find his illness difficult to hide, but he feels it reduces his chances of getting work. As he spends a lot of time just lounging around at home, the social worker has referred him to volunteer agencies. He, however, sees these as a palliative. He also doesn't want to attend the psychiatric day centre.

Whilst the case studies presented here can only be indicative of the range of employment-related difficulties social workers may encounter amongst their clients, recent research from the Association of Metropolitan Authorities suggests that they are widespread and increasingly serious. As the authors of the AMA report conclude: 'accumulated evidence in the whole sample revealed increasing and intensifying needs that are not, given current resources and practices, being adequately met . . . these needs are decisively related to the rapid and recent growth of unemployment' (Hulme and Balloch 1985).

Social work responses

How then are social workers responding to these needs and to the particularities of these cases? As we have illustrated, one of the most pronounced effects social workers feel unemployment is having on their practice is the dramatic increase in financial problems presented to them, both at intake and in their work with long-term clients. The response of social workers to this aspect of unemployment is a practical one. They may try to sort out people's financial problems and ensure that they receive all the benefits they are entitled to. This may involve negotiating with the Department of Health and Social Security (DHSS), gas and electricity boards, or firms involved in hire-purchase agreements; or they may refer people to the Citizens' Advice Bureau and to welfare rights organizations. Sometimes social workers may try to ease the financial difficulties people have, for instance by providing second-hand clothing or household equipment.

Social workers do have access to some financial resources. Under Section 1 of the Social Work Act money is available for use to prevent children being taken into care, whilst in Scotland financial resources are available 'to promote social welfare', under Section 12 of the Social Work (Scotland) Act. However, our study suggests that despite the increase in financial problems amongst clients, social workers are not making more use of Section 1/12 moneys. This would seem to be in part because there are limitations on how they can be used; but, as the following quote illustrates, obtaining these moneys is also felt to be complex and time-consuming:

'The paperwork and time spent making a case for this money is still a major mental barrier to social workers choosing to get involved . . . a case has to be made with a senior, then area, then the district manager, who has the final say. The documentation has to be signed by both senior and area officers, especially if it's large sums, say around £100 or more.'

It would seem that social workers are instead increasingly turning to charities. Some of the charities they approach provide goods such as second-hand clothing or furniture. Other charities give monetary support, although often restricted to specific groups, for instance people with health problems.

Responding to financial problems is not only a way of offering people immediate support. In some cases it is considered to be a prerequisite for other forms of support. As one of the social workers we interviewed commented:

'Working with families that are unemployed is more complex. Financial difficulties, the question of debt, are always there, whatever the other problems. It's very difficult to talk to people about themselves when they have a lot of debt or their electricity is to be cut off . . . a lot of time has to be spent sorting out debts.'

Thus, for example, in the case above of Mary and Reg (unemployed) the social worker first of all dealt with their financial problems. She re-organized their debt repayment arrangements, provided benefit advice, and obtained a second-hand washing-machine from a local community enterprise. This eased some of the housework pressure Mary felt from Reg's presence at home, and the bed-wetting of her youngest child.

Social workers may also use their counselling skills to help people with the effects of unemployment on both an individual and a family level. The social workers involved with Mary and Reg, with Norman, and with Alex spent much of their time talking about unemployment, how it affected them emotionally, what difference it made to the family relationships, and how they could come to terms with it.

The type of support social workers provide is influenced by what help people ask for. According to the social worker involved, Norman and Shirley never asked for marital help, so help with their relationship problems was not part of the support she gave them. Alex's wife May apparently rarely talked about her unemployment to the social worker. However, the support social workers give is also influenced by who is defined as the actual client. Reg and Mary were referred to the social services as a family, and in the discussions about the effects of unemployment both were involved. In contrast, in the case of both Norman and Shirley, and Alex and May, Norman and Alex were the 'clients'. The accounts the social workers in question gave of their work with these two families strongly suggest that only Norman and Alex were involved in the counselling sessions about unemployment. Few references were made to the participation of other family members.

The support social workers offer people experiencing unemployment tends to focus on financial and emotional problems. Far less support is given in relation to finding work. We found very few cases of extensive support by social workers in the search for employment. Reg and Norman found short-term employment on schemes funded by the Manpower Services Commission through their own efforts; Gail is still unemployed and according to her social worker 'isn't seriously looking for a job.' In the case of Alex, the social worker had contacted the disablement resettlement officer, but in Bill's case nothing was done. Only David received extensive support in his search for work.

If our study is any indication, social workers feel that for a large pro-portion of young people, older ex-prisoners, and those with a history of mental illness on their case-loads employment is presently not an option. Supporting these groups has become particularly problematic because, at least in theory, the pursuit of employment is central to working with them and there is as yet no clear idea about what can replace it. Whilst some of the social workers in the study were considering or implementing alternative responses like the use of group work or increased referrals to community projects, most expressed views similar to the following:

> 'As to the work you can do with unemployed clients, you're dealing with long-term depression. They're not as hopeful either about the prospect of getting employment or of changing their circumstances. I tend to think I work with positive points. This is hard to do with someone who doesn't have much belief in himself. So at the moment I'm struggling for other ways to work with these clients.'

Or, as Bill's social worker commented, 'There is little I can do with this case.'

Such statements point to another dimension of the way social workers respond to the difficulties people they work with may experience in their search for work. In Bill's case the social worker reported no support of any kind to help Bill find some form of employment. Compare this with the social worker in David's case who made use of her contacts with the careers office, Jobcentres, and local employers and who at a later stage got David a job in an old people's home. It suggests that social workers may be responding differently to the problems different client groups face. With regard to people with disabilities, older ex-prisoners, and those with a history of mental illness, there appears to be a certain degree of acceptance, albeit not necessarily conscious, that they will not find work in the 'open' labour market:

> 'In this area "normal" people feel that there is no work available. So I have also changed my attitude. I am no longer pushing my clients [people with a history of mental illness] towards jobs. I am afraid that they will fail to get a job, which makes the situation worse.'

This contrasts sharply with the way the difficulties of young people are seen. The social workers we talked to felt very strongly that the lack of job opportunities for young people was totally unacceptable. Those who indicated that they were spending more time helping people find work were invariably referring to activities with young people: 'I have close links with careers officers and spend a lot of time with youngsters. We've just slipped into accepting that there is no work for adults.'

These different perceptions seem to be reflected in the attitudes social workers have towards the various alternatives to paid employment, such as community projects, voluntary work, sheltered employment schemes, and Youth Training Schemes. These tend to be seen as more acceptable for people with disabilities, those experiencing mental illness, or older ex-prisoners than they are for young people. In the study we heard few criticisms of community projects, voluntary work, or sheltered employment schemes for the former groups. This was in marked contrast to the views of social workers on the Youth Training Schemes (YTS), which tended to be regarded as unacceptable.

Social workers' attitudes to YTS are partly a response to the negative view many young people have of these schemes (Finn 1984). As two social workers in our study commented:

'To persuade them to join YTS is a great problem. With all the YTS schemes around there must be some that are worth while, but it's a great struggle to persuade them that it's worth giving it a try.'

'Most of our kids can get on training schemes, but all we end up with is kids who are feeling fairly resentful of being made mugs of. More and more are refusing to go on schemes . . . it's passing down the grape-vine that it's a waste of time.'

Some social workers themselves also have strong doubts about YTS. They are therefore less likely to see it as an appropriate response to the un-employment of their younger clients, even though this can make it more difficult to work with them:

'When you work with youngsters, you can feel a sort of sense amongst them that there is not much point in putting any effort into training because there are no jobs at the end of the day. This makes it very hard, but it is made tougher by the fact that I don't like YTS at all. I am not prepared to push them to take up a place on a Youth Training Scheme.'

As we suggested above, there were a few instances when the social workers we interviewed were referring people to locally based initiatives focusing on unemployment. However, in general such referrals were relatively rare despite the increasing number of such groups being established. In one of our study areas more than fifty such groups are listed in a local directory, and the British Unemployment Resource Network has recently (1984) published a national directory listing more than seven hundred groups. The initiatives are as diverse as the organiza-tions and individuals involved. They provide a range of services including welfare rights and other financial advice, social support, training, personal counselling, campaigning activities, and leisure facilities. These initiatives represent a valuable resource for social workers and other service providers, but our study suggests that this resource is under-utilized. Apart from those specifically concerned with financial problems, referrals to such initiatives are not a common social work response to unemployment.

The *ad hoc* nature of social services responses

In situations where unemployment is recognized as a major cause of the problems people experience, social workers respond accordingly. However, the way they respond reflects considerable uncertainty about whether unemployment is an issue that the social services can or should take on and what they can do about it. Such uncertainty might help to explain why most of the responses are of an *ad hoc* nature, restricted to intervening in acute crises. It might also be one of the reasons why social workers appear to be ambivalent about the way they are presently responding to the effects of unemployment.

Their responses to financial problems show some of this ambivalence. As discussed, social workers are increasingly relying on charities to support the growing number of people experiencing financial difficulties (CPAG 1984, Hulme and Balloch 1985). Because of the cuts in public expenditure and limited access to internal resources, charities are regarded as the only alternative option. However, some social workers find it difficult to accept this greater reliance on them: 'Charity has certainly increased. People are now offered Women's Royal Voluntary Service "lines". I am against that. There is too much charity already. People have a right to shoes.' Additionally, there is anxiety about the fact that some charities, those distributing for instance second-hand clothing or furniture, give assistance only to people who have a referral letter or 'a line' from a person such as a social worker. Some social workers are highly critical of this procedure, not only because it places them in the role of gatekeeper, but also because of the degrading and stigmatizing effect they feel it has on them and on the people they are trying to help:

> 'We should be playing a much more active advocacy role towards the DHSS. We are getting too exhausted from fighting them all the time, and we tend to accept that the DHSS no longer provides certain payments. But we are then left in a position of having to give people "lines" to go to a voluntary organization for second-hand clothing, which is degrading both for us and for them.'

Some social workers have similar reservations about the support they may give individual clients or families in relation to the emotional and psychological impact of unemployment. Although this form of support is seen as potentially valuable, there is a feeling that counselling people is not dealing with the real problem. Unemployment tends to be seen as an economic and political problem. In the eyes of social workers the essence of the difficulty for the unemployed is not having work, and in this area many social workers feel they have little to contribute: 'People really need jobs. We have to be realistic; there are no jobs around, so what can we do?' Emotional support tends to be regarded as trivial or at best ameliorative. There is also some concern that by helping people to cope with unemployment social workers might in fact be helping to legitimize it. Some social workers feel very uneasy about being involved in such responses:

'We will be trying to help people accept unemployment. This is in complete contrast with what social work is about, prevention, intervention, and trying to cure the situation. Helping people to accept their situation is something I don't like. It means helping people to fit the system instead of changing the system.'

The *ad hoc* nature of many of the social services responses is not just a reflection of the uncertainty about how best unemployment can be integrated into social work practice. It is also related to the perceptions social workers have of the relevance of unemployment to a client's problem. There would appear to be various situations where unemployment, although present, is not seen as an issue for practice (Bridges and Campling 1978, Berglind 1984). Particularly in their work with individuals or families receiving long-term support, social workers tend to see unemployment as an aggravating factor rather than a prime cause of people's problems. As two social workers we interviewed put it:

'There would be difficulties with these families whether they were unemployed or not.'

'I am not convinced that working in an area with high levels of unemployment is any different from working in an area with low unemployment. The people we see can't cope with pressure of any sort.'

The low priority afforded to unemployment by many social workers is reflected in the failure to keep adequate and accurate records on employment status in many of the cases they come into contact with. In a small pilot project of social work involvement with employment services in 1977, the authors concluded:

'Employment problems were not generally seen as a main reason for referrals by social workers. Work was not looked at very seriously. As one social worker put it: "As a profession social workers put work low on the list of priorities. Social work reports are often sketchy on work as opposed to family background information."'

(Bridges and Campling 1978)

Since that survey was undertaken, unemployment has more than doubled in many areas of Britain, yet the situation appears to be remarkably similar. Amongst the social workers in our study the recording of employment status was also inconsistent and patchy, particularly where it concerned people other than the person defined as the client, or women. This is not to say that social workers do not respond to the problems people present to them; but it does mean that these problems are less likely to be seen as wholly or partly related to unemployment or, in a better economic situation, to the marginality of people in the labour market.

Whilst our study did not involve an exploration of the way clients perceive their own needs and the support they receive from the social services, the question whether clients share the views of social workers needs to be considered. We found some indication that clients' views of the kind of advice and support they need differ from those of social workers. In Alex Gates's case, for instance, the social worker saw volunteering as an acceptable alternative to paid work and referred Alex to volunteer agencies. Alex, on the other hand, regarded volunteering as no more than a palliative, not the advice and support he needed. Recent research from Sweden suggests that such a divergence between the client's views and those of social workers may also exist in relation to perceptions about the significance of unemployment (Berglind 1984). Berglind, who explored this issue in detail, found that

'only 13–23% of social workers saw unemployment as the client's foremost problem. And still fewer saw unemployment to be the primary cause of the client's problem. These figures are significantly under what the clients themselves give as reason for the need for economic support, just as they are lower than the figures for actual unemployment according to the clients' information. It appears, however, as if social workers in relating to the clients undervalue unemployment's importance.'

Uncertainty about the type of response presently being used within social work practice and the perceptions social workers have of the significance of unemployment to clients' problems are only two of the many factors influencing the way the social services are responding to unemployment. A number of other equally important constraints are operating. Some of these constraints are organizational. Pressure of time is particularly crucial. Social workers are very aware of the extent of unmet needs in the population and of the tendency for new 'problems' or client groups to be added constantly to their responsibilities. Other organizational constraints include the lack of financial resources, a lack of personnel, and the need to give priority to statutory obligations.

Also at managerial level there is uncertainty about what priority social workers should give to unemployment-related problems. We found amongst some managers a growing concern that increasing financial problems may be taking up too much social work time. As one manager suggested: 'So much of the work is becoming money work. I'm not sure the social services are the right people to deal with this.' The absence of clear managerial directives on unemployment and social work acts as a further major constraint.

Challenging the constraints on practice

Some of the constraints identified by social workers are real, in particular the resource difficulties, the lack of staff, and the many statutory responsibilities they have. These need to be taken into account when exploring the potential within the social services to develop responses to unemployment. However, other constraints can and need to be challenged in order to open the way to look at possible alternatives.

One issue that needs to be addressed is the view that social work responses to unemployment are bound to be ameliorative and that therefore any type of social work support is trivial, unable to deal with the 'real' problem. Clearly, the economic and political dimensions of unemployment are important, and as we have pointed out, social workers can play only a limited role here. But what about *the people* experiencing unemployment? For many individuals and families unemployment is a traumatic experience, and at this level social workers can make an important contribution to alleviate some of the worst effects. Unemployment is not the only problem that has economic and political dimensions. Work with child-care cases, the elderly, and people with disabilities, for instance, has similar dimensions, but this fact has not stopped social workers from responding. It may be that in these areas of social work the structural aspects have become less visible, or have in some way been 'defined out' to allow responses to be developed. We would not want to argue for a similar process to happen in relation to unemployment. The question is whether this is necessary. Responding to individual or family needs does not exclude the possibility of taking on an advocacy role and addressing the economic and political aspects of any of the issues dealt with by social workers.

Moreover, although the high levels of unemployment are recent, unemployment itself is not a *new* problem for social workers. In fact a substantial proportion of the social workers we interviewed made this point. To quote one of them: 'I can't say I have done [noticed an increase in unemployment amongst clients and/or family members]. Social workers are working with the unemployed all the time. I am always surprised when people have a job.' With some client groups, devising strategies to deal with the effects of unemployment and providing advice and support in the search for employment have – at least in principle – always been seen as an integral part of social work practice. If, in reality, social workers had taken these issues as seriously as this perspective suggests, there would already have been a greater sensitivity to the relevance of unemployment for the problems of clients, and more thought would have been given to clarifying the role of social workers *vis-à-vis* unemployment. Responding to unemployment would not therefore necessarily be seen, as it is by many social workers, as a *new* responsibility increasing their already heavy work-loads.

The importance of the various organizational and professional constraints will differ depending on what kind of response is being considered and whether one is thinking of improving existing practices or of developing new approaches. Time, for example, may hinder the development of totally new initiatives in the field of welfare rights; but it may be less of a barrier if the response involves taking more account of the relevance of unemployment to clients' problems in a counselling situation. And whilst some responses, such as making better use of local unemployment-related initiatives, might demand extra time in the short term, they might save time in the long term.

The same applies to models of working. We found a relatively strong conviction amongst social workers that their present client-oriented way of working is inappropriate in the context of unemployment and needs to be replaced by a community-based model. However, these models of working are not mutually exclusive; a client-oriented model can be appropriate if social workers are responding on an individual or family level. On the other hand, responding at a neighbourhood level might require community-based social work. Ideally, responses should be developed at a number of levels simultaneously.

Developing more effective responses

It is not our intention to provide a detailed strategy to deal with the problem of unemployment. All we aim to do is indicate some ways for social work to move forward, using initiatives that already exist within the social services. We will not provide detailed accounts of these initiatives but rather attempt to pull out the major characteristics that underpin them and can help to inform the development of future initiatives.

First, in order to improve service delivery to existing clients it is necessary to increase the general level of awareness amongst social workers about the relevance of unemployment to their work. In this context the systematic record-keeping of employment status and monitoring the effects of unemployment on clients and on social work practice are important. They will help to make social workers more conscious of the different groups affected, the consequences unemployment has for the individuals and families they work with, and the impact it has on their own practice. Such exercises have been undertaken in a number of social services departments and have proved valuable in improving present record-keeping and informing practice (Bennett and Barnes 1982, Nash 1983, Coles forthcoming).

Monitoring exercises may also enable social workers to identify specific, widespread difficulties and thereby facilitate collective responses directed at a particular issue. Recognition of the widespread use and criticism of the Women's Royal Voluntary Service provisions, for example, may prompt consideration of other models of providing the service. Furthermore, detailed information on unemployment is invaluable for planning services and for informing policy-makers at local and national level. It is important that social workers and their managers give much more attention than they presently do to their role as social commentators. As the author of a recent book on the future of social work argues:

'Society is denying itself the possibility of much valuable information on the problems of society and the present ways of dealing with them if social workers are constricted in their capacity for informed comment out of direct experience. To describe this sort of critical function as politically perverse or going beyond the proper function of social work is like denying doctors the right to comment on health service.'

(Walton 1982)

A second characteristic of existing innovative responses is a focus on improving ways of disseminating information. Social services departments have an important part to play in improving the availability of accurate and clear information about benefit entitlements, as well as the take-up of benefits. This means a greater involvement in welfare rights advice and possibly the production of information sheets. Another area where social services input is needed is the dissemination of information about local resources. As we have indicated, unemployment initiatives in the voluntary sector represent a potentially valuable resource for social workers. However, social workers appear to have little knowledge of local projects. Despite the long history of antagonism between the statutory and the voluntary sectors, which might be difficult to overcome, there is scope to improve the situation. If clients are to benefit from local initiatives, social workers need to make more referrals, and for this they need more information about and contact with local projects. With increased contact they might also be able to work with the voluntary sector in thinking through what responses are most appropriate.

This leads us to a third characteristic of some of the more considered responses being developed within the social services: a focus on the provision of accessible non-stigmatizing services. As described earlier, social workers have serious reservations about using services that are stigmatizing for the recipients. Some charities distributing second-hand clothing are one such example. However, partly because of the lack of other options, many social workers continue to use them. At the very least, they could nevertheless comment on the stigmatizing nature of existing statutory and voluntary provisions, including their own, and in some cases stimulate the development of alternative provisions. A good example we have identified is a small enterprise that collects and renovates furniture for distribution to social work clients. Whilst social workers themselves did not establish this initiative, the idea came from within their department. Similarly, attempts are being made to encourage the development of food co-operatives to improve the quality and lower the cost of food. Such initiatives are complementary if not alternatives to the more individually focused budget advice. Similar models of service provision have been developed in relation to welfare rights (claimant unions) and loan schemes (credit unions), whilst in some areas 'good-as-new shops', run on a co-operative basis, provide an alternative to charities. Social workers and managers may feel that they can be only marginally involved in such developments, but there is certainly scope for a greater degree of involvement than that presently existing.

Another broader issue needs to be mentioned. As noted at the beginning of the chapter, social workers in particular, and social services in general, come into contact with only the tip of the perennial iceberg of unemployment-related difficulties. The overwhelming majority of people experiencing unemployment never approach the social services, although research suggests that a majority of them will experience some financial, social, and psychological difficulties. By encouraging other statutory and voluntary agencies to provide accessible non-stigmatizing services, by facilitating the development of, and supporting, community-based self-help groups such as claimants' unions, and by fulfilling their legitimate role as social commentators, social workers can contribute – albeit in a limited way – to the well-being of this larger group of people. These activities would presumably fall within the remit of community social work, recently discussed in the Barclay Report and subsequently a topic for heated debate in the profession (Barclay Report 1982). However, it would be unfortunate, as we have argued, if client- and community-centred work came to be seen as mutually exclusive models for social work. They are not. Indeed, each grows in strength combined with the other.

176   *Unemployment*

Notes

1. Most of the material in this chapter is drawn from a wider study into the implications of unemployment for the health and social services, funded by the Health Education Council: J. Popay, Y. Dhooge and C. Shipman (1986), Unemployment and Health: What Role for Health and Social Services?. Health Education Council.
2. Although there is much discussion of the need to replace the word 'client', no generally acceptable alternative is presently available. We therefore continue, somewhat reluctantly, to use the word despite its patronizing tone.

References

Barclay Report (1982) *Social Workers: Their Role and Tasks*. London: Bedford Square Press.

Bennett, D. and Barnes, M. (1982) *Unemployment and the Social Services: A Dilemma for Planners*. City of Sheffield Family and Community Services Department, Research Report No. 10.

Berglind, H. (1984) Unemployment – A Challenge for Social Work. Paper presented to the International Conference on Social Development, Montreal, August.

Berthoud, R. (1981) *Fuel Debts and Hardship: A Review of the Electricity and Gas Industries' Code of Practice*. London: Policy Studies Institute.

—— (1984) *The Reform of Supplementary Benefit*. London: Policy Studies Institute, Research Paper 84/5.2.

Bridges, B. and Campling, J. (1978) *Employment Problems – the Social Work Involvement*. Birmingham: British Association of Social Work.

British Unemployment Resource Network (1984) *Action with the Unemployed: A National Directory of Centres, Groups and Projects*. London.

Cater, J. and Easton, P. (1980) Separation and Other Stress in Child Abuse. *The Lancet*, May: 972–73.

Child Poverty Action Group (1984) *Carrying the Can: Charities and the Welfare State*. London: CPAG/FSU.

—— (1985) *Poverty and Food*, Spring, No. 60.

Citizens' Advice Bureaux (1983) *Debt in the Recession*. CAB Occasional Paper 15.

Coles, R. (forthcoming) *Unemployment: Its Effect on Social Services*. Suffolk County Council, Social Services Department.

Crighton, S. (1984) *Trends in Child Abuse*. London: NSPCC.

Finch, G. and Groves, D. (eds) (1983) *A Labour of Love: Women, Work and Caring*. London: Routledge & Kegan Paul.

Finn, D. (1984) *The First Year on YTS: A Permanent Bridge to Work?*. Unemployment Unit Bulletin, No. 14.

Goldberg, E. and Warburton, R. (1979) *Ends and Means in Social Work*. London: Allen & Unwin.

Hulme, C. and Balloch, S. (1985) *Caring for the Unemployed: A Study by the AMA on the Impact of Unemployment on Demand for Personal Social Services*. London: Bedford Square Press.

Jahoda, M. (1982) *Employment and Unemployment: A Social–Psychological Analysis.*
   Cambridge: Cambridge University Press.
Moylan, S., Miller, J., and Davies, R. (1984) *For Richer, For Poorer?*. DHSS Cohort
   Study of Unemployed Men, Social Research Report No. 11. London: HMSO.
Nash, A. (1983) The Long Shadow of Unemployment. *Community Care*, June.
Strathclyde Regional Council (1983) *Report of Research in Linwood.* Talbot Initiative
   Group, Report of Director of Social Work, Appendix III. C. Madigan, Paisley
   College, Department of Politics and Sociology.
Walton, R. (1982) *Social Work 2000: The Future of Social Work in a Changing Society.*
   London: Longman.

10. Discouraged workers? The long-term unemployed and the search for work

Sarah Buckland and Susanne MacGregor

At the Conservative Party Conference on 10 October 1985, Lord Young, Secretary of State for Employment, claimed that one-third of those currently counted as unemployed are 'not looking for work'. He also referred to the fact that 1.4 million people are now officially 'long-term unemployed'. The implication seemed to be that the long-term unemployed were to blame for their situation. They were not trying hard enough to find work. In support of this, Lord Young pointed out that the largest number of long-term unemployed live in the South East of England where 'employers can't find labour'.

Whilst such mystification reigns in public discussion of long-term unemployment, the private lives of the unemployed and their families are becoming increasingly impoverished and ever more remote from those of their more affluent fellow citizens who still have jobs to go to. In this chapter we provide a platform for their views and show how people faced with the consequences of long-term unemployment try to find ways of getting by. They try to develop strategies to deal with the problems that surround them, and they often show an ingenuity and resilience at variance with the pathetic image often portrayed in public debate.

It seems to us more likely that the 'disincentive to labour' has its base in the job market, the wage system, and the tax and social security systems, than in any special psyche or character of the long-term unemployed. The semi-official categories of 'long-term unemployed' and 'discouraged, demoralized workers' mask a wide variety of men and women with a range of needs, interests, skills, problems, practices, and styles of living that cannot be reduced to such simple codes. They are people, not mere units of labour or unemployment statistics.

A note on the research project

The information in this chapter is drawn from a research study conducted for the Department of Health and Social Security (DHSS) between 1981 and 1983. This was an assessment of an 'upgraded' re-establishment centre (REC) in South London. Re-establishment courses run by the DHSS are designed to revive the will to work, to restore the habit of getting up and going to work, and to give men confidence in their ability to hold down a job under normal conditions. These courses differ from those of the Community Enterprise Programme or the Community Programme, run by the Manpower Services Commission, in that it is assumed that men sent on them have lost the work habit and the motivation to work – that is, that they are 'discouraged workers'.

The course we looked at was a specially 'upgraded' one, a trial exercise based primarily on the Wider Opportunities Courses then run by the Manpower Services Commission. At Wider Opportunities Courses, men and women were asked to undertake work projects to test their aptitudes and abilities. Following this, effort was directed to finding them suitable work or referral to trade training.

It was hoped originally that applying these methods to long-term unemployed, discouraged workers would improve their job chances. Over time, however, it was increasingly recognized that the unemployment situation was worsening and that upgrading re-establishment centres was unlikely to produce any great success in job placements. It was hoped instead that transfers and placements on to full trade training courses – the Training Opportunities Programme (TOPS) in particular – might increase. The upgrading of RECs and the secondment of Manpower Services Commission instructors on to their staff was tried experimentally with this object in mind.

The men referred to this London re-establishment centre had been selected by unemployment review officers at local DHSS offices as suitable cases.[2] Only men were referred. None received more than his normal supplementary benefit in return, other than free lunch and help with travel expenses. Attendance was in principle voluntary; indeed, more of those referred chose not to attend than did attend. However, some felt that there was an element of compulsion involved in that they were afraid they might be viewed unfavourably by the unemployment review officers if they refused and felt that they might then be under scrutiny, even that their benefit payments were at risk.

The research study involved the collection and analysis of administrative records on all 349 referrals to this course made between November 1981 and July 1983. We have information on 327 men referred in this 21-month period; 134 attended the course and 193 did not.

Forty-two men attending the course between January and July 1983 were interviewed at the re-establishment centre at the beginning of the course, and those still attending after six weeks were subsequently re-interviewed. The men were interviewed again in their homes approximately three months after the end of the course. Interviews with a group of thirty-two men who were referred but decided not to attend were carried out in their homes.

Some case histories

In this chapter we set out the views of some of the men on this re-establishment course in South London about opportunities for work, the experience of unemployment, and the relevance of available courses. What do they want? What do they think would help them to sort out the situation? To spell out their replies in detail we present three selected case histories.[3]

Case 1. Mr Collins

Mr Collins was in his twenties, married with two children of school age. He had not worked for two years. He felt that the reason why he had been unable to get a job was because of his prison record, and that this always went against him in interviews with prospective employers: 'sometimes, being interviewed and it's going all right, but as soon as you tell them, all the smiles go away. . . . It always comes up when they ask why you left your last job.' Prior to this current spell of unemployment he had been unemployed for only the odd month, and had mainly moved straight from one job to the next.

Both Mr and Mrs Collins felt that unemployment had placed a strain on their relationship as well as on their children. Mrs Collins considered that her husband was harder to live with than when he had been working. The major problems that they identified were these: Mr Collins being at home far more than when he was working and so 'getting under his wife's feet'; lack of money; and a lack of what they called 'legitimate' money, i.e. having to claim social security and not being able to earn a living for oneself.

The difficulties created by a lack of money featured in almost all cases, but were of particular concern to Mr Collins: 'Having no money; nowadays you've got to have it. If you go out, you've got to have money. The kids don't understand you can't pay it out. Money. It all comes back to money.' They found it very hard to manage on their income. There was never enough to get them through the second week (benefit was paid fortnightly), although they always made sure that they had enough food to feed the children. Two years earlier they had had their electricity cut off for failure to pay the bills, so they now had a pre-payment meter. They could not afford a telephone. This had prevented Mr Collins getting a job that he had applied for, as the employer required him to be available by telephone for emergency call-outs. Mr and Mrs Collins owed £200 for loans they had taken out. They were paying these back regularly, although only a portion of the required payments. For some months Mrs Collins had been working part-time cleaning but she had left this job two weeks earlier because, she claimed, her employer had been very unreliable in paying her wages. The strategies and resources available for this couple to deal with poverty were limited. They never bought new clothes and relied on gifts from friends. Mr Collins did all his own repairs and maintenance around the house as well as on their car. If they needed help they felt they could turn to their family, in particular to Mr Collins's mother.

Mr and Mrs Collins said that they could never afford to go out for a night 'down the pub', but that unemployment had not had any effect on the friends that they mixed with, except that Mr Collins tended to see far more of them than when he had been working. Some of their friends were unemployed, while others were working; he sometimes helped out one of his friends who had recently 'gone self-employed'. In this way Mr Collins did have access to the informal economy, although any involvement was only peripheral and did not have a significant effect on their resources. They were both keen for Mr Collins to find 'legitimate' employment, and to stop having to accept money from social security, but they felt the opportunities available were limited, and this had been one of the reasons why Mr Collins had decided to attend the course at the re-establishment centre.

Mr Collins: 'When you go to sign on and then get a cheque at the end, it's not the same as getting a wage; you don't feel you've bought anything yourself.' Mrs Collins: 'We're round each other too much – could break a marriage up. If he goes and works at least he could say I worked for this and this. You're looked on like dirt around here if you're on social security.' Mr Collins felt that the course would teach him new skills, and help him to know what type of work he would be better at doing. By the sixth week of the course he felt that it had helped a great deal and boosted his confidence in his own abilities, as well as increasing his chances of finding work:

> 'I think this is the best type of help you could get, because you know you come here and it gets you up in the morning at the same time on a regular basis. It does help you; well, it helps me. It depends on what sort of attitude you have . . . if you've got the right attitude, like myself, you can learn something. I'm coming here 'cause I want to learn, and I hav' learnt.'

His wife had reservations initially about the value of the course, as she doubted whether it would help him to get a job, but by the sixth week his instructor had raised the possibility of his attending a TOPS course, which they both felt was a good idea. Mr Collins was keen to go on such a course, and took some of the maths books home with him to work on in the evenings. He was, however, unsure as to whether he would be able to achieve the standard required, particularly as he had not done any maths since leaving school at fifteen: 'I want to do it [TOPS] and I'm interested in doing it, but until I start doing it I don't know what it will involve.'

Mr Collins's determination to find work was reflected in his 'job search'. During the six months prior to attending the course he had been looking in newspapers and asking friends about jobs several times a week. He had never given up looking for work, always hopeful that something would turn up. However, he had had only half a dozen interviews out of all the jobs he had applied for since becoming unemployed. His most recent job application had been made shortly before starting the course. While on the course he had applied for several jobs and obtained an interview for one; but he was not offered the job.

At the time of the follow-up interview three months after leaving the course, Mr Collins had not succeeded in gaining a place on a TOPS course, because, he asserted, his maths had not been fast enough. He was now less optimistic about his chances of finding work than he had been when on the course, and had applied for only one job since. He was considering the possibility of setting up in business, and wondered whether he could get an enterprise allowance, but felt that there was no way he could raise the capital required to qualify for it.

Case 2. Mr Black

Mr Black was in his mid-twenties, married with three children, and his wife was pregnant. He had worked for only two weeks in the past two years, and his wife had not worked since before they were married five years ago. When asked why he felt he had been unable to find work, he said that it was because he had not got a lot to offer anybody as he had no skills on paper, although he felt he was capable of doing the work.

The worst thing for Mr Black about being unemployed was the lack of money to live on. Although unemployment had affected his relationship with his wife, and this did cause arguments, he thought the main problem was being unable to buy the things that they needed and wanted: 'The biggest difficulty is not being able to do the things that most families do. Everybody gets pretty cheesed off, and I get ratty. I don't like struggling. . . . Stupid things affect me, like seeing someone who's got better things.'

Mr and Mrs Black said that they tried to lead as normal a life as possible, as if Mr Black was still at work; so he went out most days. Mrs Black said that she would not be able to cope if he was at home all day. Mr Black used to go to the pub frequently when he was working and knew many people, but he had lost contact with them because he could no longer afford to go out drinking. All his contacts now are unemployed, he said, as he 'can't keep up with the ones who have got money'. Although he sees more people now than when he was working, because none is in work he does not get to hear about any jobs that are going.

Mr and Mrs Black said that their flat was gradually looking tatty and that they could not afford things that their friends could, and they did not have any money to buy the things that they needed. Mr Black had been convicted of theft in the past, but his wife said that he did not steal any more because she was 'tired of being knocked up by police at six in the morning'. She said that all their friends stole, and there was always one of them getting arrested. Yet the decision not to steal placed Mr Black in a position where he felt that he could not provide adequately for his family.

When Mr Black was first interviewed he said that they owed £500 for the rent and that they found it difficult to pay for the gas and electricity. He said that they went to bed early to save gas, and they tended to buy cheaper foods when they shopped. They used to swap things with their friends and always bought second-hand clothes and shoes. On occasion, when they were particularly short of money, they used to tell the electricity board that they were going away for a couple of weeks. The electricity men would then come to empty the meter (as they lived on a 'high risk' estate), and so the Blacks would get some cash back (the rebate). Christmas was very important to them and they used to save £3 a week towards it. They said that they would do anything to make Christmas good for their children. Mr Black's mother sometimes helped out at Christmas and other times, as she did not want to 'see her son back in gaol'. But, being on only a pension herself, 'it wasn't easy'.

Mr Black had become very disillusioned with his search for work prior to attending the course, and at one stage he gave up looking for eight months, feeling that 'it was all a waste of time'. The last job application he had made was over a year before. He felt that the only jobs he had any chance of getting did not pay enough for him to be able to support his wife and children. The only advantage he could see in working was the money, so if the job did not pay enough he saw no point in applying: 'now I would turn round before the interview started and ask, "How much do you pay?" There's such an output of money needed these days.' He was against applying for family income supplement: 'It's like working on the dole, just another form of government aid; a political cheap-labour scheme.'

When Mr Black had first become unemployed, he had looked regularly for work and he said that he practically lived in the Jobcentre, but he had since realized that without further skills he stood little chance of getting a better-paid job. This was the reason he had given for wanting to attend a re-establishment centre and, he hoped, to go on to do a TOPS course:

'I didn't have my arm up my back. [It was] something to do during the day, as opposed to soldiering on for £10-a-week jobs. . . they won't pay money for a good labourer, so I need to do it [TOPS] for the family to get more money.'

On attending the course Mr Black found that it was not what he had expected, but he was slowly learning the proper way to do things: 'I thought I'd come in and do it all in one day. He [the instructor] slowed me down, making me into a tradesman.' Although he said that he enjoyed the course, he saw it as being 'Maggie Thatcher's conscience money' to occupy the unemployed, 'same as YOP schemes, another form of cheap-labour scheme, isn't it?'

His wife was unhappy about his being on the course, as she missed him being around if she needed him. She also felt it wrong that he did not get any extra money for attending. By the sixth week of the course he felt less confident about his chances of getting a job doing bricklaying, despite being more confident that he would be able to do such work should he get a job. He felt that the course had helped him and given him the incentive to try to go on to do another course, possibly at evening classes. While he was on the course he was looking for work much more frequently, scanning advertisements in the evening paper every day. Mr Black said that the course had changed his attitude to work: 'Before, it used to be how fast can you do things, but not how good. I can't get used to the fact that I have to do things slowly . . . it's frustrating.' However, Mr Black thought that employers would think of him as a layabout if they knew he had attended a re-establishment course.

By the time of the follow-up interview Mr Black did not feel any more hopeful of finding employment (although he had applied for some jobs since leaving). Without proper training there was little prospect for him in the future. Mr and Mrs Black both felt that the one thing that would help them would be to move away from the estate where they lived, which had a reputation for thieving and robbing. When an employer knew you lived there, that 'told against you'.

Case 3 Mr Jeffries

Mr Jeffries was in his thirties, married with two children at school. At the time of the follow-up interview he was working full-time, but before attending the course he had been unemployed for one and a half years. He thought the reason why he had been unable to get work prior to the course was because of the circumstances in which he had left his last job. He said he walked out following a row with his employer, who had wanted to sack him for taking time off work due to illness. He had worked for the company for two years and thought they had treated him unfairly.

In this case lack of money and the strain on the family came up again as a major consequence of unemployment:

'Financial problems are the worst, I think. I'm used to a much higher state of living, I suppose, plus it does put a strain on the home. I don't enjoy unemployment. The times when you get a bill in and can't pay, you get worried, you're bound to.'

When Mr Jeffries was unemployed the family constantly found it difficult to make ends meet. They said that they managed well considering their circumstances but they had had to cut back on the food they ate. His wife had two 'book clubs' (a form of delayed payment) to pay for the children's clothes and for Christmas presents. They did not owe money for bills, but found it a continual struggle. The only way they could get by was if Mr Jeffries took on casual work. They had had a wide circle of friends, but had lost contact with many. They were unable to afford to go out with them. In spite of this it was a friend who had offered him the job that he was in at the time of the follow-up interview.

When Mr Jeffries lost his last job, he worried about the lack of money and his chances of finding work: 'I went through that stage of feeling very depressed because of the way I lost my last job. I got over it. I don't worry as much now as at the beginning as to where to get money.' Initially, he looked for work frequently, regularly visiting the Jobcentre. But as time wore on this became more of an effort, so he looked less often. He stopped using the Jobcentre. At one stage he stopped searching for three or four months because, he said, he got 'in a rut', and he just felt down and useless: 'Life gets on top of you.'

Prior to attending the re-establishment centre Mr Jeffries was regularly looking for work. The family were moving to a new area, so he had been spending time travelling around and enquiring about work. When he started the course he had applied for a job only the week before. Although he was initially reluctant to attend the course, feeling that he was under pressure to do so, Mr Jeffries thought that he might gain something from attending. When asked half-way through the course what he had enjoyed most about attending, he said that it was the companionship, mixing with others in a similar position to himself: 'Being amongst another group of chaps in the same position, you realize it's not as bad as you think. It's nice to get back in a workshop and socialize. I like the companionship.' At the follow-up interview he again mentioned companionship as a positive feature of the course: 'The community spirit was good, having people around; you miss that when you're unemployed. You don't mix with the same type of people.'

After six weeks on the course Mr Jeffries felt more confident that he would get work and be able to hold down the job. He felt that the work experience and routine of working had been of value: 'When you're out of work you lose confidence. It's nice to get that back. As you get older you lose confidence quickly.' However, even while on the course (and despite staying for over thirteen weeks) Mr Jeffries had reservations about its use: 'You're playing at work and, when you know there's nothing at the end of it, it's demoralizing.'

After leaving the centre he felt that, although the course did help people to get back into a routine, this was not of much use to him. All that he felt he had gained was a little more confidence in his abilities: 'I, personally, have not gained a great deal, except probably a bit more self-confidence. I think in the end it's a disappointment to know I got nothing out of it except work experience.'

Ironically, despite spending three months 'training' in the engineering workshop at the centre, the job he eventually found was as a trainee carpenter, work that he had never considered doing before. A friend had offered him this job, because one of his staff had left. The work was new to him, and he was being trained on the job at a low wage, with the added expense of having to buy tools for the trade. He said he was £10 a week worse off than when on benefit (partly due to being on emergency tax), and that he would no longer be able to get free school meals for his children. He was also having to work long hours. He felt, however, that it was worth the hard work and financial difficulties because it gave him a permanent job with the prospect of increased pay once he had proved that he was capable. Being unable to drive, he was having to rely on lifts from others, or on public transport, but was hopeful that this too would change, as employment would enable him to pay for driving lessons. When asked whether he was considering claiming family income supplement he replied: 'I don't know really, I don't like claiming for things. I've never been one for that. It's a case of pride. Money you have in your pocket you like to have earned.'

Consistencies and variations in the experience of long-term unemployment

The people who are likely to become long-term unemployed in South London are not all noble heroes or respectable labourers afflicted by cruel circumstances. Some do, indeed, fit this image, but others are less talented. In a society that sets out to reward talent and ability – however these come to be defined – the direct consequence is to take away from those who are seen as less able. The men we talked to are just ordinary people with the vices and virtues, the failings and saving graces, of the rest of humanity. They are more likely, however, to have acquired few skills, no qualifications, and some handicap or disadvantage that makes getting a job more difficult. These may range from the relatively trivial, like tattoos and bad teeth, to more severe problems, like 'trouble with your nerves'.

One man, for example, had been admitted to a mental hospital on a compulsory order twenty years previously when he threatened his father and he had then spent twelve months in treatment. He tended to be aggressive and touchy, he was 'proud' and somewhat inflexible. This man annoyed his wife because he refused to look for work in London: 'You end up paying half your wages in fares.' These disadvantages had not, however, prevented him from holding down his last job for over two years, but he had had to give it up when he developed dermatitis (from working too closely with resin). Others, particularly the younger men, seemed to start off on leaving school with perhaps a rather too casual attitude to getting work: 'I didn't expect it to be so difficult.' Spending a lot of time at first 'hanging around' and working on his bike (his first love; he would love to be a motor-cycle mechanic), one young man gradually realized that he would not be able to get a job. Now nineteen years of age, he had never had a job and was not 'attractive to an employer'. Another nineteen-year-old similarly had had only one job, at a bakery, since leaving school with no qualifications. He lost that after a year when he was found smoking in the production room.

There were some people who had problems to cope with that were just as pressing as getting a job. A young single man of twenty-two, whose last job was stacking supermarket shelves overnight, lived at home with his parents. His father was chronically sick and unemployed, and his mother 'has a problem drinking and taking pills'. He felt very depressed about being unemployed:

> 'Sometimes I feel like curling up in a corner. . . . The worst thing is when you write off and you hear nothing from them. When I was first unemployed, I had a little bit of hope, but not a lot now. If you think about it too much you crack up.'

An older man of forty-four, single and shy, had been in and out of institutions all his life. His mother was mentally ill, and he was brought up in care from birth. He 'couldn't cope alone', his welfare officer commented. He had a drink problem and had been fined many times for being drunk and disorderly. He was, in fact, receiving treatment for depression and attending a day hospital three months after leaving the course.

Another very hard-working man, not at all lazy, having learnt how to make windmills on the course, spent all his time at home enthusiastically making them. They were stacked up in his bedroom, and he hoped to be able to sell them later at a profit. This man could not read properly but he would like to learn a trade and go on a course. When times were better he had been able to find work – just as the so-called unemployables of the 1930s found work during the war, and in the 1950s the number classified as unemployable dropped. This same man had worked as a driver for many years till following an accident he had been demoted on his heavy-goods-vehicle licence, so he could drive only lighter vehicles. The fairly common occurrence of losing a driving licence (sometimes, it should be said, through drinking and driving), often the only paper qualification a man has, can be enough to catapult a man into long-term unemployment.

In spite of the sort of problems we have indicated, about one-half of the men on this course were thought by the instructors to be people they would themselves employ. Those they would not employ were usually considered so because of poor time-keeping rather than their lack of effort. And given the cynicism about the course shown by some men – 'You work hard all week for dole money' – it cannot be assumed that they all tried as hard as they would in a 'real job'.

What sort of work would they like and what was it like to be un-employed? Gardening, bricklaying, car mechanics, these were all popular options. 'Anything would do', said one man with a criminal record. He would take any job but he did not try for jobs where handling cash was involved. 'There'd be no point,' he said. 'It's in my past, but they don't let you forget it. It's like having a number tattooed on your head.' He thought that 'Jobcentres are a dead loss' for finding work.

When you are out of work you do not fit in. 'Your friends are working, going out, having a good time. You feel left out,' said one eighteen-year-old. 'Even my girl-friend has a part-time job at Boots.' TOPS courses are 'packed out', said one man, who wanted to be a mechanic but saw little chance of being successful. Getting on to a TOPS course was many men's ambition: 'to learn the things you didn't learn at school'. One man had been going to night-school to learn basic maths to try to catch up. His last job had been clearing tables at the Royal Festival Hall. But after a time out of work, 'You lose all hope of finding a job'.

'You get in those long queues, waiting half an hour to an hour. You get fed up.'

'I did have friends when I was working. But if you haven't any money you lose your friends. Nobody wants to know you when you haven't got nothing.'

Tension builds up at home for the unemployed. One man, married for nineteen years, found things were getting difficult 'due to the bills'. He and his wife now slept apart: 'The marriage is breaking up.' He had four children, two still at home, and desperately wanted to have a qualification and a job. Bricklaying, carpentry, being a handyman, these all appealed. But 'most big firms are looking for youngsters with O- and A-levels now'. He had seen council houses that needed doing up, and felt that he 'could do that', given the chance. He was ashamed being out of work and tried hard to keep up appearances. This man said he wanted a job so he could 'come off public assistance'.

One man who had plenty of ideas about the type of course that would be useful said, 'When you're unemployed, you've no status. People think you're useless. They think they're superior to you.'

Almost all hated being unemployed. But 'I've resigned myself to it,' said one man. 'It's getting to be a way of life.' A discouraged worker, perhaps; certainly demoralized. But 'No one likes being out of work'; 'lack of money, lack of independence, the monotony' – these were mentioned time and again. One man, whose mother had died two weeks earlier, got by because his dad helped him out. He had given up looking for work: 'I felt it was flogging a dead horse.' He does not tell people he is unemployed. He pretends he has a job. He would like a job gardening or working in an old people's home doing odd jobs. Nearly all the men could think of useful things they could be doing if only they were given the chance.

All these men had felt the need at some stage to seek alternative ways of raising money to alleviate the financial hardship of unemployment, in addition to using the more officially acceptable strategies of borrowing money and cutting back on everyday expenses. But the majority did not often have the chance to get casual work since one key effect of unemployment is to isolate people out of work from those in work.

The effects of unemployment were, however, the same for all the men: loss of confidence; strain on relationships; disillusionment; and a feeling of helplessness and isolation. All the men disliked being dependent on the state and saw attendance at a re-establishment centre as a possible light at the end of the tunnel. Mr Collins and Mr Black were hopeful that training might bring increased job chances and the possibility of better paid jobs, but as it turned out for them there was nothing at the end. Mr Jeffries found work, and possibly the course did help indirectly, but without his own contacts, he, too, might still have been unemployed. The job did not provide him with immediate relief from financial hardship, but it gave him the hope that he was searching for.

What, then, could be done to improve things? All the men emphasized that their main aim was to get a job. The prospects are not encouraging, however. The latest report (in November 1985) from the Confederation of

British Industry, although optimistic about increased order books, rising manufacturing output, and low inflation, expects little impact to be made on unemployment in 1986. Industry alone is likely to shed a further 120,000 jobs in the next two years.

For the long-term unemployed, at the back of the queue, some specific help in finding work is increasingly needed, just to help them compete on more favourable terms with others out of work. But what kind of help? Most of the men we spoke to had little time for Jobcentres: 'Jobcentres are a waste of time. It's always the same jobs up on the board.' Newspapers were of little use, some thought: 'By the time you've rung up the job has gone.' But when someone else helps by looking out for a job in the paper and pointing out the ones that are relevant, this can be valuable. Help in applying, from relatives, friends, or officials, was appreciated. Most of those who found work did so after being put in touch with a vacancy by someone they knew. Just having someone backing you up makes a difference: 'My mum wrote to the hospital for me. They put my name on a waiting-list for porters.' Having a reference from someone respected, like an instructor on a course, might make all the difference.

Some way of being put in touch with available jobs earlier seemed to be needed. But 'If you turn up, that's your best chance. If they see your face and what kind of man you are, they may offer you a job. On the phone they don't know what you're like.' Help with the costs of looking for work would also be valuable: 'I spent £7.00 in one day getting on and off buses'; this man went out every day looking for work. 'Last week I walked from Bromley to Croydon, but no luck.' The lack of available jobs made it an uphill road:

'There's not much about in Brixton or South London. It's either messy jobs, not proper jobs, or the other end – there's nothing in the middle.'

'There are quite a few jobs at £50 or £60 a week, but by the time you've paid tax and £20 rent that's no good. I'd need £70 to £75 after tax for it to be worth while.'

For those who feel discouraged and demoralized, a course that increased self-confidence has a part to play: 'I enjoyed the course. I felt I'd done something useful for once'; 'You get a certain satisfaction out of making something and completing it.' Courses would be worth while if you got a job out of it, but also 'a bit more self-respect'. If you are working, 'You feel better in yourself, a lot more confident.' But this man added, 'I know I'm not going to get a job. No one's going to employ me. I'd never stand a chance. I've been out of work so long. There's no light at the end of the tunnel.' Courses are useful too because they take you out of the house: 'It gets too much if you and the wife see each other all the time'; and 'a course can help you get back into a routine'. They are especially useful for school-leavers, most thought, 'for the young fellers, keeps them out of trouble, stops them thieving'. The quality and interest of the instructors mattered a lot: 'The standards they set . . . if they seem more active in helping you, that's good. Some places you go to you spend a lot of time standing around doing nothing.'

But most had reservations:

'I've been on several courses. They all said they'd help me find a job or I'd be able to train. But they didn't do a thing. I gained nothing from them – except a bit more experience. I'm not going to go on any more.'

'These kinds of courses would be more useful if you went on them when you're first unemployed. I don't think it'll help me now. I've tried everything.'

Most emphasized that 'You should be properly paid if you go on a course.' They resented 'doing so much for so little. It's no incentive to try if you only get dole money at the end.'

Some were more hostile:

'The government is wasting money on these schemes. They'd be all right for those straight out of school. It would show them what work is all about. But for anyone who's done a job before, they're useless.'

'The course would be OK if you were guaranteed a job at the end. But it's hopeless as it is. They send you from one place after another, and there's no job at the end.'

Similarly, 'There's no point in these courses if there's nothing at the end.' It was not that the men were against training as such but against training that leads nowhere: 'I'd like to get into computing, but she said I'm too old' (at forty); 'I tried to get into a Skillcentre, but they said I'd been unemployed too long.' However one man added, 'If they paid you, people would be queueing up to go on these courses.'

The men who felt positive about attending a training/rehabilitation course most frequently mentioned three reasons for this: that they could obtain training or learn something; that they were fed up and wanted to get out of the house; and that it might improve their chances of getting a job. Those who were not so keen mentioned that it was unlikely there would be a job for them at the end; that there was not enough choice of type of work available; and the lack of additional money for attending. Of all the features that they would think important on any course or scheme, three were most commonly mentioned: the guarantee of a job at the end; variety of work; and the chance to learn a new skill. Help in finding work was additionally important: 'It's never enough until I get a job.'

We talked to men who did not attend the course as well as to those who did. Those who had turned down the offer said they did so because there was no point in it, because there was no job at the end; they did not like the choice of work available; and that attending cut down the time available to look for work or to do other things. One of these men, who was forty-six, had worked all his life as a builder's labourer and was depressed to find people now thought him too old. He would sit up till two in the morning teaching himself computing using his Sinclair home computer. The feeling of being useless and discarded was the main consequence of being unemployed for him. He was financially protected because his four sons, his daughter, and his wife were all in full-time work. But he thought it was 'bloody horrible to treat someone like this at my age. I don't think I'm too old at forty-six.'

On the whole, those who did attend found it of some value: learning new skills; acquiring new knowledge; revising maths; getting into the routine of working; increased self-confidence. In addition, they mentioned getting a reference, the opportunity to get on to a TOPS course, making friends, and simply helping to pass the time.

What should be done?

Our intention, in this chapter, has been to demonstrate the contrast between the formulas and clichés pronounced at the highest level and reports from below. Looked at from the bottom up, things appear very different.

The Manpower Services Commission's report on long-term unemployment (MSC 1982) concluded that substantial numbers of those aged over fifty would never work again. Those who are unemployed for long periods of time need help in maintaining self-respect, coming to realistic job expectations, and finding the self-confidence and energy to look for another job. The Community Enterprise Programme was thought valuable because it jolted the long-term unemployed out of lethargy and increased their effort to find work; it provided them with recent work experience to offer an employer, and provided them with something to do, this being valuable in itself. The MSC Corporate Plan (1982–6, paras 5–7) concluded that

'short of permanent work, temporary unemployment programmes provide the most effective help. They enable long-term unemployed people to obtain a reference from a recent employer . . . are of great psychological and social value to the participants themselves and can create assets of long-term value to communities and individuals.'

David Donnison (1981) has argued in addition that the long-term unemployed are socially isolated. They must have 'opportunities for meeting, for making things, for seeking advice, for taking social and political action and asserting their identity and rights.'

Taylor has reminded us of 'the scandal of Britain's hit-and-miss training system' (Taylor 1982: 112) and stressed that 'we need to give a high priority to training adult workers and to giving young unqualified people a basic grounding in the tools for survival in the harsh labour market of the eighties' (1982: 114).

In spite of these conclusions, the view that the current unemployment figures reflect 'inadequate job search' continues to serve as a powerful and attractive device for those wanting to explain away the rising toll. While recognizing the attempts that have been made with the Youth Training Scheme and the Community Programme, with the government's failure to provide either adequate training or to make any impact on the total figures of the unemployed, the gap between the two worlds – the world of labour and that of unemployment – grows ever wider. Where in the past re-establishment courses or other forms of training and rehabilitation might have bridged the gap they now fail to do so. And whatever schemes are devised to prepare men for work, if the work is not there at the end, all talk of training is just a cruel joke. For the general labourers who form the majority of those referred to re-establishment centres, what is needed is the creation of more jobs. The government recognizes that this is a problem, but its latest response – a £20-a-week subsidy for the first six months when employers take on out-of-work people at low wages – is more likely to lead to cuts in wages and the replacement of one worker by another drawn from the register of long-term unemployed than to any net addition to the total of jobs available.

The last word, however, should be left to one man whose comment sums up the situation succinctly: 'I'd be wasting my time at my age training. It'd be like teaching an old dog new tricks. I don't want retraining in computing. I want a job I can do.'

Notes

1. The research study on which this paper is based was supported by funds from DHSS. The opinions expressed here are, however, entirely our own.
2. The role of unemployment review officers is to review the cases of claimants who are most frequently unemployed 'without good reason' and those unemployed for six months or more. This entails assessing the claimant's capacity for employment both as an individual, including past work experience and current and future work expectations, and in relation to the work available

in the locality. They also review claimants who 'appear not to be making positive efforts to obtain work'.

3. In presenting the case-histories, names and personal details have been altered or omitted to protect the identity of individuals.

References

Donnison, D. (1981) The Emergence of an Issue. *New Society*, 27 January :153.
Manpower Services Commission (1982) *Long-Term Unemployment*. London: HMSO.
Taylor, R. (1982) *Workers and the New Depression*. London: Macmillan.

11. Young people: from school to unemployment?

Leo B. Hendry

It is ironic that International Youth Year (1985) was also a year of serious unemployment among young people. Unemployment is perhaps one of the most serious concerns facing the industrialized world today. In economic terms the cost of unemployment, both to the individual and to society, may be extremely high. Manufacturing industry is in the middle of a massive restructuring process, which has had a profound effect on the labour market. In all major industrial countries, including our own, former methods of mass production are being discarded, or drastically modified. Computers are now beginning to control products from the moment of conception until they are sold to the consumer. Since these new methods are more efficient they are, in a capitalist society, quite irresistible. This on its own reduces employment opportunities, but there is more to it than that. These new methods have less and less use for unskilled or semi-skilled workers, and so many young people leaving school with few qualifications are having little success in the labour market. Thus unemployment has other effects far beyond the obvious economic consequences: it may influence the individual's self-esteem and total life-style. As the Scottish Council for Community Education (1981: 1) stated:

> 'There seems to be general agreement that the traditional patterns of working and leisure life will undergo profound change – are indeed already doing so to an increasing degree – under the impact of technological development. . . . It is suggested that many young people already living will never have paid employment of the traditional kind. It is irrefutable that very many people will find themselves with vastly increased amounts of what has been regarded in the past as "leisure".'

If the scenario is accurate, education, for both work and leisure, is inevitably an area of growing concern. With such a backcloth in mind, this chapter explores young people's personal and social development in modern society, and examines the roles of school, work, and leisure in their socialization towards adulthood. It then analyses the various effects of unemployment on today's adolescents, and suggests implications for the educational system as we move towards the 1990s and beyond.

Young people and society

What are the central issues in the adolescent's life? From the physical and physiological changes that herald the teenage years, the adolescent has various personal and social tasks to achieve. There are at least six tasks to be attempted across the adolescent years (see Hendry 1983 for elaboration):

(1) developing a self-identity in the light of physical changes;
(2) developing a gender identity;
(3) gaining a degree of independence from parents;
(4) accepting or rejecting family values;
(5) shaping up to an occupational (or unemployed) role;
(6) developing and extending friendships.

These six tasks are encapsulated in the notion put forward by Erikson (1968) that the chief task of adolescence is identity formation. According to Erikson there are eight psychosocial crises extending through the individual's life-span. He believed that the search for identity becomes especially acute during adolescence as a result of rapid changes in the biological, social, and psychological aspects of the individual, and because of the necessity for occupational decisions to be made, ideals to be accepted or rejected, and sexual and friendship choices to be determined.

Lewin (1970) has argued that adolescents, in passing through childhood to adulthood, are in a 'marginal' position and are entering a 'cognitively unstructured region'. Their sense of competence and ultimately their self-concept and future personal identity depend on how well expectations are accepted and processed into personal life-styles. If these behaviour patterns fit the requirements of roles encountered at school, at work, in heterosexual relationships, and in community life generally, then the outcome is satisfactory. Alternatively, if they fail to gain structure in their personal identity, confusion and conflict may result (Erikson 1968).

More recently Coleman (1979) has outlined a 'focal' theory of adolescence relating to self-image, parental relationships, peer relationships, friendships, and larger group situations. Based on his empirical data he showed that these relationships changed as a function of age, and that concern about different issues reached a peak at different stages in the adolescent process. In general, anxiety over heterosexual relationships declines from a peak around thirteen years; fears of rejection from peers are highly important around fifteen years; while conflict with parents climbs steadily in importance from thirteen to fifteen years and then tails off.

Clearly the patterns overlap. Different issues come into focus at different times; but simply because an issue is not important at a particular age does not mean that it may not be critical for some teenagers. Such a theory may provide a resolution between the amount of disruption implicit in adolescence on the one hand, and the relatively successful adaptation among most adolescents on the other. The majority of teenagers cope by dealing with one issue at a time. Adaptation covers a number of years attempting to solve one issue, then the next. Thus any stresses resulting from the need to adapt to new modes of behaviour are rarely concentrated all at one time. Those who, for whatever reason, do have more than one issue to cope with at one time are most likely to have problems of adjustment.

For most adolescents, personal and social development across the teenage years is relatively tension free, with fairly easy social adjustments, although there is a minority for whom this is not true. Further, evidence for the existence of a stressful period in the relationships between young people and adults seems greatly exaggerated (Bandura 1972, Fogelman 1976). Where morality, political views, religious beliefs, or sexual attitudes are concerned, adolescents appear to be largely in agreement with their parents (e.g. Rutter *et al.* 1976, Coleman, George, and Holt 1977). Conflicts between the generations would appear to centre upon mundane day-to-day issues and facets of behaviour such as dress, hair-style, noisiness, tidiness, and punctuality.

Thus the findings of Roberts (1983), HMSO (1983), and others discredit to some extent any theory of a generation gap in terms of values. Many young people today appear rather to accept adult models in their social environment and develop life-styles commensurate with the values of their subcultural background and upbringing. But since children may be reared in a social milieu that is quite different from that of their parents' generation, individuals have to carry with them into society the stamp of their own particular family life-style 'tailored' to present social requirements and reshaped because social forces may have begun to initiate wider changes in behaviour, values, and norms in society.

Adolescence, then, is a period of transition and adjustment. The young person is required to respond to the forces, both internal and external, that shape the emergent adult. The internal pressures involved have often been evinced as reasons for the emotional turmoil and stress experienced in the teenage years; but there is some evidence that these 'storms' are more apparent than real for most adolescents.

The external pressures on the adolescent often give rise to a high-profile youth culture seemingly opposed to the traditional life-style and values of the previous generation. Again, this vision of the 'opposition' of youth may be overstated. Parental values and norms seem to be transmitted fairly steadily across the generation gap, despite the separation in appearance and activities bolstered by commercial interests. Thus the key elements in the adolescent's progress towards adulthood in modern society may be seen in terms of both absorption and adaptation, and it is therefore important to question the functions and effectiveness of various social agencies that contribute to the young person's social and educational development. We might ask if our schools, in preparing our young people's vocational and leisure interests, are offering opportunities to acquire the social and intellectual skills necessary to cope with adolescence in modern Britain.

Young people, school, work, and leisure

Over the past twenty years a relatively high percentage of British adolescents have appeared eager to leave school at the earliest possible opportunity and to be indifferent or even hostile towards the values of school and the processes of schooling. Many years ago Morton-Williams and Finch (1968) painted a general picture of the contrasting qualities of 'early leavers' and the pupils staying on beyond the minimum leaving age. They described 'early leavers' as having less favourable home backgrounds, being less inclined to have academic interests, being more inclined to resent school disciplines, being less identified with school values, occupying their leisure time less satisfactorily, being more easily bored, and giving their parents more cause for anxiety. Carter has argued that 'there is this substantial hard core of young people to whom the idea of remaining at school is abhorrent . . . and [this is] based in a sub-culture and a social system which rejects school and all it is presumed to stand for' (Carter 1972: 61–2).

A study by Hendry and McKenzie (1978) has shown that, since the raising of the minimum school-leaving age to sixteen years in the 1970s, comprehensive schools still broadly contain two groups of pupils very similar in characteristics and attitudes to the schoolchildren in Morton-Williams and Finch's (1968) investigation. Pupils' pro- and anti-school subcultures with their sharply different values, attitudes, and aspirations seem as firmly entrenched in comprehensive schools as they were in selective and non-selective schools.

It can be suggested that such a situation is no longer appropriate in the changing modern world. There is an increasing awareness of the fact that both for employment and for other aspects of life in the adult world young people of all kinds require many competencies, abilities, and qualities other than the cognitive academic skills that are emphasized in schools. Thus Ryrie (1981) questioned whether, if academically able children are given opportunities in keeping with their type of ability, the same can be said of the less academically able children. Are the varied gifts and potentials of such children – of whatever background – recognized, valued, encouraged, and developed in such a way as to allow them to grasp the opportunities of life as fully as possible? The answer would seem to be that within our schooling system they are not. He further suggested that there is good reason to believe that the basic reason why the varied potential of young people is not developed in our schools is that skills and abilities other than academic and cognitive ones are not sufficiently valued and respected. If this view is correct, he claimed, we are unlikely to achieve a more appropriate approach to the non-academic youngster, or to provide an education system that is relevant to people and society today and in the future. We should accord a greater respect, dignity, and importance to the varied and usually not very academic potential of many young people.

The 'inappropriate' nature of what is taught in many secondary schools is well illustrated by the aspirations and awareness of their future displayed by working-class pupils in Willis's (1977) and Corrigan's (1979) case studies. These working-class pupils saw secondary education as a 'confidence trick' and were totally disengaged from it. They behaved in the school by 'playing the system' in order to gain some personal control over the school organization. Such opposition involved an inversion of the values held up by school authority (such as diligence, deference, and respect); these behaviour patterns became antithetical as conducted by the 'lads'. Their opposition was expressed mainly as a 'style'. Popular criticisms of education are based on the feelings of many pupils and their parents that 'School by its compulsory nature is a sentence which must be served before the real business of life can begin' (Weir and Nolan 1977: 109).

Yet the link between schooling and occupation (and the qualities associated with an employee's role) have been continually stressed in works on education. Stanley Nisbet said, in *Purpose in the Curriculum* (1957: 25): 'Few would deny that preparation for an occupation is one of the tasks of education. . . . occupation is a role which gives the individual a real and tangible place in the community.'

Coming closer to the present, views can be seen as changing somewhat, although the inherent link between the educational system and occupation is still present: 'The logic of automation . . . is not that it creates armies of unskilled workers, but that it makes the unskilled redundant' (Entwistle 1970: 10).

Clearly, education has continued to reflect an emphasis on the value and importance of work. While the modern school may additionally emphasize education for leisure, it is still preparation for leisure within the context of work. Secondary-school education has been seen by many pupils, teachers, and parents as being primarily a preparation for work. Like government vocational training schemes, this emphasis helps only to reinforce assumptions about the centrality of work to the human life plan, and by implication increases the individual's social and psychological dependence on it. However, as Hargreaves (1981: 199) indicated:

'Very little of our secondary education is strictly vocational; schools are more orientated towards public examinations than towards jobs. Yet for those who leave school at sixteen, a job is the natural next step, one that has been awaited with eagerness for it signifies independence and adult standing. . . . by calling them "qualifications" teachers made examination results seem vocationally relevant and examinations could be used as a pseudo-vocational incentive for adolescent pupils to work hard and behave well in school. When employment is then denied to the young school-leaver with his or her scroll of "qualifications" the reaction is naturally one of shock and disappointment, personal crisis and social dislocation.'

Other studies (e.g. Weir and Nolan 1977, Ashton and Maguire 1980) suggest that many young people are pleased at the prospect of putting their schooldays behind them. Thus on closer examination we find a profound ambivalence exhibited by adolescents towards work. Carter (1971) has argued that many adolescents are not particularly interested in a future job or jobs but rather in 'the status and perquisites of a young worker'. Murdock and Phelps (1973) have suggested that many adolescents attempt to resolve tensions, monotony, or boredom perceived in school or work situations through the creation of particular styles of leisure pursuits which reflect social class differences. Hence, in our society, leisure has normally been structured and given meaning by its relation to working time. Parker (1983), for example, sees leisure as a time of freedom bounded by the constraints of work and non-work commitments.

It can be argued that the importance of leisure has become more apparent in recent years because of shifts in the work–leisure balance in society and of the spectacular increase in unemployment, particularly among young people. Unemployment creates a great deal of 'free' time, but the equation of 'free' time with leisure time has been strongly disputed (e.g. Hendry, Raymond, and Stewart 1984) because unemployment unties the traditional work–leisure 'package'.

It has been suggested by Leigh (1971) that education for leisure attempts 'to increase both the true range of choices available and the ability of the individual to make effective and significant choices'. But the majority of schools provide leisure education in very similar ways, usually through a mixture of curricular and extra-curricular activities, with the addition of schemes such as the Duke of Edinburgh Award Scheme, which allows young volunteers to develop skills and hobbies and to offer community service for which they are assessed and awarded 'bronze', 'silver', and 'gold' grades. Hence the activities that educators often see in terms of the leisure lives of pupils are sports, games, art, music, and practical subjects such as woodwork, metalwork, and technical drawing – which, even though they may have a vocational bias in a narrow sense, are useful for do-it-yourself and recreation. Often these subjects are also offered to pupils in extra-curricular time.

Yet in designing leisure education programmes schools may well reject ways in which adolescents actually spend their leisure time simply because these do not conform to the school's view of how leisure should be 'profitably' used. Thus it has been found that the range of extra-curricular activities that the vast majority of schools provide, in order to substantiate their claim of providing leisure education, is in fact pursued by only a minority of adolescents – mainly middle-class, academically able pupils (e.g. Hendry 1983).

It is clear, therefore, that school influences provide important constraints and opportunities for young people's leisure. A recent survey of all secondary schools in one Scottish region and a case study of one school (Hendry and Marr 1985) have shown that there were few differences between schools in terms of the organization of leisure education despite considerable differences in location and size. Much greater differences emerged, however, when schools were asked to state the aims of, and their attitudes towards, leisure education. There was no doubt that a variety of objectives was being set, as the comments of school staff in Hendry and Marr's study (1985: 123–24) illustrated. One headteacher wrote that he disagreed 'with the effectiveness claimed of the leisure concept in schools. The normal operation of the school in its curriculum should pay heed to the usefulness of all subjects for private time.' The same headteacher concluded 'that gathering to socialize is a very acceptable form of leisure', and that every pupil had 'a democratic right, which ought to be respected, to not be involved'. Another headteacher of one of the newest schools in the region suggested that separate leisure education provision within the timetable could be positively harmful, particularly if a lot of time has to be spent in travelling. Much better, he suggested, 'to make pupils aware of the leisure possibilities within their normal curricular activities. Why not, for example, make a transistor radio in science?' This head put forward a most telling argument against a specific time allocation for leisure education when he stated that such provision could help to 'legitimate youth unemployment' by diverting demands for political action.

These statements were in stark contrast to the more traditional views that were adopted by many respondents. An assistant headteacher in one of the largest schools in the region stated that 'leisure is a timetabled subject' and that 'leisure is compulsory'. Another head adopted a rather different line in that he felt that leisure education was not part of the school's function:

> 'I have to say that I am not greatly interested in the idea of leisure programmes elaborately occupying much of the school day – even if unemployment is to grow! We have already too many masters to serve, too little time in which to serve them, too few teaching staff genuinely interested beyond their subject speciality, too many parents demanding, justifiably in my opinion, that we should use our time and resources to do for their children what nobody else can do.'

A diversity of approach to the question of leisure education was clearly evident in the schools surveyed. Physical education, sport, and extra-curricular activities were nevertheless seen by most schools to be self-evidently worthwhile leisure pursuits, and figured prominently with schools' leisure provision.

All schools reported an extensive range of available extra-curricular activities. But despite this range, the regional survey and the case study both provided evidence (as do other studies) that only about one-third of pupils were regularly involved in such activities; more than half were completely non-participant. In their leisure time away from school the most popular activities for the mid-adolescent years were socially oriented pursuits, together with a considerable amount of televiewing, and few of these activities could be directly related to school influences.

Schools explained non-participation in school-based leisure activities in terms of the 'shortcomings' of the pupils rather than of the possible deficiencies of schools' approaches. Non-participation was seen to stem from such factors as pupils' limited ability, laziness, and lack of identification with the school, rather than from an inappropriate programme on the school's part. Further, it has been argued that the low level of participation in schools' extra-curricular activities is somewhat misleading in that the influence of the school may in fact lie dormant for a number of years.

Within the transition from school to society it has been suggested that the decline in participation after leaving school is a temporary state of affairs. The Wolfenden Report (1960: 25) defined it as

'the manifest break between, on the one hand, participation in recreative activities, which is normal for boys and girls at school, and, on the other hand, their participation in similar (though not necessarily identical) activities some years later when they are more adult.'

This has become known as the 'Wolfenden gap'. But the success of school-based approaches has to be seriously questioned in the 1980s, particularly in relation to the reported low rate of post-school participation (e.g. Emmett 1977, Hendry and Marr 1985). This has been explained by reference to a number of factors such as over-emphasis by schools on sports; value judgements and ideologies, particularly concerning the 'profitable' use of leisure time; lack of true choice for adolescents; and the inappropriateness of schools as a source of leisure education.

What is being argued here is that the 'official' school curriculum serves to reinforce the centrality of the work ethic in society. Additionally, there is an at least tacit acceptance by schools of the increased leisure time available to school-leavers, mainly due to a societal shift in the work–leisure balance, and of the attendant problems of youth unemployment. This conflict for schools seems often to be resolved by the introduction of programmes of leisure education. Such programmes remain profoundly unsatisfactory because they do not displace the centrality of the work ethic. Indeed, the form they take can act to enforce the 'hidden' message that unemployment is a transient, 'unnatural', but often self-inflicted phenomenon.

Young people and unemployment

'What is your job? remains the most illuminating question to ask about someone met for the first time. . . . An occupation is a socially recognized set of work activities . . . it therefore implies . . . a place in the social division of labour.'

(Brown 1978: 55–6)

Paid employment is still a major factor in defining the parameters of human life for many of us. While work is central in giving structure to the individual's life, it is also important as a key element in popular culture. Trade unions may agitate for increased leisure, but they will also demand the right that everyone should have employment. The idea of constructive unemployment, or work outside the traditional bounds of employment, continues to be rejected for more than purely financial reasons. Both the cultural framework of Western capitalism and the status of self-esteem of the individual lean heavily, although increasingly precariously, on the concept of work. This helps to explain why, even though work is frequently unpleasant, boring, and alienating, it is still firmly held to be preferable to unemployment. Jenkins and Sherman (1979: 2) summed up this paradox:

> 'Yet whether skills become outdated or not, whether people start to feel inadequate at work or not, they do feel they have to work – and not just for the money. The work ethic is so deeply engrained in British and other industrialized societies that it has acquired a value in itself even though it is widely regarded as unpleasant.'

Hence work can provide a variety of satisfactions, including achievement, recognition, responsibility, and intrinsic pleasure. Work also imposes a time structure, and provides opportunities for social interaction and for the development of identity and self-esteem (e.g. Kelvin 1981). Jahoda (1979) listed five basic needs that are met by the structured framework of employment:

(1) Work provides a true structure for the day, the week, and the year.
(2) Work implies regularly shared experiences outside the family.
(3) Work links the individual to goals and purposes that transcend his or her own.
(4) Work defines aspects of personal status and identity.
(5) Work enforces activity.

Conversely, to be unemployed, as illustrated by various contributors to this book, places the individual outside this accepted, taken-for-granted system. It puts in question one's capacity to carry responsibility for oneself, let alone for one's dependants.

The demise of large-scale, labour-intensive, and repetitive work has far-reaching consequences in altering the relationship between work and leisure, the time available for each dimension, and the role of schools in preparing young people for such a leisure existence. Hargreaves (1982) has suggested that the secondary-school curriculum should be built around the twin themes of 'community' and 'leisure', while the Alexander Report (1975) recommended lifelong learning, the development of a sense of community, local participation in decision-making, and attention to the quality of leisure and living.

Young people without jobs tend to be those with fewest academic qualifications, and they tend to come from families of manual workers in which other people are also unemployed (Holland 1979, Raffe 1983). It may be that some of these factors emerge while adolescents are still at school. Holland (1979: 150) noted that 'Manpower Services Commission studies show that half of those young people who are unemployed have stayed away from school, other than for reasons of sickness, in their last two or three years and that 1 in 3 have done so more than once.' In general terms, the type of adolescent who, during times of relatively full employment, changed jobs frequently after leaving school may be particularly vulnerable to longer periods of unemployment as the overall rate of youth unemployment has risen. Thus attitudes formerly found to be associated with frequent job changing may currently be associated with unemployment among young people. On this point Carter (1966) reported that higher rates of job changing were associated with 'a refusal to accommodate to discipline', lower academic ability, and immaturity.

How true are these descriptions in the present-day context? In offering 'hard facts', Raffe (1983) has provided us with trends in youth unemployment from the mid-1970s to the 1980s. Discussing the current situation, he wrote: 'The association between qualifications and employment remains strong. Although unemployment rose among qualified school leavers, they retain their relative advantage over the unqualified' (1983: 16).

The pervasive influence of unemployment reaches beyond those adolescents actually out of work. In Hendry, Raymond, and Stewart's (1984) study, pupils about to enter the job market seemed fully aware of the problems of finding a job, and the school's emphasis on this aspect of unemployment stressed the importance of work in the eyes of the pupils. Their reaction to the immediate future was realistic; they were aware of the problems that might lie ahead in the job market, but there was no indication that the fear of unemployment had destroyed their confidence. However, their knowledge of the experiences of unemployment did not appear to have come from the classroom. Very few pupils stated that there had been any discussion of life on the dole or how to cope with large amounts of free time. Further, pupils tended to see future day-to-day living and leisure patterns in terms of the sort of opportunity that only a job could provide. A selection of quotations helps to give a flavour of how unemployment was viewed from the school:[1]

'Your friends around you having jobs while you yourself are on the dole and having nothing to do and no day pattern.'

'Getting on everyone's nerves sitting around doing nothing . . .'

'Having no money to buy clothes . . . to go out with your friends.'

'Not having anything to look forward to when you get up in the morning.'

The impact of unemployment on adolescence is complex and far reaching. It was apparent that pupils about to enter the job market were fully aware of the problems of finding a job. The school's emphasis on this aspect of unemployment stressed the importance of work in the eyes of pupils. As Hargreaves (1981: 200) wrote:

> 'Effort soon becomes associated with "work", which becomes associated with the imposed official curriculum; in its turn that curriculum is instrumental to the passing of examinations, which in their turn are instrumental to the acquisition of paid employment. In this lesson, which even the "least able" pupils learn so very thoroughly, resides that powerful dichotomy between work (high effort, boredom, low autonomy, discipline and constraint, seriousness, competitive individualism, long-term goals) and leisure (low effort, relaxation and idleness, passivity, pleasure, non-seriousness, immediacy, spontaneity, freedom, social co-operation).'

Schools did not seem to have helped pupils to develop skills and attitudes necessary for a leisured existence. Could the reason be one advanced by Hargreaves (1981: 203)? 'It is quite easy to see special leisure-based courses for pupils destined for the dole queues, or educational grants, or Youth Opportunity Programmes, as modern instruments of social control.'

Sports and hobbies – the sort of leisure activities encouraged by the schools – were not considered by young people to be important to their future leisure, a fact backed up by the low carry-over effect of school leisure activities among the school-leavers. Parker's (1971) work on the sociology of leisure emphasized the interdependence between work and leisure, and this relationship determined the attitudes school-leavers have towards leisure: 'You can only have leisure when you're working – you'd enjoy yourself more in your free time if you're working.' Unemployed adolescents felt that they were being excluded from the more 'adult' leisure of their employed contemporaries:

> 'I'm too old for youth clubs now.'

> 'You can't go out with your mates when they're working; they've got more money than you've got.'

> 'You need more money at a time when you haven't got any.'

> 'Having nothing to do . . . you end up spending more.'

Similarly, unemployment had an indirect but powerful effect on working adolescents, creating feelings of insecurity about their jobs and forcing them to remain in jobs that some admitted to finding unpleasant and unsatisfying. Simon (1978) has pointed out that enthusiasm for working life tends to evaporate quickly on leaving school. This was reflected in the cynical attitude to work expressed by the employed school-leavers inter-viewed by Hendry, Raymond, and Stewart (1984). There was little intrinsic satisfaction in working: work was acceptable only as a source of money, as a chance to be with friends, and as an alternative to the boredom of unemployment. Additionally, most of the employed group interviewed saw the value of leisure in terms of escape or relaxation from work, and they tended to make more use of commercial leisure activities, while the unemployed adolescents made more use of cheaper entertain-ments like youth clubs and 'hanging about'. There was also some indication that those with more demanding jobs pursued more demanding leisure.

Unemployment, as argued earlier, redefines the individual's con-ception of leisure time. Being workless does not necessarily involve an increase in leisure time, but an extension of free time: two totally different concepts. Free time was more acceptable, however, provided the ex-perience was shared with friends. An interviewee said: 'Sometimes it gets boring when your mates are working, but it's not so bad when you've got company . . . it's O.K. then.' One teenager who had left school without a job and then had a few months' experience of employment before becoming redundant summed up the effect of this experience on his attitude to money: 'When you just left school it seemed like a lot of money they were paying you . . . not now, though.'

The absence of work confuses the meaning of leisure. As two un-employed school-leavers put it: 'Two days off when you're working, you need it then. Now, you just spend most of your time in bed. You're not tired so you can't sleep – so you just walk about half the night.' And: 'There's no difference between the end of the week and the rest of the week . . . It's only like a weekend if you've got any money.' Additionally, some unemployed youngsters had difficulty in describing the exact nature of their daytime experience: 'When your giro comes through, then you get up early in the morning, then you have a good time'; 'It's only leisure when your mates get off work'; 'It's just like working . . . only you're not doing anything.'

Pupils in the schools often referred to the unemployed as 'layabouts' and 'hooligans'. Interestingly, about one-quarter of the unemployed teenage boys in Hendry and Raymond's (1983) study mentioned that unemployment leads to boredom, and that this in turn leads to thoughts of exciting and possibly delinquent activities. There is some evidence (e.g. Murray 1978) that periods of youth unemployment can lead to the development of unco-operative and disenchanted attitudes. When this feeling of early failure is coupled with unofficial discrimination, as in the case of ethnic minorities, the consequences can be very disturbing.

But there was no sense that the unemployed blamed themselves for their situation or were conscious of having low status in the eyes of society. As one pointed out, the workless state was 'like seven Sundays, not even seven Saturdays'. Some adolescents who were not career oriented, or who were without experience of a work pattern and increased spending power, found the unemployed life-style little different from the passive leisure they had been familiar with as pupils. While a job might be welcome in the future, by seeing the experience as a 'holiday' from the constraints of work a few adolescents had given their period of un-employment some meaning. As one said: 'It [being unemployed] might get boring later on. . . . It's not great when you've no money, but it's OK when you've got some cash. I'm not that interested in turning up [at work] all the time.'

Unemployment also appears to have hidden consequences in re-inforcing traditional sex roles. Some girls impose a structure on their day by turning to domestic chores and becoming the family's unpaid servant girl, while several boys used the rituals of 'signing on' and 'job-hunting' to re-create the single-sex street-corner groupings so noticeable in the 1930s (Jahoda, Lazarsfield, and Zeisel 1933). The question of sex dif-ferences is important in that the decline of work should not mean that women find themselves constrained by domestic roles while the develop-ment of alternative life-styles is available only to men.

Kelvin (1981) has suggested that unemployment is becoming an accept-able aspect of young people's self-perceptions and self-identity as more and more adolescents fail to find a niche in the job market when they leave school. It is nevertheless possible to suggest that unemployment creates a structureless, confused time-state for some adolescents within which leisure, with all its concomitant social opportunities, vanishes. Thus the major impact of unemployment on adolescents may be its ultimate effect on the transition from adolescence to adulthood: 'When a boy or girl personally accepts the label 'unemployed' the subjective environment changes; it becomes a state of inactivity and lassitude, where personal powers cannot be adequately used or expressed' (Kitwood 1980: 238–39).

A retrospective but recent look at unemployment came from one girl who was involved in a Youth Opportunities Programme placement. She spoke graphically of the importance of work as a social context for making friends:

'It's hard to remember what I did when I was unemployed, there was nothing definite. . . . I went shopping down the town, but always on my own . . . it got very lonely; there was no way of making friends when you're unemployed. I'm getting out with people in the evenings more often now that I'm working.'

(Hendry and Raymond 1983: 34–7)

By interpreting the effects of a variety of factors, which may combine to create an overall positive or negative effect, an understanding of particular individual reactions that shape the experience of youth unemployment may be possible. There is an immediate paradox: a number of these factors have the potential either to cause distress or to provide support. This point is illustrated in *Figure 1*, which shows how different orientations of the same factor can (theoretically) have a positive or a disruptive influence on the individual unemployed adolescent.[2]

Figure 1 Factors influencing the experience of unemployment

− Negative orientation		+ Positive orientation
Low, guilt, self-blame	← SELF-IMAGE →	Defensively high
Devalued, low	← ASPIRATIONS →	High
Isolation	← SOCIALIZATION with peers →	Contact with peers
No freedom, low structure	← TIME USE/STRUCTURE →	Structure, purpose, self-responsibility
Pressure, stress	← FAMILY →	Support, sympathy
Not 'adult', frustrating	← LEISURE →	'Appropriate', acceptable
Not useful	← EDUCATION →	Helpful, useful
Rejected, hostility	← YOUTH Training Schemes →	Involvement
− Negative orientation		+Positive orientation

None of these social or psychological factors explains by itself why one young person copes well with unemployment while another drifts into despair. A time structure to the day or week can be purposeful or it can be stifling; families can be sympathetic or they can be pressurizing; informal community-based education can be helpful while school education may be seen as irrelevant by adolescents; peers can be supportive or socially constraining; aspirations towards finding a job can be maintained or they can collapse; and self-image can be kept defensively high during a long period of unemployment or it can be low in the apparently supportive atmosphere of a Youth Training Scheme course (see Hendry and Raymond 1985 for an elaboration of these apparently contradictory elements in youth unemployment).

These aspects must then be seen in relation to the dynamics of time without work for, as Gurney (1980) made clear, the key problem facing the unemployed school-leaver is not the trauma of job loss, but the frustration and identity confusion of having entry into adult work delayed. The next step is thus to consider how these factors can work in combination with each other. Coleman's (1979) focal model of psychosocial issues in adolescence explains how some young people can find the

Figure 2 Time and the factors involved in unemployment

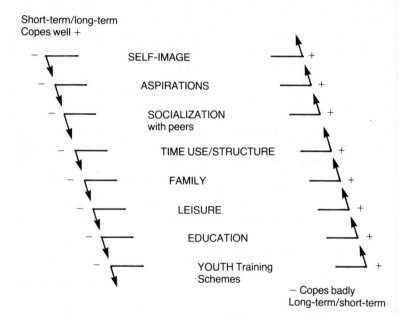

Short-term/long-term
Copes well +

SELF-IMAGE

ASPIRATIONS

SOCIALIZATION
with peers

TIME USE/STRUCTURE

FAMILY

LEISURE

EDUCATION

YOUTH Training
Schemes

− Copes badly
Long-term/short-term

teenage years stressful, while the majority cope well. Sources of stress, like identity crisis or role development, rarely occur at the same time; they can usually be dealt with separately and cause the adolescent little or no distress. Sometimes several sources of stress affect the adolescent concurrently, making it increasingly difficult to cope with the pressures.

Similarly, the unemployed adolescent will usually undergo a mixture of positive and negative experiences. As *Figure 2* suggests, it is only when a number of negative factors impinge on the individual concurrently, and cumulatively, that unemployment becomes an ordeal like other adolescent crises proposed by Coleman. Often the influence of several positive factors can allow the unemployed youth to cope relatively easily with the experience. For instance, a number of negative factors – low self-image, low aspirations, and family pressures – would be likely to increase in a period of unemployment. In other cases a supportive family, enjoyable leisure, and good time structure create the potential for an individual to cope with unemployment even after a fairly lengthy period without work.

It is being suggested that these apparent paradoxes may be resolved by interpreting the experience of unemployment for young people in terms of positive and negative 'trade-offs'. Rather like Coleman's (1979) theory of adolescent focal issues, the reality of the process of unemployment can be viewed as a series of different psychological and social issues hitting the individual sequentially. Problems occur when several issues overlap. These factors, in combination, produce the elements around which coping strategies develop or a growing state of distress emerges in the face of unemployment.

Young people, unemployment, and the educational system

Our concern for those who do not cope, and our interest in those who do, must be based in an acknowledgement of the fact that we are not just observing the casualties of a current hiccup in the structure of the labour market. If, and when, economic recovery allows an escape from the present recession, the gap between desire for work and the opportunity for employment may still not narrow. Job-sharing, informal work, and changing patterns of leisure are likely to be part of a necessary adjustment to a decline in the net amount of employment available. Nevertheless, Jahoda (1979: 314) suggested that 'Human ingenuity could invent new social institutions which could meet the needs normally satisfied by employment. . . . if current institutions no longer meet these needs, new institutions must be created.'

One such development of our social institutions has been the creation of holistic education. Holistic principles of lifelong education have been conceptually and methodologically developed over the last twenty years (OECD 1975). Within this style of education the emphasis is placed upon an active participation in learning. And, of particular relevance to the present argument, the purpose of holistic education is not only focused on work and employment activities, but also involves learning in leisure, through leisure, and for leisure: 'Individuals develop an understanding of self, leisure, and the relationship of leisure to their lifestyles and the fabric of society' (Mundy and Odum 1979: 2). As Hargreaves (1981: 205) has written:

'Perhaps today we are ready for John Leigh's (1971) insights that the primary skills in which schools must train young people are social organisational ones. . . . They are skills which relate to groups of people whatever activity they are pursuing. . . . the task of education is to steer and recombine these ingredients to make a society where education, work and leisure have new meanings and new relation-ships.'

It is possible that the notions of 'activity' and 'responsibility' should become prime ingredients of an educational skills menu. But part of the difficulty lies in the fact that attempts to encourage adolescents to be active and responsible and to initiate their own learning activities within an institutional context have often been profoundly disappointing (Nisbet and Shucksmith 1984).

Yet relatively minor changes can substantially affect pupil attitudes. For instance, Rutter *et al.* (1979) found surprising scope for secondary schools to organize themselves in ways that evoked positive responses from their pupils. Schools with similar pupil intake varied greatly on outcome measures of school behaviour, attendance, delinquency, and academic attainment. The differences were due to the way the schools organized teacher–pupil relationships and enhanced pupils' motivation. But it seems likely that some more fundamental reorganization of curricular aims is also called for.

Jonathan (1982: 87), in discussing unemployment and education, argued that:

'Once we discard the exploitative model of mindless work as a necessary evil and acknowledge that, for the individual, work has a cultural as well as an economic function it becomes obvious that preparation for life cannot be seen as a choice between "educating for leisure" or "training for work".'

And Hargreaves (1981: 208) stated:

'Perhaps the concept of leisure has outlived its usefulness and can be discarded; certainly the concept of work will have to be transformed and disconnected from paid employment. Perhaps it would be easier to speak of "ways of life" or "lifestyles".'

We return once again to the theme that what is lacking for adolescents is some element in their education that transmits to them the skills necessary to evaluate themselves and their needs so that they can make after-school choices from amongst a set of alternatives, according to their circumstances. This idea can be generalized more widely to the educa-tional processes available to young people in developing competencies required in modern society. Raven (1982: 54–5) has made the point that the qualities most urgently required for operating organizations in our society effectively fall into three broad areas:

'1 Human resources; value-laden competencies: These include qualities like initiative, leadership, and the willingness to observe the way our organization and society work and think out the implications for one's own behaviour.
2 Perceptions and expectations relating to the way society works, and one's own role in that structure: Under this heading are included such aspects as people's self-images, the way they think their organizations work and their own role and that of others in those organizations, their understanding of organizational social climates which make for innovation, responsibility, and development. . . .
3 People's understandings of what is meant by a number of terms which describe relationships within organizations – terms like leadership, decision-taking, democracy, responsibility, accountability and delegation.'

Raven further argued that the implication for education is that:

'Educators need to help people to think through some of the issues. . . . they need to help them think about how their organizations should and do operate, and about their own role and the role of others in these organizations and in their society.'

It could perhaps be argued that such an integrative move may be essential if the curriculum is to retain any relevance for the increasing number of pupils who may leave school to face unemployment. Weir and Nolan (1977) indicated how closely pupils and their parents associated the relevance of education with the ability of school-leavers to find employment. The removal of the prospect of employment for many young people could lead increasing numbers of adolescents to reject an academic or vocational curriculum. As Hartley (1985: 96) wrote:

'Hitherto, there was little need to formalize the hidden curriculum because its subliminal messages were, for the most part, effectively assimilated. In the main, pupils were adequately socialized by the hidden curriculum to fit into society. Now, however, it appears that pupils cannot be assumed to have acquiesced either in the formal goals of education or in their justification. When teachers justify schooling in vocational terms, the message is questioned by children who know full well that academic credentials are no guarantee of a job, and this will be especially so of low achievers. The meaning of schooling must therefore undergo change, and it is no accident that it is the schooling of "young people" which has acquired problematic status because it is they who are questioning the legitimacy of the educational messages which they receive (Gow and McPherson 1980).

But there are risks in simply moving towards an experiential pupil-oriented learning programme. If we are in the process of shifting from a 'collection' (traditional) curriculum to a more 'integrated' (progressive) code (e.g. Bernstein 1977) with an emphasis in the classroom on self-direction, self-control, and flexibility on the part of pupils, its parallel in their future world of work would be a shift from a highly bureaucratic management style to one informed by the human-relations school of management. Such school processes would, therefore, be detrimental preparation for the work processes presently in operation in society.

A similar argument can be offered in relation to social and leisure skills. Mundy and Odum (1979) have proposed an 'enabling' approach that aims to develop a person's ability to think through, evaluate, and make his or her own decisions and choices regarding leisure while understanding the impact of his or her choices upon his or her own life and upon others in society. Thus Mundy and Odum favour the learning of decision-making and evaluative/social skills. Such training, they argue, would allow pupils to

'develop a cognitive, conscious awareness of their own behaviour and beliefs . . . establish criteria for leisure issues and decisions . . . and develop skills related to enriching self-determination, pro-activity and meaningful control over their own leisure lives.'

(1979: 8)

But schools have tended to concentrate on providing short-term recreational and activity skills rather than equipping pupils with such attitudes and social skills that may enable them to organize, select, and participate in chosen leisure pursuits in post-school years.

In short, education for children in our schools appears to include no political polemic whatsoever that will enable them to analyse their own predicament in a society which increasingly locates failure in the 'self' and asks the young person merely 'to cope'. In reinforcing the work ethic and a continuing vocational 'impulse' within the curriculum, moreover, there is an implicit future acceptance of the 'employee's' role (and its attendant characteristics) by many pupils. The removal of entrepreneurial initiative and corporate-management strategies has received recent royal comment. This system stresses the fact that the unemployed state is based on the individual and his or her ability to adapt to it, thereby removing any consideration of the wider social issues involved. Buckminster Fuller (1970) recommended that 'We must give each human who is or becomes unemployed a life fellowship in research and development.' He added that, given these fellowships, 'many who have been frustrated during their younger years may feel like going fishing. Fishing provides an excellent opportunity to think clearly; to review one's life; to recall one's earlier frustrated and abandoned longings and curiosities. What we want everyone to do is to think clearly.' Would we wish anything less than clarity of thought in all aspects of their life by our young people?

The British government's responses to youth unemployment have continued to address an alleged mismatch between school-leavers' capabilities and occupational requirements in the service and high-technology sectors – which, it is claimed, contain the best hopes for future job creation. Hence the case for Britain's Technical and Vocational Education Initiative, the Youth Training Scheme, and the Sixteen to Eighteen Action Plan. However, educational solutions to the disappearance of jobs for adolescents are yielding diminishing returns (Bates *et al.* 1984). Young people in Britain are now being given more vocational advice, work experience, and generic skills than ever before. Traditional academic syllabuses are being replaced by up-to-date technical and vocational courses. These attempts to tighten the bonds between schooling and job requirements and to strengthen young people's vocational orientations are problematic. The new technologies that are displacing labour may require more highly educated and trained designers, technicians, and managers; but the pace at which ordinary workers can be discarded seems to be running well ahead of the need for longer vocational preparation.

Only improved employment prospects for young people in our society permit the maintenance of current educational plans and prospects, establishing as they do closer and closer links between schooling and job requirements. On the other hand, continuing youth unemployment makes it likely that adolescents will perceive the offerings of the educational system (at all levels) as increasingly ineffective in providing them with the means and qualifications to secure a desirable place in the labour market. The consequences of this are the creation of a new caste system in society – 'the new leisured class' (i.e. the unemployed) and 'the new (technocratic) working class' – and the possibility of increasing social unrest, urban rioting, and economic 'destabilization'. The hope for our educational institutions is that they become catalysts of positive change towards the future. Young people need therefore to be helped to prepare for a wide range of leisure activities and social strategies in conjunction with preparation for a viable working life: skills relevant for handling the work of a highly technological society and crafts and skills unlikely to be replaced by the computer. This combination of approaches might give them a good basis for finding use for a shorter working day or week; or for occasional periods of unemployment; or possibly for a shorter working life. But to prepare them in the expectation that their lives will simply be leisured (i.e. unemployed) or occupied (i.e. working) is naïve and un-justified as we approach the twenty-first century.

Notes

1. All unreferenced quotations by young people are taken from Hendry and Raymond (1983).
2. I wish to acknowledge the help of my co-researcher, Martin J. Raymond (Scottish Health Education Group), in designing the models presented in Figures 1 and 2, and to thank him for permission to publish them here.

References

Alexander Report (1975) *Adult Education: The Challenge of Change.* London: HMSO.

Ashton, D. N. and Maguire, M. J. (1980) The Functions of Academic and Non-Academic Criteria in Employers' Selection Strategies. *British Journal of Guidance and Counselling* 8: 146–57.

Bandura, A. (1972) The Stormy Decade: Fact or Fiction?. In D. Rogers (ed.) *Issues in Adolescent Psychology* (2nd edn). New York: Appleton-Century-Crofts.

Bates, I., Clarke, J., Cohen, P., Finn, D., Moore, R., and Willis, P. (1984) *Schooling for the Dole.* London: Macmillan.

Bernstein, B. (1977) *Class Codes and Control* (3). London: Routledge & Kegan Paul.

Brown, R. (1978) Work. In P. Abrams (ed.) *Work, Urbanism and Inequality in UK Society Today.* London: Weidenfeld.

Carter, M. (1966) *Into Work.* Harmondsworth: Penguin.

—— (1971) *Home, School and Work.* London: Pergamon.

—— (1972) The World of Work and the ROSLA Pupil. *Education in the North* 9: 61–4.

Coleman, J. C. (1979) *The School Years: Current Views on the Adolescent Process.* London: Methuen.

Coleman, J. C., George, R., and Holt, G. (1977) Adolescents and their Parents: A Study of Attitudes. *Journal of Genetic Psychology* 130: 239–45.

Corrigan, P. (1979) *Schooling the Smash Street Kids.* London: Macmillan.

Emmett, I. (1977) Decline in Sports Participation After Leaving School. Unpublished draft report to the Sports Council. London: Sports Council.

Entwistle, H. (1970) *Education, Work and Leisure.* London: Routledge & Kegan Paul.

Erikson, E. H. (1968) *Identity, Youth and Crisis.* New York: Norton.

Fogelman, K. (1976) *Britain's Sixteen Year Olds.* London: National Children's Bureau.

Fuller, R. B. (1970) *Operating Manual for Spaceship Earth.* New York: Pocket Books.

Gow, L. and McPherson, A. (1980) *Tell Them From Me.* Aberdeen: Aberdeen University Press.

Gurney, R. M. (1980) The Effects of Unemployment on the Psycho-Social Developments of School-Leavers. *Journal of Occupational Psychology* 53: 205–13.

Hargreaves, D. H. (1981) Unemployment, Leisure and Education. *Oxford Review of Education* 7 (3): 197–210.
—— (1982) *Challenge for the Comprehensive School.* London: Routledge & Kegan Paul.
Hartley, D. (1985) Social Education in Scotland: Some Sociological Considerations. *Scottish Educational Review* 17 (2): 92–8.
Hendry, L. B. (1983) *Growing Up and Going Out.* Aberdeen: Aberdeen University Press.
Hendry, L. B. and Marr, D. (1985) Leisure Education and Young People's Leisure. *Scottish Educational Review* 17 (2): 116–27.
Hendry, L. B. and McKenzie, H. F. (1978) Advantages and Disadvantages of Raising the School-Leaving Age: The Pupil's Viewpoint. *Scottish Educational Review* 10 (2): 53–61.
Hendry, L. B. and Raymond, M. J. (1983) Youth Unemployment and Lifestyles: Some Educational Considerations. *Scottish Educational Review* 15 (1): 28–40.
—— (1985) Coping with Unemployment: Some Psycho-Social Factors. Unpublished report to the Scottish Educational Department, New St Andrew's House, Edinburgh.
Hendry, L. B., Raymond, M. J., and Stewart, C. (1984) Unemployment, School and Leisure: An Adolescent Study. *Leisure Studies* 3: 175–87.
HMSO (1983) *Young People in the '80s.* London: HMSO.
Holland, G. (1979) More than Half our Future: Sixteen- to Nineteen-year-olds in Employment. *Oxford Review of Education* 5 (2): 147–56.
Jahoda, M. (1979) The Impact of Unemployment in the 1930s and the 1970s. *Bulletin of British Psychological Society* 32: 309–14.
Jahoda, M., Lazarsfield, P. F., and Zeisel, H. (1933) *Marienthal: The Sociography of an Unemployed Community.* London: Tavistock.
Jenkins, C. and Sherman, B. (1979) *The Collapse of Work.* London: Eyre-Methuen.
Jonathan, R. (1982) Lifelong Learning: Slogan, Educational Aim or Manpower Service?. *Scottish Educational Review* 14 (2): 80–92.
Kelvin, P. (1981) Work as a Source of Identity: The Implications of Unemployment. *British Journal of Guidance and Counselling* 9 (1): 2–11.
Kitwood, T. (1980) *Disclosures to a Stranger: Adolescent Values in an Advanced Industrial Society.* London: Routledge & Kegan Paul.
Leigh, J. (1971) *Young People and Leisure.* London: Routledge & Kegan Paul.
Lewin, K. (1970) Field Theory and Experiment in Social Psychology. In R. Muuss (ed.) *Adolescent Behaviour and Society.* New York: Random House.
Morton-Williams, R. and Finch, S. (1968) *Enquiry 1: Young School-Leavers.* London: HMSO.
Mundy, J. and Odum, L. (1979) *Leisure Education.* New York: Wiley.
Murdock, G. and Phelps, G. (1973) *Mass Media and the Secondary School.* London: Macmillan.
Murray, C. (1978) *Youth Unemployment: A Social-Psychological Study of Disadvantaged 16–18-Year-Olds.* Slough: NFER.
Nisbet, S. (1957) *Purpose in the Curriculum.* London: London University Press.
Nisbet, J. D. and Shucksmith, J. (1984) The Seventh Sense. *Scottish Educational Review* 16 (2): 75–87.

218   *Unemployment*

Organization for Economic Co-operation and Development (1975) *School and Community*. Paris: OECD.

Parker, S. (1971) *The Future of Work and Leisure*. London: MacGibbon & Kee.

—— (1983) *Leisure and Work*. London: Allen & Unwin.

Raffe, D. (1983) Youth Unemployment in Scotland Since 1977. *Scottish Educational Review* 15: 16–27.

Raven, J. (1982) Education and the Competencies Required in Modern Society. *Higher Education Review* 15: 47–57.

Roberts, K. (1983) *Youth and Leisure*. London: Allen & Unwin.

Rutter, M., Graham, P., Chadwick, O., and Yule, W. (1976) Adolescent Turmoil: Fact or Fiction? *Journal of Child Psychology and Psychiatry* 17: 35–56.

Rutter, M., Maughan, B., Mortimer, P., and Ouston, J. (1979) *Fifteen Thousand Hours: Secondary Schools and their Effects on Children*. London: Open Books.

Ryrie, A. C. (1981) *Routes and Results*. London: Hodder & Stoughton.

Scottish Council for Community Education (1981) *Community School in Scotland*. Edinburgh: SCCE, Atholl House.

Simon, M. (1978) Young People's Attitudes to Work. In C. Murray (ed.) *Youth in Contemporary Society*. Slough: NFER.

Weir, D. and Nolan, F. (1977) *Glad to be Out?* Edinburgh: SCRE.

Willis, P. (1977) *Learning to Labour*. Farnborough: Saxon House.

Wolfenden Report (1960) *Sport and the Community*. The Report of the Wolfenden Committee on Sport. London: Central Council of Physical Recreation.

12. The effect of unemployment upon the employed: a new realism in industrial relations?

Roderick Martin

Unemployment is a profound personal concern for men and women out of work, involving major economic, social, and often personal problems. But it is also an issue for the employed, as workers, voters, and parents. As workers, employees face the possibility of dismissal or redundancy, and probable unemployment, at least for a period; as voters, citizens determine the political complexion of the government, and the political priority accorded to reducing unemployment; as parents, employees are concerned about the employment prospects of their children. The level of unemployment is determined by the operation of the system of production, and by the decisions of employers and the employed, not by the unemployed themselves – although precisely who is unemployed may be influenced by the individuals themselves. Understanding unemployment therefore involves understanding the system of production and the behaviour of the employed, not of the unemployed – as Beveridge emphasized in the title of his pioneering work on unemployment, *Unemployment – A Problem of Industry*, published in 1909.

Overall accounts of the economic factors that influence the level of unemployment are available elsewhere, for example in the collection of papers edited by Greenhalgh, Layard, and Oswald (1983; see also Routh 1984). This chapter is concerned with a narrower issue: the effect of high levels of unemployment in the 1980s on British industrial relations. Unemployment in the UK rose from an annual average of 5.3 per cent in 1979 to an annual average of 13.1 per cent in 1984; in January 1985 unemployment stood at 13.9 per cent, or 3,341,000 men and women according to the Department of Employment's relatively narrow definition of the unemployed. In the North of England 17.8 per cent of the 'working' population were not employed, and in the region with the lowest level of unemployment, the South East, 9.7 per cent were out of work. What effect has the rise in unemployment had upon workers in employment? Has the rise in unemployment led to a new sense of 'realism' on the shop-floor?

To answer this question the present chapter focuses upon four issues: wage determination, strike action, the scope of collective bargaining, and the organizational strength of the trade union movement. In brief, the rise in unemployment has not led to major changes in industrial relations; the employed have been partially insulated from the effects of unemployment. Most importantly, the real earnings of the employed have continued to grow, rising more rapidly than the rate of inflation and than increases in productivity.

The influence of unemployment upon earnings

The first priority of the Thatcher government's economic strategy, at least until 1985, has been to reduce the rate of inflation. Increases in unemployment have been an unfortunate by-product of measures designed to reduce inflation. The government has been concerned to restrict the growth of the money supply, even if high interest rates, a reduction in investment, and lower employment levels have resulted. Containing inflation involves controlling two pressures: the level of demand, and wage increases above the level of increases in productivity. High levels of unemployment may help, or result from, attempts to achieve both objectives.

The trade-off between inflation and unemployment has been a central issue for economic research, at least since the publication of the 'Philips curve' in 1958. Philips appeared to demonstrate empirically that increases in the level of unemployment resulted in a decline in the rate of increase of money wages (Philips 1958). Subsequent research has developed the concept of an 'expectations augmented' curve (Routh 1984, Graham in Morris (ed.) 1985).[1] There are four general ways in which the level of unemployment might directly affect the process of wage determination: (1) by influencing managers' objectives from the bargaining process, or (2) their ability to resist pressure; by influencing workers' objectives (3), or (4) their ability to exert pressure.

The level of unemployment might lead managers to lower their wage offers, or to lower their sticking-points in the negotiating process. This would be justified by their perception of the lack of alternative job opportunities for workers who leave the firm as a result of discontent with the wages offered, wage trends in other companies, or anticipation of a further fall in demand for the firm's products. The level of unemployment might also increase management's ability to resist union pressure, for example through easing labour supply and making threats of dismissal more realistic.

The level of unemployment might also lead workers to lower their earnings objectives. This would be justified by the declining level of demand for the firm's products and the danger of making the firm uncompetitive. The rate of increase in earnings achieved by comparative wage reference groups might also be expected to decline, making lower levels of increase acceptable as 'fair'. A decline in the rate of increase in the cost of living would also make lower wage increases acceptable. Moreover, workers might realize that management's ability to resist pressure had increased, and that there was little point in striving for unrealistic objectives. Even if workers' objectives remain unchanged, workers may be unable to exert bargaining leverage upon employers because of higher unemployment levels; employers might be able to dismiss workers and secure replacements; they might be able to supply customers from stock because of increasing stock levels; they might welcome a strike as a way of reducing supplies to the market and reducing operating costs; and unemployment might increase divisions amongst workers, making it difficult to maintain unity during conflict.

Increasing unemployment might also reduce inflationary pressures indirectly. Within the enterprise, unemployment might facilitate management initiatives in improving the efficiency of work organization, leading workers to accept changes in methods of production, or being unable to resist increases in work intensity. Problems of labour management and labour discipline would be eased by making the threat of the sack more realistic than it had been in the 1960s; dismissed workers would find it more difficult to secure jobs, and employers would find it easier to secure replacements. Increased productivity would result, providing a non-inflationary source of increased earnings. Moreover, the difficulty in finding new jobs might lead to reductions in labour turnover, leading to lower recruitment and induction costs, and a more experienced work-force: there would be less loss of time in on-the-job learning. The quality of labour should therefore rise. Outside the enterprise, high levels of unemployment might increase the efficiency of the labour market by reducing the time taken to fill vacancies, and by having available a more qualified recruitment pool with the greater availability of surplus labour.

Empirical research confirms that some of the expected trends have developed. For example, the level of labour turnover has fallen compared with the 1970s; with high unemployment, workers are more reluctant to give up their jobs voluntarily (although the take-up of special voluntary redundancy schemes remains high). However, more importantly, aggregate data on changes in earnings and in the level of pay settlements do not support the view that unemployment leads to a decline in real wages. Despite a steep rise in the level of unemployment, and predictions of continuing increase, the level of earnings of the employed population has continued to increase faster than the rate of inflation throughout the 1980s, as it did throughout the 1970s. Between 1978 and June 1983 earnings rose by more than 90 per cent, and prices by 69 per cent; in manufacturing industry, where redundancies have been heavily concentrated, earnings rose by 85 per cent for men and 75 per cent for women. This represented a faster rate of increase in real earnings than in the mid-1970s: between 1973 and 1978 average weekly earnings rose by 117 per cent, whilst prices rose by 109 per cent (Batstone 1984). According to Department of Employment figures, real earnings have continued to rise throughout the 1980s: between January 1983 and January 1984, for example, average weekly earnings rose by 7.1 per cent, although the Retail Price Index rose by only 5 per cent. Between 1981 and 1984 the average hourly earnings of full-time male manual workers rose by 25.58 per cent, and of full-time female manual workers by 26.19 per cent; the Retail Price Index rose by 23.54 per cent. Over the same four years unemployment rose from an annual average of 10.5 per cent in 1981 to over 13 per cent. Part of the increase in real earnings is due to a change in the occupational composition of the labour force; throughout the 1980s low-paid and low-skilled workers have lost their jobs more than skilled workers, resulting in an inevitable rise in average hourly earnings. However, the level of settlements has also more than kept pace with inflation. Evidence from the Confederation of British Industry (CBI) Pay Databank, based upon settlements in eight sectors of manufacturing industry, indicates a rise in the level of real earnings for 1979–84 (Gregory, Lobban, and Thompson 1985). The level of take-home pay would, of course, be higher than reported to the CBI since take-home pay would include overtime and bonus payments. After dropping slightly in 1982, the average number of hours worked by male manual workers has increased, to 43.4 hours in 1984, indicating a significant increase in overtime working. In short, a large and continuing rise in the level of unemployment in the 1980s has not been associated with a decline in the real level of earnings, or in pay settlements below the rate of inflation.

Unemployment has been especially heavy amongst manual workers. In 1981, for example, the unemployment rate was 12.3 per cent for manual workers, compared with a rate of 5.2 per cent for non-manual workers. However, the CBI Pay Databank indicated that the cumulative increase in pay settlements over the period 1979–83 was exactly the same for both manual and non-manual workers, 42.9 per cent.

Overall changes in the level of unemployment have only a limited effect upon changes in the level of earnings or pay settlements. Nor is this surprising, for two major reasons. First, the limited substitutability of the unemployed for the employed. The view that levels of unemployment will substantially and directly influence the rate of increase in earnings depends upon the substitutability of unemployed labour for employed labour; if employed labour is different in kind from unemployed labour the threat posed to the employed is very limited. In any circumstances there is likely to be a difference between employed and unemployed workers: employed workers have already acquired relevant skills and experience; at the minimum, new recruits would require training. As the costs of training increase, or as the significance of specific job-related experience increases, the costs of substituting recruits from the unemployed for the presently employed increase. Moreover, the quality of existing workers – in terms of motivation, commitment, intelligence, and competence – is already known. Research into the unemployed indicates that they are significantly different from the employed: the unemployed are younger (and older) than the employed, they have lower levels of education, they are less likely to be skilled, they are more likely to have had a disrupted work history (Sinfield 1981). There are thus several differences between the employed and the unemployed that indicate that the employed are not easily substituted by the unemployed.

Secondly, there are alternative ways in which firms could reduce their labour costs. Economic pressures could lead to firms spreading the same amount of work amongst existing workers, resulting in maintaining levels of employment but reducing productivity and real earnings, or to reducing employment levels to match declining demand. For the individual firm reducing the size of the labour force increases productivity, and may reduce the overall cost of labour. Increasing productivity through reducing the number of workers also eases industrial relations problems, where the number of workers is reduced through natural wastage and slowing down recruitment: firms can maintain levels of earnings for existing workers despite tightening product markets. In the early 1980s manufacturing industry responded to declining demand by reducing employment levels more than proportionally; the increase in productivity in 1981–82 was the result of producing almost the same level of output with substantially fewer workers, not increasing output with the same number of workers. The increase in productivity involved a large increase in the number of redundancies, and a sharp rise in unemployment.

Overall, the unemployed cannot easily substitute for the employed. The analogy between a reservoir of water and a reservoir of labour is misleading. However, the unemployed could influence the behaviour of the employed even if they could not substitute for them in general. This would occur if managers and the employed believed that the unemployed could substitute for the employed, even if the belief was mistaken; bargaining behaviour is based on belief, not 'reality'. This belief might occur because of political and media attention to the level of unemployment. The salience of high general levels of unemployment might persuade workers that there were unemployed people willing and able to carry out their jobs. Such political and media attention is especially persuasive to union leaders, who are concerned about the overall level of jobs available to their potential union members. In the short-term the employed might believe that they were substitutable by the unemployed: but in the face of day-to-day experience the belief is likely to be short-lived.

The level of change in real earnings is affected more by company-level factors than by the overall level of unemployment. Several pieces of research have shown the lack of fit between local labour-market factors and changes in factory-level earnings (Robinson 1970). Workers can be paid very different rates for the same job in the same local labour market. Workers' earnings are linked to the economic performance of the company (or establishment, or profit centre), to the customary rate for the job, and to nationally negotiated changes, not to changes in the supply of labour as measured by the level of unemployment (at least in the short run). Comparative wage reference groups are also likely to be firm-based rather than locality-based (much less nationality-based), especially for non-craft-workers (Willman 1982). This is partly because of the visibility of different groups; groups within the firm are more visible than groups outside. It is also a result of management policies, especially the development of 'internal labour markets', the practice of filling higher-level vacancies from within the firm, not from the external labour market. Internal labour markets are a means whereby employers increase employee commitment, reward employees for the acquisition of firm-related skills, and reduce labour turnover (Doeringer and Piore 1971). Such labour markets involve restricting points of entry into the firm. The development of internal labour markets was associated with the spread of company and plant-level collective bargaining in the 1970s, and with the spread of job evaluation schemes as a means of rationalizing pay structures (Brown 1981). The growth of internal labour markets designed to increase management flexibility in using labour within the firm inevitably reduces management's ability to respond to changes in the availability of candidates for specific jobs from outside the firm.

The effect of the general economic situation is not via the level of unemployment, but via changes in the level of demand for the firm's products. Wages respond at one remove to changes in product markets, not directly to changes in labour markets. Earnings in establishments producing goods for which demand remains high, or where there is a low level of price elasticity (i.e. changes in price do not feed through proportionately into changes in demand), may thus be expected to rise, regardless of overall changes in the level of unemployment. The level and pattern of demand are of course affected by the level of unemployment; in so far as high levels of unemployment reduce demand they might be expected to influence the rate of increase in earnings. But high levels of unemployment will have a differential effect upon the pattern of demand, since unemployment is concentrated in particular sectors of the population, with particular patterns of consumption. It is more likely to affect the market for second-hand Ford Cortinas than for new Jaguar XJ6s. High levels of unemployment operating through the product market would thus be expected to result in a widening of the dispersal of earnings between companies and between industries serving different markets. This is largely confirmed, and pay settlements have become more widely dispersed. In the 1979–83 period, settlements were consistently higher in companies in the food, chemicals, and paper industries, and consistently lower in companies in metals, mechanical engineering, and textiles. The importance of product market changes is reflected in the growing importance of 'ability to pay' arguments in the 1980s.

Pay settlements are influenced by the collective bargaining system and by workers' expectations as well as by product market situation. Where bargaining is carried out at industry level the collective bargaining system exerts a pressure towards uniformity, in comparison with company or with plant-level bargaining. Centralized bargaining decelerates the effect of product market changes upon earnings, reducing the rate of decline that might be expected in competitive product markets. Workers' bargaining behaviour is influenced by expectations of future patterns of product market demand, not by the present level of demand. Pressure for increased earnings will be greater where demand is expected to pick up than where it is expected to decline.

Changes in product markets in the 1980s have reinforced trends towards the segmentation of the labour market, which developed in the late 1960s and 1970s for other reasons. The labour market is divided into at least two segments, a primary segment and a secondary segment. The difference is partly one of industrial sector – as in the contrast between the chemicals industry, operating in a primary labour market, and textiles – and partly one of occupation – as in the contrast between maintenance workers and sub-assembly workers in the same firm. Jobs in the primary sector are in large enterprises and provide relative job security, salary progression, and promotion opportunities; entry is restricted. Jobs in the secondary labour market are in smaller companies, with little employment security, no regular salary progression, and no regular promotion opportunities. Workers in the primary sector are partially insulated from competitive pressures. Secondary workers are more likely to find themselves unemployed than primary sector workers. Equally, the unemployed are more likely to obtain jobs within the secondary than the primary sector. The difference between the primary and secondary labour market is increased by legislation designed to restrict the operation of employment security legislation in small enterprises.

High levels of unemployment are more likely to affect earnings in the secondary than in the primary labour market. Employers face more severe competitive conditions, and workers possess less bargaining power. Moreover, the jobs involving lower levels of skills associated with the secondary labour markets are more accessible to the unemployed; the skills and qualities required for jobs in personal services, for example, are more widely distributed than those required for electronic maintenance work. Real differences in skill requirements are reinforced by differences in union coverage, and effectiveness. However, even in the secondary labour market employers have not secured major wage reductions amongst existing employees, and have not generally pursued a policy of paying new employees lower rates than existing employees, for reasons of prudence as well as equity. Instead, wages in the competitive secondary sector have been reduced by the entrance of new firms, which have been able to recruit workers without paying the level of wages paid by existing firms. 'Real' wages have become more flexible during the current recession, especially in the 'competitive' sector, and this flexibility is greatly enhanced by the entrance of new firms. Economic conditions, however, will have to worsen considerably before nominal wages fall in existing firms, except in certain severe cases (Kaufman 1984: 110). Policies designed to stimulate the creation of new firms in the competitive sector will have the overall effect of reducing earnings in the secondary labour market.

In short, the unemployed are a reservoir for the secondary labour market, not for the labour market as a whole.

The 1980s have seen a widening of the gap between the primary 'core' labour market and the secondary labour market. There has also been a widening gap between the core employed labour force and the unemployed. This is partly a matter of wage bargaining processes, in which increases are linked to changes in productivity, or in the earning of comparative wage reference groups, or in the cost of living, but not to the poverty line. Unemployment and supplementary benefits are not up-rated proportional to the cost of living, much less to changes in the level of productivity or increases in earnings. The effects of this difference are reinforced by competitive pressures in the secondary labour market, which operate to reduce the cost of the services used by workers in the primary labour market. The economic fortunes of workers employed in the primary labour market improve as a result of the pressures operating upon workers in the secondary labour market; competitive pressures in retail distribution improve the standard of living of manual workers, as well as of bankers.

Unemployment and strikes

A second way in which high levels of unemployment might affect the employed is through their effect on strike action. Workers will be reluctant to go on strike if there are a large number of unemployed workers available to replace them. Strike action has declined since the 1970s; the number of days lost through strike action declined between 1980 and 1983, only to rise sharply in 1984 and 1985 with the miners' strike. The number of strikes has also declined compared with the 1970s; according to Department of Employment figures, 2,703 strikes began in 1977, and 2,080 in 1979, compared with 1,330 in 1980, 1,338 in 1981, 1,528 in 1982, 1,352 in 1983, and 1,154 in 1984. In some industries, for example the railways in 1985, workers have voted against strike action against the recommendations of their leaders, or have refused to go out on strike when called.

The reduction in industrial action is due to several factors, and is not simply the result of high levels of unemployment. One reason for the decline in industrial action is the shake-out in manufacturing industry in 1980–81, which led to the closure of many plants in sectors that had high levels of industrial action, and a reduction in the size of the labour force in the plants that survived. Fewer workers are now employed in historically strike-prone industries, leading inevitably to a reduction in the number of days lost. Secondly, the continuing high level of pay settlements in the 'core' manufacturing sector has meant that the incentive for strike action is less. Strike action in the secondary labour market is less common because of competitive pressures, the small size of firms, and the difficulties of union organization. Thirdly, industrial action has occurred in sectors of the 'core' where settlements have not kept pace with the rate of inflation, for example in the Civil Service and amongst teachers; the strikes have sometimes been widespread, but not national, partly because of increasingly sophisticated strike tactics designed to reduce the high costs of strike action and partly because of the hesitations of the groups involved in undertaking strike action due to professional commitment. Finally, Batstone suggests that industrial action short of strike action has been increasing:

'workers may over the last five years [1978–83] have resorted to more "subtle" forms of industrial sanction rather than the high risk tactics of the lengthy strike – hence in only 3 per cent of plants have there been four or more strikes of more than a day or shift duration in the last two years, while about three times this proportion have experienced an equal number of short strikes or other forms of industrial action.'

(Batstone 1984: 293)

(Strikes involving fewer than ten workers, or lasting for a day or less, are excluded from Department of Employment (DE) figures. DE figures would therefore overstate the decline in the number of strikes if there had been a move to strikes lasting less than a day.)

Unemployment and the scope of collective bargaining

A third way in which the level of unemployment might affect the behaviour of employed workers is through a reduction in the scope of collective bargaining. In the 1970s managements agreed to negotiate with unions over a wider range of issues than in previous years, primarily at plant level. There was a particular growth in bargaining over levels of output and manning (Storey 1980: 129). Managements might be expected to attempt to reassert their managerial prerogatives and cut back on the range of issues negotiated, believing that trade union power was weakened by high levels of unemployment. Some managements have reasserted 'the right of management to manage', especially in the public sector: Sir Michael Edwardes at BL, Ian McGregor at British Steel and the National Coal Board. However, it is easy to exaggerate this trend. The spectacular attempts to reassert management control have largely been in the public sector, where managements have been able to incur massive costs from strike action because of government support (no private employer could have stood the costs of the 1984 dispute at the Department of Health and Social Security (DHSS) in Newcastle, or the coal-miners' strike in 1984–85).[2] Batstone's survey of personnel managers in manufacturing industry indicated that a fifth of employers had reduced the range or amount of bargaining between 1978 and 1983, a quarter had increased it, and half had made no change (Batstone 1984: 274). Managements require the co-operation of workers on a day-to-day basis, and hesitate to disrupt working relationships, unless there is a crisis; this hesitation is even more pronounced where managements anticipate an increase in economic activity and a possible revival of worker bargaining power. Worker co-operation is even more necessary when management is attempting to change working practices. In short, the change in the scope of collective bargaining in the 1980s is unlikely to have been dramatic.

Unemployment and trade union organization

A fourth way in which high levels of unemployment might affect the employed is through their effect upon the trade unions as institutions. High levels of unemployment might weaken trade unions at shop-floor level and at national level. At shop-floor level workers may be increasingly reluctant to take up union office because of the fear of management hostility, or may carry out union duties cautiously. According to the Workplace Industrial Relations Survey carried out in 1980, 44 per cent of establishments employing manual workers had shop stewards; and in 74 per cent of such establishments (which recognized trade unions) each steward represented an average of twenty-nine workers (Daniel and Millward 1983: 34). Evidence from the comparable 1984 survey is not yet available. Batstone concludes that about a fifth of employers have attempted to put unions in their place by curbing the activities of shop stewards, mainly in plants where steward influence had reached very high levels in the 1970s (Batstone 1984: 260). But there has been no widespread disintegration of steward organization; indeed, management moves to increase employee involvement may increase the overall importance of the shop steward, as the leader of the work group, although this would not be formally linked to union office. Batstone suggests that steward influence may have declined in a minority of plants where steward influence had previously been very high, but only to more average levels. The degree of steward influence had remained resilient overall.

High levels of unemployment may also reduce the significance of the union at national level. Union leaders may be demoralized by their failure to reduce the level of unemployment, or to advance the interests of the unemployed effectively. Despite criticisms of government ineffectiveness in dealing with unemployment, and the rhetoric of the Campaign for Jobs, union leaders have not made a significant impact on the problem of unemployment. High levels of unemployment create divisions within the labour movement, between the employed and the unemployed, and between workers in the primary and secondary labour markets. The union movement is faced with the conflict between increasing wages and maintaining employment levels – deciding how far wage restraint is an effective means of generating employment. Moreover, unemployment obviously results in a drop in the level of union membership, despite the existence of special sections for unemployed members; the number of union members dropped from 13,289,000 in 1979 to 11,338,000 in 1983.

High levels of unemployment have created major problems for the national-level trade union leadership. But the demoralization of the unions at national level is due to more than the continuation of high levels of unemployment. It reflects government hostility, internal organiza-tional difficulties, the poor political performance of the Labour Party, and occupational change – the decline of extractive and manufacturing industries reducing the significance of historically dominant manual unions. Moreover, the priority given to the unemployed by employed members of the labour force is low in day-to-day practice, as the growth in overtime earnings in 1985 indicates.

Conclusions

In the mid-1980s Conservative politicians and a wide spectrum of journalistic opinion have argued that the power of the trade unions has been broken. According to the *Sunday Times*, 'the Thatcher years have tamed Britain's unions to an extent most experts said was impossible a decade ago . . . the unions have been cut down to size' (*Sunday Times*, 1 September 1985). Government legislation (continues the argument) has made union leaders responsible to their membership, and the member-ship has obliged union leaders to follow realistic policies in the face of high levels of unemployment. Such realism has led to reduced pressure for inflationary increases in earnings, fewer strikes, and less willingness to follow militant shop stewards.

This view of the relationship between union leaders and their members is seriously misleading. Union leaders were aware of the penalties of losing touch with their members before the Conservative legislation of 1980, 1982, and 1984, and union members are not consistently less militant than their leaders, especially when their own interests are involved. More importantly for the present argument, such views exaggerate the change in union members' views brought about by unemployment, as trends in earnings, strikes, collective bargaining, and union organization indicate.

High levels of unemployment have led to anxieties amongst union members. The trade union movement has undertaken a Campaign for Jobs. All three major political parties see unemployment as the major political problem. The Labour Party and the Social Democratic/Liberal Alliance have made reducing unemployment their major political priority throughout the 1980s. By late 1985 even the Conservative Party was beginning to stress the need to reduce unemployment (rather than the need to reduce inflation). However, the concern with unemployment is not wholly reflected in day-to-day industrial relations; unemployment has had less effect upon the behaviour of the employed than the 'new realism' analysis suggests.

Unemployment remains a profound personal problem for the un-employed, as explained elsewhere in this book. But the effect of unemployment upon the employed is indirect, through its effect upon product market demand. Where product market demand remains high the effect upon the employed is limited. Throughout the 1980s the recession was very steep in 1980–81, but economic activity has picked up since 1981. The steep recession in 1980–81 had a marked effect upon the level of pay settlements; since 1981 the level of settlements has slowly risen. Recession has affected different industries differently, and the engineering industry has been affected particularly severely. Settlements in the engineering industry have been consistently low throughout the 1980s. Where firms have retained their position in the product market, real earnings have continued to rise, despite overall high levels of unemployment. Similarly, the extent to which work-group power has been destroyed remains limited. Only a limited number of employers have explicitly attemped to roll back the influence of trade unions on the shop-floor. Work-group power may have declined elsewhere, without specific management action; but the overall level of bargaining remains higher than in the late 1960s. At the national level the trade unions have experienced a major loss of influence and prestige. The government has refused to discuss economic issues with the Trades Union Congress (TUC); the movement has been split by employer intransigence both in the private sector (as in the *Stockport Messenger* dispute in 1983)[3] and in the public sector (as in the coal-miners' dispute of 1984–85); the level of union membership has declined; internal squabbles, as over the policy of refusing government money available under the 1980 Employment Act for ballot expenses, have produced public ridicule; the TUC and individual unions have experienced severe financial pressures.

Nevertheless the 1980s have not led to the collapse suggested by the *Sunday Times*. The density of union membership remains above the density achieved in the early 1970s, despite changes in the occupational structure that have led to the decline of the highly unionized manufacturing industry (and public services) and the expansion of the private services sector, with low levels of union membership. Improvements in the electoral position of the Labour Party increase the morale of the whole labour movement, including the trade unions. The result of union ballots on the political levy in 1985, in which all unions that have so far balloted have voted to continue the levy, indicates a continuing commitment by the union membership, as well as the union leadership, to political action. Although some well-publicized strike ballots have gone against executive recommendations for strike action, notably the National Union of Railwaymen ballot on industrial action against the introduction of driver-only-operated trains in August 1985, the majority of ballots have endorsed official recommendations for strike action. The trade union movement may have been weakened in the 1980s, but its influence has been far from destroyed.

The major reason for the resilience of union power despite high overall levels of unemployment lies in the lack of substitutability of the employed for the unemployed. As noted earlier, there are major demographic differences overall between the employed and the unemployed. The unemployed are younger (and older) than the employed, and less skilled, and they are concentrated in particular labour markets. The level of unemployment in the Department of Employment travel-to-work areas in January 1985 ranged from a low of 4.9 per cent in Winchester and East Leigh to a peak of 39.3 per cent in Strabane; it is impossible to cycle to Winchester from Strabane. The general lack of substitutability is especially marked in large-scale manufacturing industry, where throughout the 1970s employers increased the use of internal labour markets, thus segmenting the labour market, reducing access to the primary sector, and at the same time reducing ease of substitution. The demand for labour in the 1980s recession has been met by reductions in external recruitment and internal transfer – before carrying out redundancies – further widening the differences between the employed and the unemployed.

High levels of unemployment have weakened the bargaining power of trade unions. But the effects of unemployment have been less than many commentators assert. Most importantly, high levels of unemployment have not brought the rate of increase in earnings down to the rate of increase in productivity. Unit labour costs are continuing to rise, although at a lower rate than in the early 1980s. Nor has unemployment led to a general transformation of industrial relations at company and plant level. Recession has provided an incentive and an opportunity for managements of firms in economic difficulties to increase productivity by reducing the number of workers, reorganizing methods of production, and in some cases reforming industrial relations; but the impact of reducing demand is too great upon profits and investment, as well as upon employment, for it to provide the basis for a long-term strategy. Firms facing fewer competitive pressures have made pay settlements significantly above the rate of inflation.

The unemployed themselves have been unable to make a major impact upon government policy. They remain a minority, tied by economic position and history to the Labour Party, with little political leverage on the Conservative Party. The employed are deeply worried by unemployment, as reflected in opinion poll findings, but they have not launched an effective campaign to reduce the level of unemployment, or to prevent a worsening of the economic position of the unemployed. Significant improvements in the position of the unemployed will, however, be brought about only by the action of the employed.

Notes

1. In the 1977 edition of the same volume Graham explained why the Philips curve appeared to fit the British experience between 1861 and 1913, but not experience since 1945: 'at that time conditions were fundamentally different from the present. Markets were more competitive, labour was less well organized, unified, and cohesive in wage bargaining, and above all neither firms nor employees expected governments to pursue full employment policies. As a result bankruptcies and loss of jobs were seen as real possibilities' (Graham in Morris (ed.) 1977: 200) – an unexpectedly prophetic comment.
2. Proposed changes in shift-work arrangements at the DHSS led to a strike by 555 computer staff in May 1984. The strike ended in January 1985 with a compromise agreement. The strike by the National Union of Mineworkers against pit closures began in March 1984 and ended in March 1985, after the loss of more than 26 million working days. The National Coal Board effectively secured the closure of some pits on 'economic' grounds, but without an agreement from the mineworkers.
3. The *Stockport Messenger* dispute arose in the newspaper-printing industry when the National Graphical Association (NGA) withdrew its members in protest against Eddie Shah's recruitment of non-union labour for a subsidiary, despite a pre-entry closed shop in the industry. Following extensive legal action the NGA was fined heavily, and its members failed to secure reinstatement.

References

Batstone, E. (1984) *Working Order: Workplace Industrial Relations over Two Decades.* Oxford: Blackwell.

Beveridge, W. H. (1909) *Unemployment – A Problem of Industry.* London: Longmans.

Brown, W. (ed.) (1981) *The Changing Contours of British Industrial Relations.* Oxford: Blackwell.

Daniel, W. H. and Millward, N. (1983) *Workplace Industrial Relations in Britain.* London: Heinemann.

Doeringer, P. and Piore, M. J. (1971) *Internal Labor Markets and Manpower Analysis.* Boston: D. C. Heath.

Graham, A. W. M. (1977) Inflation. In Derek Morris (ed.) *The Economic System of the UK.* Oxford: Oxford University Press.

Greenhalgh, C. A., Layard, P. R. G., and Oswald, A. J. (eds) (1983) *The Causes of Unemployment.* Oxford: Oxford University Press.

Gregory, M., Lobban, P., and Thompson, A. W. J. (1985) Wage Settlements in Manufacturing 1979–83: Evidence from the CBI Pay Databank. Mimeo.

Kaufman, R. T. (1984) On Wage Stickiness in Britain's Competitive Sector. *British Journal of Industrial Relations* XXII (I): 101–11.

King, J. E. (1980) *Readings in Labour Economics.* Oxford: Oxford University Press.

Morris, D. (ed.) (1977) *The Economic System in the UK.* Oxford: Oxford University Press.

—— (ed.) (1985) *The Economic System in the UK* (3rd edn). Oxford: Oxford University Press.

Philips, A. W. (1958) The Relation between Unemployment and the Rate of Change of Money Wage Rates in the United Kingdom, 1861–1957. *Economica* XXV: 283–99.

Robinson, D. (1970) *Local Labour Markets and Wage Structures*. London: Gower.

Routh, G. (1984) Industrial Relations, Unemployment and Inflation. Brighton: University of Sussex. Mimeo.

Sinfield, A. (1981) *What Unemployment Means*. Oxford: Martin Robertson.

Storey, J. (1980) *The Challenge to Management Control*. London: Business Books.

Willman, P. (1982) *Fairness, Collective Bargaining and Incomes Policy*. Oxford: Clarendon Press.

Part 4
Looking on

13. From here to there – alternative routes to work

Stephen Fineman

We can examine society from the viewpoint of those who no longer feel they belong. We then learn a number of things – for example, what it is like to be an 'outsider'; the passions and problems of feeling disenfranchised; not part of the normal run of things. We can also produce an image of some of the assumptions and rules that bind the fabric of social relationships, an unusual glimpse at those forces that lead to the construction of individual realities and meanings – principles rarely questioned and, for most people, only dimly recognized.

Unemployment, as addressed by the contributors to this book, offers such perspectives and insights. This concluding chapter will bring together, in general format, some of their positions. The major source of its data already rests in this volume; however, I will also attempt to develop what has been presented to indicate where our analyses might take us. The chapter is divided into two sections. The first section highlights some of the content-themes of the book; the second looks towards possible directions and change.

Section 1. The outsiders

It is hard to resist the conclusion that the unemployed remain apart from 'normal' society in several different ways.

Firstly, and most obviously, they are in a country where many more people are in, rather than out of, employment. The relative positions of these groups lie in stark contrast to one another. In our media-slick society it is not difficult for those amongst the hardest core of unemployed to detect that a massive chunk of Britain, mainly in the South, remains buoyant and prosperous, while many other areas suffer high unemployment, sometimes of more than 30 per cent. Recent figures produced by

Newcastle University show that in September 1985 forty of the fifty most prosperous towns were in the South, prosperity indicated by a combination of employment, population change, and car ownership (Green and Champion 1985). In observing Consett in County Durham, one of Britain's most industrially depressed steel regions, Chester and Tigh reflect on the 'very real problem of whether to prepare children for work or for play, or simply to improve their expertise as benefit claimants' (1985: 29). It would be surprising to encounter such a dilemma amongst the suburban families of the Home Counties.

But being unemployed, in a poor area, should not necessarily mean a lack of community or a *sense* of alienation. Does not the local community form a supportive, warm network, a source of strength in the face of adversity? In part: there are accounts of flourishing Centres for the Unemployed, self-help groups, extended credit by shopkeepers, and sympathetic building societies. Furthermore, friends and kinship ties can emerge as one of the few effective forms of job location.

At best, though, this seems to operate patchily. The image of a stoic, even jolly, working-class community courageously rising to meet its chronic unemployment both romanticizes and trivializes the effects of joblessness. As Bostyn and Wight point out (Chapter 8), poverty and lack of spending power divide an already beleaguered community. They split off those few who have money from those who do not. They emphasize the relative helplessness of people who have developed a life-style and value system around consuming and know of no other. Money provides the only legitimate entrée to reciprocated exchanges that are the substance of social life. Symbols of worth – the car, furniture, particular foods, the pint of beer – are intrinsic to rituals of display, courtship, manliness, housewifery. But they are also the symbols of employment. They reflect the proper order of things and are clung to, even in the absence of work. Things are to be bought, not made oneself. To engage in a work surrogate may be a form of treachery, an admission that there will be no proper employment again.

Given the awesome grip of a financially based economy from which the unemployed cannot, and often do not want to, escape, subcultural patterns of survival emerge. Some are sad, others are ingenious. Our contributors have illustrated this point in various ways. There is a twilight zone where the desperate vehemently defend their 'survival' crime – in terms sometimes aggressive, often cynical. This is where money and goods emerge from deals conducted with a skill that compares well with more 'legitimate' entrepreneurial activity. Some, however, progress little beyond a crude and rather dangerous attempt to bypass the gas or electricity meter. But even this may be worth trying when the alternative prospect is no light or heat, and when living 'is a full-time job'.

The oppressive effect of not earning a living permeates the consciousness of the unemployed in both the working and middle classes. There is, to repeat, no cohesive community of unemployed. Apart from the reasons already mentioned, some mobility *within* a population sector – people moving in and out of jobs, families with members unemployed at different times – will add to the fragmentation of an unemployed 'community'. As a consequence the unemployed begin to feel very much on their own, especially as time without work increases. It can be difficult for them to convey the sheer force of the effect of no longer being financially creditworthy in a society that builds many of its transactions, in one way or another, on cash. It is an experiential gap that can exasperate the jobless. They *know* what it is like. However, the people who retain the political clout, the employed – who form the real pressure groups for change – either do not know or, if they do (having been unemployed themselves), are now far more concerned with protecting their own security. There is something of a 'catch 22' in this process.

Without work people can feel poverty and deprivation, a physical and emotional world that is distant from that of those whose comfortable life-styles continue uninterrupted. This presents a sombre irony for jobless professionals who once commanded a substantial salary, some of whom helped to execute others' unemployment. For the newly qualified, the highly skilled entrants to the job market, unemployment offers no celebration. For them, the promised rewards of study and impecunious living have vanished.

So the effect of being unemployed and poor is problematic, to say the least. Social security payments can help pay a bill or two, but they are rarely sought as a replacement for earned income. Indeed, just about everything associated with the dispensation of state aid appears to fuel a mixture of anger and resentment amongst the unemployed. It can feel like a demeaning hand-out to the inadequate. Its bureaucracy provides an ideal focus for pent-up frustrations, so any challenge to defraud may stem as much from the *frisson* of doing something effective against a legitimate target as from a genuine need for more money.

As individuals move into long-term unemployment (even by probably conservative official figures, more than 40 per cent have now been jobless for over a year, and half of this group for over two years), chronic financial difficulties are matched by social and psychological ones. Any initial feelings of shock, resentment, or even hope for a more exciting future have given way to a pervasive sense of rejection after repeated failures in the job market. This brings home the chilling fact that Roderick Martin (Chapter 12) has emphasized: the unemployed are, by and large, no substitute for the employed. Where the unemployed (blue and white collar) may find intermittent work is around the fringes of the corporate

giants, providing services ranging from cleaning and driving to professional marketing and design. This, though, represents a minefield of
insecurity where small businesses have a tendency to falter and fail. It also
offers little prospect for absorbing the huge numbers once employed in
our mass-production, 'low tec' industries.

A vast proportion of the long-term unemployed remain outside of all
forms of employment. Time-markers become more diffuse as one day
drags into the next. The personal imposition of routine and self-directedness, alluded to by David Fryer and Stephen McKenna (Chapter 4), can be
eroded with each new week, each new month without work. It seems that
a sense of future, however limited, is crucial to psychological health. We
may look ahead to starting work, finishing work, meeting colleagues,
resting at weekends, socializing, and exchanging anecdotes. We may not
look forward, in a positive sense, to all of these, but they do provide an
ebb and flow of experience, a predictable *variation* in which to pace our
time and our lives. Some of us will be more inventive than others in
substituting one marker for another, in creating alternatives – or even in
living in relative isolation. But few of us, it seems, find effective ways of
permanently replacing what was once the solid *structure* of work. Few of
us, it appears, want to.

'Leisure, free time, unlimited fun': such is one image of life without
work. In practice leisure turns out to be something that people buy into, in
one way or another. There is an entrance fee to the leisure pursuits that
many of us enjoy. We have here yet another commodity that has to be
purchased. The annual holiday , drinks in the pub, the bottle of wine for a
dinner-party, the costs of a car, the do-it-yourself materials, the gifts, the
television and video rental, the cinema, bingo, or theatre tickets – all have
to be afforded. Also, for many of the people described in this book, they
have to be *seen* to be afforded, and much may be sacrificed in attempts to
maintain that impression.

But such endeavour can soon feel rootless. Leisure has rested symbi-
otically with work. Destroy the job, and leisure is set adrift. It does not
mean the same any more or fulfil the same function. This can be a very
unsettling realization for the job loser who fast turns to those leisure
pursuits that he or she has known to be satisfying and purposeful. Even
sharing occasions with friends or acquaintances who are employed feels
different – uncomfortably so. This underlines Leo Hendry's point
(Chapter 11) that we do not school our children, our potential un-
employees, towards leisure outside the context of work. Indeed, perhaps
we do not educate and skill them towards leisure beyond the rather
restricted curricula and confines of the school.

Unlimited 'free' time can turn out to be more of a shackle than a
liberation. It can appear daunting to those who believe that they have all,

or a good part, of a working lifetime ahead of them. In late career a job loss can be construed as an early retirement, which may be welcome if funds and plans are adequate; even better if activities outside of work have been developed and well rehearsed as the major source of structure and satisfaction. A person in this position is mentally prepared, and skilled, for retirement; the old routines are rapidly replaced. But unpreparedness is perhaps a more likely situation: a sense of interrupted business, of being ejected from a community, of loss of control over the present and the future.

Making meanings

Some of the psychological reactions to unemployment bear a marked resemblance to the effects of 'sensory deprivation', a condition keenly observed by psychologists in their laboratories during the 1960s. Human beings (like many other beings) do not take kindly to having their routines violently disturbed. They become distressed as social contacts are reduced. The less they are able to interact with other people and things, the more stress they experience. Contact with a responsive world is extremely important to provide a frame of reference, to know who and what one is.

There is a compelling similarity between the confusion, lethargy, and depression that sensory deprivation can bring and those very same states reported of, and by, the unemployed in this book. We have accounts of the workless who live in grey, shabby surroundings; people whose lives are diminished socially and psychologically. But these same accounts also illustrate how bored and disaffected people will sometimes create activity to provide an immediate sense of action, result, and above all, control. The vandalism, theft, and fraud observed by Jeremy Seabrook (Chapter 2) and Anne-Marie Bostyn and Daniel Wight (Chapter 8) may be viewed in this light. They are active attempts to make meaning, to feel an *agent* in society, experiencing the rewards – even if fleeting – of effort. If work and leisure are untenable, then such action makes sense – even if we, as critical observers, do not like the sense. We like it even less when there is physical violence towards another person. Yet, before blaming the unemployed for their fate, their actions, or both, we should be mindful that 'normal' self-control is something that can best flourish in normal social circumstances.

Keeping it in the family

We are reminded, by David Clark (Chapter 6) in particular, that an individual's stresses and struggles in unemployment are rarely located in a social vacuum. There are immediate family ramifications. Families, though, are more than a single, tidy sociological unit, as most of us who are in one will know. Some will be starting up, full of excitement and apprehension. Others are relatively mature, with older children and fairly firm rules and roles. Still others are adjusting to middle age and sickness, perhaps including members of the extended family under the same roof. There are broken families and divided ones, recriminative and supportive ones. It is perhaps the family that is the first institution or unit to feel the full force of an individual's job loss.

The loss of the major source of income to a family can challenge a whole variety of transactions that spun around the nucleus of one person's job. Who gets money for what, and from where, can be immediate questions to face. This might not be too much of a headache if redundancy payments have been generous, if there are no children to support, and if local kinship ties are active and supportive. It helps, also, if the *local* labour market has a little to offer the persevering applicant, whether husband or wife. David Clark sketches this scenario, along with some less happy ones. For example, some families are already in debt, trying to cope with ill health, have few helpful local contacts, and between them have little to offer an already depressed labour market. For single parents, who are the sole source of care and income for their family, the burdens of joblessness can be intolerable – especially for women, who are more disadvantaged than men in the job market.

Yet it is noteworthy how, on the whole, family organization proves to be relatively conservative and inflexible in the face of the pressures of unemployment. What seems to happen is that the old rules and roles, the pre-unemployment rituals, get replayed, even sharpened, in circumstances that have now changed – sometimes drastically so. This may be beneficial, at least to one party. Thus Jean Hartley describes (Chapter 7) how the home-centred, caring wife of the thrusting, career-oriented manager continues her ministrations after the man loses his job. She echoes her husband's reactions, suppressing her own wants, taking on board his problem as hers to solve. Meanwhile she continues with her home duties and child care, as before. My own study of a similar population (Fineman 1983) also revealed this pattern; but I also encountered couples whose inability to communicate and share before unemployment continued after the event. Not surprisingly, recrimination and marriage break-up were one outcome. Some wives realized how much they were an appendage to their husband's career only when they found themselves unable to fill the yawning gap that joblessness had created. They then found themselves helpless observers of their husband's plight and their own inadequacy. Again, the old roles play themselves out.

We find that the traditionally segregated male and female roles generally become reinforced during unemployment. It is against the background of employment (together with broad cultural expectations) that roles are determined and fixed. In this way, the timing and cooking of meals, the chores and maintenance jobs in the house, the ways and places different members of the family can socialize, who gets the children to school, who does the shopping, the use of weekends – all get sorted out, with various degrees of angst. This is a relatively complicated process, much of it progressing on the basis of tacit understandings. Not surprisingly, when unemployment hits the family there is an inclination, at least initially, to wish to carry on as if things have not changed. So, as David Clark and others have observed, customary male and female roles continue as before. There is little sharing of household tasks, despite the availability of the husband. Indeed, the man's presence can generate more housework for the woman, while threatening the use of space and time that was previously just hers. Generally, one gains the impression that these issues are faced, not with a sense of impending liberalization or renegotiation, but with resignation, agitation, and stress.

There is much within the structure of families to reinforce old responses to new problems. The 'bread-winning' male is still a resilient feature of both the working-class and the middle-class family. Dual careers and role swapping have grown, but they remain a relatively unusual form of family arrangement. They represent, in a minority of cases, one eventual *response* to unemployment, sometimes aided by increased awareness from the women's movement. Yet the woman as a domestic supporter to her working husband clearly dominates the family accounts in this book. Such values lie deep, to the extent that, as Claire Callender observes (Chapter 3), the working housewife will resist the label 'unemployed' when she loses her job, deferring to males in the queue for work.

Section 2. Deliberations and directions

In many respects the contributions to this book can be read as a social commentary. The commentary is focused through a variety of professional lenses by authors concerned as much about understanding what is happening to people without work as about ways in which things might be different and better. This raises questions about the value stance of social enquiry, and about the extent to which the investigator should use his or her intimate familiarity with a topic to raise issues hinted at in, or even beyond, the data. One view, reflected in fair measure in this volume, is that a social science that purports to study important facets of the human condition, but fails to offer at least some translation and speculation about where such insights might lead, is 'copping out'. It is perhaps understandable that to the eye of the innocent observer the traditional social scientist's cautious quest for illusive laws of human conduct appears as Nero fiddling while Rome burns.

What, then, has this book to offer in directions for amelioration or change? Each author has addressed this in his or her own way. Rather than repeat what has already been said, I would like to draw out some themes that strike me as important.

Sticking-plasters and work

This book essentially reproduces certain realities of those who live in a social system where paid work is what most people do for most of their lives. It is also what the unemployed want to do, but cannot. They then find themselves, in effect, designated as potential employees, awaiting new work opportunities. To help them on their way they are lifted into a looking-for-work system that offers them retraining, some financial support, and job agencies. Some will also receive soothing words. All will have heard that, contrary to rumour, their government is concerned about them. But they will also have received the firm impression that their fate rests ultimately in their own hands. Thus it is an entrepreneurially driven, initiative culture that determines the position of the unemployed. This is important because it assists in supporting another rhetoric – that of 'creating real jobs', a slogan that sounds plausible and popular. However, as the long-term unemployed have testified, they feel marooned in a stagnant pond. New work, new and usable skills, and new initiatives form no part of their world. Nationally, though, this produces no massive political problem, no substantial politicization by the unemployed. As Moon and Richardson shrewdly observe of government help for the unemployed:

> 'the direct responses to unemployment are rather like placebos, possibly having no long-term curative properties but performing the essential function of enabling the patient to come to terms with what could turn out to be an incurable disease. . . . These policies have been backed up by use of the "numbers game" and by certain changes in attitudes to unemployment (which cannot be directly linked to government policies), and have produced a great political success for the present government: public expectations have been lowered, and unemployment is more widely accepted as being here to stay.'
> (1985: 182)

This analysis may be substantially correct. It is consistent with a social policy that aims to restore social control by cutting public expenditure and reducing real wages. It is then 'necessary' to tolerate unemployment. But the disease metaphor could be worth stretching a little further than Moon and Richardson intended. Some diseases are highly contagious and can soon affect the healthy. We can then place the afflicted in quarantine. Our divided country and isolated communities, our poor and depressed families, may be so regarded. A good placebo fools its patient into acceptance or 'health'; a poor one – training for those who cannot relearn; temporary, demeaning jobs; job agencies with no work; social security payments that humiliate or stigmatize – can serve to hasten the progress of the disease. The 'medicine' will be rejected, or ejected.

We help the unemployed by sticking on plasters and offering them bottles of different coloured medicines. These come in the form of a variety of programmes and packages to enhance or develop education or skills, develop communities, and provide Jobcentre services. They are backed up by social security payments, including special grants to those eligible. Social services departments, the police, the Probation Service, and medical practitioners are expected to accommodate unemployment-related issues as part of their normal business and with their usual knowledge and skill. Within these national networks are a range of local initiatives that include trade-union-sponsored Centres for the Unemployed, local authority community schemes, local job-creation ventures, and the work of the churches and charities in counselling and practical help for the unemployed. For those who seek private guidance services, there is now a growing industry of post-redundancy consultants – entrepreneurism indeed!

All such efforts, regardless of motive, offer something to the un-employed they reach. Some people fare well and find a new direction, even a 'proper' job. This, perhaps, we should be thankful for. But one picture that emerges from this book is that the support offered can often dramatically fail to engage with the full social and psychological realities as experienced by the unemployed. Worse still, it can serve to underline their feeling that, through no fault of their own, they are no longer regarded as 'proper' citizens. In an employment-centred, industrially focused, financial economy, the non-working are akin to waste. They are not counted as producers of wealth, so there is a resistance to counting them at all. In this scenario, the unemployed may soon learn that they are being offered placebos by the state, and that 'care' can take the form of empty rhetoric.

Within this overall context, and if we are listening to the voices of the unemployed, we are left with a number of possible and overlapping routes to consider. A primary one is to seek imaginative ways of enabling individuals to gain work and income, and to support such initiatives with a thorough review of our systems of education and training. Another track is to offer better 'treatment of the symptoms' through more integrated and contingent support for the unemployed. More radically, we might examine the premise, so deeply rooted in our social system, that the mass-employment economy and the consumerism ethic, to which the unemployed are tied as much as the employed, are the most desirable way to 'the good life'. All such routes, which are by no means exhaustive of the possibilities, must be viewed against a backcloth where most people are 'all right, thank you', in that they have a job. Small changes, by bureaucratic tinkering, are likely to be more acceptable and less threatening to them than social revolution.

Jobs and income

The preface to a recent report on unemployment by the European Foundation for the Improvement of Living and Working Conditions (1985) includes the views of representatives from the trades unions, the employers, and the governments of five European countries, including the United Kingdom. The unions argue for the creation of more private and public sector jobs, to be helped along by reducing working hours, extending holidays, and lowering the pensionable age. They are of the firm conviction that employers think only in terms of profits and investment in profitable activities, instead of investing in jobs. They also assert the need for education and training throughout life. This last point is also echoed by the employers, but they are anxious about any help for the unemployed that neglects what they see as the crucial issue: structural changes that will stimulate private sector growth. Here they speak of measures to 'increase the flexibility of the labour market' by reducing minimum wages; reducing social security benefits, 'which are not always an incentive to look for and accept work'; easing hiring and firing; and creating greater work-force mobility. Thirdly, the governments' position: this is presented as a fairly bald statement affirming the primary role of the private sector in generating employment growth, and a demand for an evaluation of the 'effectiveness' of other measures that purport to help the unemployed.

Thus the contestants line up, in perhaps predictable formation. They all (as do the main political parties) emphasize different levers to pull, but within the old rules of the market economy. The implied goal of full employment remains essentially unchallenged. Spending public money on jobs for their own sake is viewed with scorn, interest, or enthusiasm, depending on the guiding political ideology. But, as we have seen from the perspectives of the unemployed themselves, political and corporate ideology is many miles away from their personal and family struggles. This gap has yet to be bridged. In no sense do our leaders present a firm vision of a society where rewarding jobs may lie outside of conventional business enterprise or large employers. Our faltering economy is seen to require repair, not remodelling.

If employment acts so powerfully as a psychic glue, holding people together in aim, purpose, and time, then of course we must look for more of it and create more jobs. Currently, the political question then becomes 'At whose expense?' Do we wait for the magic of market forces and entrepreneurism, or do we intervene by wealth redistribution, or do we do a bit of both? The contributors to this book alert us to some of the personal and social costs of a social policy that regards high unemployment as the necessary bitter aftertaste of the restorative medicine. Such costs get higher as the awaited cure recedes further and further into the distance. For many individuals and families it is likely that any return to employment after a long period of joblessness will leave some indelible marks. While getting back to work may be better than unemployment, an economic recovery is not necessarily synonymous with a social and psychological recovery (see Fineman forthcoming for a discussion of this point).

Political imagination is most limited, however, in grasping the implications of a large, permanent pool of unemployed. This comprises not just those with outdated skills, but people at all points of career for whom there are not enough jobs to go round – and may never be. While some might eventually find alternative routes to work, assisted by special schemes, many others seem unlikely to. For them, the need for cash to weld together their lives and families has not diminished. The rules about transactions in society have not changed just for them.

Yet one sign of a civilized community is perhaps the way it helps enrich, rather than impoverish, its unemployed. If we grudgingly offer minimal payment to our jobless, in the mistaken belief that it is the only way of keeping them interested in work, then we must take some responsibility for family strife and survival crime. If we continue to parade the glories of consumption and material possessions then we should not be too surprised when our chronically unemployed become fixated on their lost capacity to consume and trade. If we cannot supply them with a job to join in the purchasing game, then maybe we should be more generous with the consolation prize. Even better, perhaps, that we organize our tax system to ensure that a basic income is something that everyone is guaranteed. This could be one bold step towards eliminating the poverty trap, while removing the stigmatizing bureaucracy through which the unemployed now have to justify their right to a survival income. A sense of security is a sound psychological basis from which to develop new ways of helping oneself, seeking paid employment, and creating work.

What counts as 'wealth' in our society, and the nature of financially rewardable endeavour, is germane to the shape of future work and income. We could generate rather different principles of wealth distribution if we considered more closely what we mean by wealth. Wealth accounting is currently based (crudely speaking) upon the exchange of *certain* products and services for money, in which so-called 'market forces' determine the amount of money. The principles of wealth creation are based on what human effort, 'work', produces. Where and how such wealth is eligible for money exchange are, though, an altogether more arbitrary affair. Thus a woman may offer her services as a nanny, and get paid – presumably because this is a worthy service in society. Yet her service to society in rearing her own children, and doing family housework, is not seen as producing the sort of wealth for which we, society, through our elected agent, government, should offer financial reward or credit. The end-point of this logic is that working at, say, selling shoes or designing clothes is more valuable to our 'commonwealth' than working at bringing up children and creating a home. Thus a woman (or a man) who wishes to devote time to a house career is not rewarded with money. It is a 'job' that is not counted – but it could be.

We have commentators who have addressed this form of argument when speculating about different scenarios of work (e.g. Jones 1982, Watts 1983, Handy 1984, Robertson 1985). For example, we might move towards a world where different sorts of occupation, in a number of different settings, become the norm: the career is neither uni-directional nor unbroken, and unemployment becomes a less meaningful category. Selling services from home, part-time production work, sabbatical periods, continuing education, sharing child care with a working partner, job sharing, and periods of travel could all form the colourful patchwork of a career. Leisure is no longer in stark contrast to work, and the annual holiday is replaced by a year in which holiday activities fall naturally between phases of work. Traditional family roles become blurred as available work, in and out of the home, for money or for love, has to be shared around. All such moves would need to be buttressed by the state, providing for greater financial and health security for part-time workers of both sexes. One would also expect highly accessible, state-funded crèches.

Education and training

One point of convergence between politicians, industrialists, and unionists is that the shape of education influences the shape of 'employ-ability'. They will argue, however, about appropriate curricula, and how far educational objectives ought to reflect occupational ones. The position of the unemployed school- and college-leavers portrayed in this book is fairly clear: 'What was it all for?' For them, our educational system has continued to issue tickets of educational proficiency – secondary-school certificates, technical diplomas, degrees – as implicit or explicit passports to jobs, even when the individual teacher or lecturer knows that, for many young men and women, such qualifications no longer ensure access to work. The average school-leaver has little conception of how a life may be built outside the contract of employment, other than being on the dole. One educational response to this has been to turn inwards, creating greater pressures on the students to do even better academically and to improve their chances in the ever-shrinking job market. This process feeds the sense of anti-climax amongst those who leave education well qualified but still find it impossible to get work.

Such a scene raises important issues about the role of our educational system in channelling people towards specific occupations. While the rhetoric of the educational establishment may include statements about 'generally preparing the young for life', in practice this soon becomes translated into specific, occupationally relevant material such as 'scientist', 'engineer', 'linguist', 'teacher', 'builder', 'mechanic', 'welder', or 'soldier'. We make a business of *channelling* our children, on whom we impress the language of jobs, especially *a* job. But this is a risky strategy in times of occupational turbulence.

We may better serve our pupils and students through curricula that are freed from job-tags and emphasize a far broader spectrum of skills and knowledge for living. Central here would be engaging activities aimed at fostering self-awareness, creativity, independence of thought and action, interpersonal skills, and an appreciation of others' perspectives. These could be focused to provide a keener sense of the world 'outside'; its politics, pitfalls, and avenues to survival. This would not obviate some of the traditional educational matter, such as literacy and numeracy, and features of arts and science, but it would place it all in a very different, and exciting, context. Each level of education could embrace these principles in its own way. The net effect would be to ensure a better armour for those who step from the school or college gate into the void of unemployment; and, of equal significance, it should create far more flexible, self-sufficient individuals to meet the specific training requirements of available employment, self-employment, and occupational changes in a fast-moving world. It would also seem appropriate that formal education introduces to the student an appreciation of informal learning: that people develop knowledge and skills vicariously by 'doing things' outside institutional learning settings. If self-help is important, then so is learning by experience. Our further education establishments could assist in the development of such experiences by providing continuing supportive resources.

If we are moving towards the creation of new jobs, new forms of occupation outside of conventional employment, and, for some, a life without regular financial remuneration, then an underpinning educational initiative is imperative. To continue to educate under the sole justification, as the student may see it, that the point of it all is a well-paid job, can turn out to be a cruel sham.

An educational perspective also directs our attention to the question of learning and retraining for the unemployed in later career. Retraining, on the face of it, appears a plausible and caring way of helping the unemployed; and for some it clearly works. But for others it can look a little like an unthinking, 'knee-jerk' response of the sort: 'If old skills are defunct, we must graft on the new.' Many people who have reached mid- or late career before unemployment have been settled into a specialist corner of the world of work. They have probably been rewarded for their stability, even loyalty, but their company-sponsored training has been modest or negligible – a point starkly made in a recent report by the Manpower Services Commission (1985). The so-called 'unskilled' unemployed have held jobs in which their hands and wits have seen them through. Their proficiencies have developed through on-the-job experience, not special training. All such people have, if anything, been socialized away from formal relearning and training. Hence retraining can be a tough experience for some, impossible for others, and, for yet others, an irrelevancy if there is no obvious likelihood of a job afterwards.

Training and other support, then, to be meaningful to the unemployed, have to be viewed beyond a package prescription and carefully tailored to the social and psychological position of the unemployed individual. The relevant dimensions that have been highlighted in this book are as follows.

* Unemployment can mean something different to a person in early or mid-career than to a person in late career. It can also be a very different experience if one is black, female, infirm, or of foreign origin. All face problems, in varying degrees of severity, about the shape and meaning of their lives.
* Unemployment directly after school, college, university, or other study can bring its special disappointments and stresses.
* Many jobless women, of working-class and middle-class backgrounds, see their position as less consequential than that of unemployed males. The married will seek to support their husband in his job search. However, women are certainly pleased to have a job when they see it is their turn in the queue.
* Many families respond to unemployment in the terms they understand best – the language and patterns of their usual relationships. These can be ill-matched to their new circumstances. Some families will carry additional burdens because of poverty, sickness, children to care for, separation of partners, and lack of mobility.

* For the young and mid-career unemployed (especially), there is a strong belief that there is no effective substitute for a 'real' job. Leisure, temporary work, and voluntary unpaid work are all seen as reinforcing their displacement in society.
* The desire to gain paid work is undiminished amongst the unemployed. This appears to be more a reflection of the ethic to consume than of some noble form of Protestantism. The propaganda of consumption and materialism continues to reach the eyes and ears of the unemployed. Through such a milieu social positions and mores have become defined and deeply imbedded in community behaviour. The unemployed can very soon confront an acute problem of how properly to express themselves outside of the cash nexus.
* The jobless are restricted in what they can realistically aim for. Initially, though, they have little sense of being substantially different from a normal job applicant. Later they will feel very different. If they get a job it is more likely to be through personal contacts and casual encounters than from job agencies or advertisements.
* One consequence of the loss of the male full-time job is a shift of responsibility to the woman to meet both the household and the material needs of the family. Department of Employment figures indicate that a considerable proportion of new jobs are part-time and come into this category. They are poorly paid and fall below the threshold of employee-protective benefits (a financial saving for the employer).
* Many older, unskilled people may never work again. Nor may many older, highly skilled people. Their expertise is no longer required.

With these points in mind, support for the unemployed – towards work or towards living without work – has some formidable psychological and social issues to face. We may choose to ignore them, to sit back and blame the victims for their predicament, perhaps to make a few palliative gestures. Alternatively we may shoulder fuller responsibility, attending to the here-and-now human consequences. We do have programmes of support, some designed with specific unemployed groups in mind. Nevertheless, individuals can soon find themselves shuffled from agency to agency, and from one overburdened department to another. Many of their problems can end up falling between agencies, and they soon reach a position of disbelief about any 'official' overtures of support. If there is any central message about support from the experiences of the unemployed in this book, it is that it needs to be simple, accessible, comfortable, non-stigmatizing, and related to their individual and family needs.

At first sight this looks like a task for social services departments. While social work skills may be suitable, the local authority social services department seems inappropriate for a number of reasons. Social workers are themselves confused about their role and appropriate response to unemployment (see Yvonne Dhooge and Jennie Popay, Chapter 9, and a report by Balloch *et al.* 1985). They are also part of a fairly cumbersome organizational apparatus where, generally speaking, clients have to go to them first, or be seen at home *in extremis*. This can be received as a stigmatizing process. Social workers provide a service that generally does not reach, or is not wanted by, the middle class. In addition, as was poignantly evident from a recent study of my own, social workers themselves could well do without a further extension of their often overloaded role (Fineman 1985).

We are left, then, with a challenge of how to present a community service to the unemployed that gives them what they desire of support during jobless periods, but without adding to the plethora of bureaucracy that many of them now face. This challenge is particularly problematic for a government committed to reducing public expenditure.

In memoriam?

As jobs pass away, the fabric of social relationships becomes frayed. We can try to tighten the weave by creating more jobs, exploring different formulas for 'work', and easing the path for those seeking work: a strengthening of our Welfare State. Within this picture, though, is an image of people still schooled towards 'getting a job in an organization' and to be dependent upon institutions for goods and services. Material consumption can become an end in itself. Jobs, at all levels, tend to reinforce such an orientation, through which other social and psychological dependencies arise. The unemployed, understandably, cannot lose their instinct to consume what others produce; most cannot survive without doing so in our society. And here lie some of the more uncomfortable questions to confront. If we are finding it so difficult to accommodate the growing numbers of unemployed within our culture of the employed, then maybe it is the mass-employment/consumption ethic that requires our prime attention. Meanwhile, we will no doubt continue to move around its perimeter making adjustments here and there. This is necessary, but unlikely to be sufficient.

References

Balloch, S., Hume, C., Jones, B., and Westland, P. (1985) *Caring for Unemployed People*. London: Bedford Square Press/National Council for Voluntary Organizations.

Chester, L. and Tigh, C. (1985) Consett Has Seen the Future – and It's Workless. *Sunday Times Magazine*, 15 September: 24–32.

European Foundation for the Improvement of Living and Working Conditions (1985) *Activities for the Unemployed: United Kingdom*. Dublin: Shankill.

Fineman, S. (1983) *White-Collar Unemployment: Impact and Stress*. Chichester: Wiley.

—— (1985) *Social Work Stress and Intervention*. Aldershot: Gower.

—— (forthcoming) Back to Work: Wounds and Wisdoms. In D. Fryer and P. Ullah (eds) *Unemployed People: Social and Psychological Perspectives*. Milton Keynes: Open University Press.

Green, A. and Champion, T. (1985) Discussion Paper No. 72, Centre for Urban and Regional Studies, University of Newcastle.

Handy, C. (1984) *The Future of Work*. Oxford: Blackwell.

Jones, B. (1982) *Sleepers, Wake! Technology and the Future of Work*. Brighton: Wheatsheaf.

Manpower Services Commission (1985) *Challenge to Complacency*. Sheffield: MSC.

Moon, J. and Richardson, J. J. (1985) *Unemployment in the UK*. Aldershot: Gower.

Robertson, J. (1985) *Future Work*. Aldershot: Gower.

Watts, A. G. (1983) *Education, Unemployment and the Future of Work*. Milton Keynes: Open University Press.

Name index

Subject index